EXECUTIVE ECONOMICS

Ten Essential Tools for Managers

SHLOMO MAITAL

THE FREE PRESS

THE FREE PRESS
A Division of Simon & Schuster Inc.
1230 Avenue of the Americas
New York, NY 10020

Manufactured in the United States of America

10

Library of Congress Cataloging-in-Publication Data
Maital, Shlomo
    Executive economics : ten essential tools for managers / Shlomo Maital
        p.   cm.

    ISBN 978-1-4516-3159-3

    1. Managerial economics   I. Title.
HD30.22.M34   1994
338.5'024658 — dc20   94–10300
                                                              CIP

For Sharona, Temira, Ronen, Iris, Tal, Yochai, and Noam,
with love

and to all my students, past and present,
with gratitude

Contents

Preface   *vii*

1. Cost, Value, Price: Three Pillars of Profit   1

2. Hidden Costs   21

3. Tradeoffs: Pain versus Gain   41

4. Do You Know Where Your Costs Are?   65

5. People, Knowledge, and/or Machines   87

6. From Volume to Variety   117

7. Racing Down the Learning Curve   139

8. Markets and Demand: How to Listen
    to Your Customer   169

9. Calculated Risks   205

10. Competing by Cooperating   227

Notes   255
Acknowledgments   269
Index   271

Preface

Once upon a time, in 1967, I sought to join a tribe known as the Econ, a generally peaceful and mildly underachieving band found all over the world and numbering some 80,000 in North America alone.[1]

Time-honored initiation rites made me prove my worthiness for membership by doing a very difficult task—take some familiar, everyday event or behavior and analyze it using Greek letters, also known as "math," in a way that no one could recognize what I was trying to say.

The elders of the Econ tested me with two fearful questions.

- Does he know what he is talking about?
- Does he know whether what he is saying is true?

"Yes" answers flunked you. "Maybes" got you probation. Firm "nos" got you into the tribe.

I made it. I was successful enough to be accepted as a full-fledged Econ. I spent 17 happy years with them, rising through their ranks, teaching their young, and initiating others in the revered rites of mystification and obfuscation.

One day, by chance, I met some members of a larger and more prosperous tribe known as the Exec. The Exec, I discovered, are practical, hard-headed, tough, and smart. Unlike the Econ, who spend most of their time spinning tales, the Exec work hard and are often subject to intense pressures. Their job is to tell large numbers of people what to do and how to do it.

Unlike the Econ, if the Exec do not speak and think clearly and do not perform well, the result is disaster—layoffs, lost jobs, and wasted resources. Execs that do succeed create nearly boundless amounts of wealth, income, and jobs, for those who work for them and for themselves. Execs who fail create misery and poverty.

I learned that in their youth, Execs often have contact with Econs and are sometimes asked to study a little of the Econ's lore. But in general, the Exec's memories of the Econ are not happy ones. There are barriers of language, culture, and purpose. Most Execs are happy and relieved when they can say good-bye forever to their Econ instructors. Some Execs even employ Econ as company storytellers, but wisely ignore them.

In 1984 I was asked to teach the language and logic of the Econ to a group of Execs at MIT. The Execs themselves were not overjoyed with this idea, but for some reason the elders of both my tribe and theirs thought it was necessary.

The shock of the Exec's culture was for me like a stinging cold shower. The Exec kept asking me, So what? Why should I learn this? How can we use it? How do you know what you are telling us is true? How can it help us Execs make better decisions?

Never before had I encountered such a challenge. Younger members of my own tribe were usually too polite to ask such questions. Their purpose was to find out, as quickly as possible, what they needed to know, say, and do in order to become an Econ like me. Their main objective in life was to learn whatever it was I told them well enough to repeat to other Econs.

But the Execs had a different goal. They wanted to find out, what (if anything) do the Econ know that can help us make our companies more profitable and more competitive?

To be perfectly honest, I had no idea.

With the help of the patient Execs, I learned. The process took many years and it is far from complete, but at long last there is a glimmer of light. I discovered that the lore of the Econ *is* of value to the Exec. It can *indeed* help their companies do better. The tales of the Econ, when properly framed and explained, can help Execs build and implement better competitive strategies and achieve more profitable operations.

Formally, I am still an Econ, and always will be. But secretly, I harbor deep respect and admiration for the Exec and what they do for society. As a mark of that respect, I decided to create a written record of my experiences in teaching them. This book is the result.

I dedicate it to the cause of peace and understanding between the two, often fractious tribes, in the fervent hope that one day, the Exec and the Econ will live together in harmony, goodwill, and mutual respect and understanding, all over the world.

Cambridge, Mass.,
August 1993

EXECUTIVE
ECONOMICS

Chapter One

COST, VALUE, PRICE:

The Three Pillars of Profit

In 1984 I was asked to teach economics to a group of seasoned managers with scientific and engineering backgrounds in the MIT Sloan School of Management's Management of Technology M.Sc. program. In one class, a young woman—a senior manager at IBM—asked me politely but firmly, "why do I have to know this?" My response was pitifully lame—something like, "well, because... because it's economics, and this is an economics course."

For me, that question was an epiphany. I encounter it often when facing her equally challenging successors. Generally, I try to ask it before they do.

Most master's programs in management require candidates to take at least one course in economics. It is considered self-evident that managers, whose job it is to hire labor, borrow capital, acquire technology, and buy materials to make goods and services, need to know microeconomics, the discipline that studies precisely that. But while obvious to their mentors, the relevance of economics in its current form is often not so obvious to the managers or would-be managers themselves. It is not obvious to working managers that the subject matter of conventional economics is either relevant or useful. This is true, despite the fact that among the CEOs of America's largest 1,000 companies, economics was their second most popular major in college (after engineering).[1]

Most of my manager-students had over a decade of practical experience in business. They challenged me repeatedly to demonstrate the utility, relevance, viability, and applicability of the theories I taught them. For far longer than I would have wished, I drew a blank in proving to them the added value of economic concepts as tools in business decisions. It took me a decade of on-the-job training, teaching economics as a management tool to managers in the United States, Europe, and Israel, and recently serving as a consultant, for my manager-students and clients to educate me sufficiently so that I could write this book. To be honest—another decade would not have hurt.

After about five years of teaching managers, I wondered whether anything that I taught them had proved useful, after they left the classroom and returned to their companies and jobs. I wrote to 150 former Management of Technology students and asked them to rate on a scale of one to six each of the 30 economic concepts I had taught them, in terms of how useful it had proved in their day-to-day decisions. I learned from their responses that the parts of micro-economics they used most were those that helped them understand costs—including "hidden" or opportunity costs (see chapter 2), marginal costs, sunk costs, and learning curves—and the links between the costs of production, the value of their products, and the prices they get for them.[2] Later generations of managers have confirmed this finding. It is reflected in the fact that the first seven chapters of this book deal in one way or another with costs—in contrast with most microeconomics texts, which usually race to discuss demand after a polite introduction, even though demand, I believe, is a subject where economics has relatively little to communicate to managers.

HOW MANAGERS USE ECONOMICS

My results echoed those from a broader survey of how managers use economics, undertaken in 1982 by Guisseppi A. Forgionne. He canvassed a random sample of 500 corporate executives drawn from the 1,500 largest American corporations. Forgionne found that fully 70 per cent of the executives said they make use of most of the basic economic concepts of cost (such as economies of scale, cost functions, and learning curves, all of which will be discussed in later chapters), price (supply and demand, marginal-cost pricing) and value. Some 86 percent of the respondents said the major benefit in implementing economic concepts in decision making is that "the analysis generates useful data, and... forces the decision maker to define the problem clearly and concisely." Yet, *more than half cited "poor communication" between economic specialist and manager, and nearly 60 per cent complained that "inadequate data are a barrier to implementation [of economic tools]."* This, despite the fact that most managers literally drown in data, spewed out endlessly by costly, sophisticated management information systems.[3]

Clearly, the Exec need a travel guide to the curious land of the Econ, and a basic dictionary. And in a sense, this book *is* that travel diary, an account of what I learned in my decade-long journey among the Execs. My hike along the path of applying economics to business decisions began with the deep conviction that somehow, economics was a powerful tool for managers. It was the insightful comments and criticisms of hundreds of experienced managers delivered in classrooms through over a decade that strengthened that conviction and led me to write this book.

The thinker and essayist Ralph Waldo Emerson was known to despise small talk. He liked to greet friends and visitors with the question: What have you learned since we last met? This book is a response to Emerson's question: What have I learned since that day in class before a group of independent-minded managers who refused to swallow theory for the sake of theory alone? It is built on the belief that economics, a venerable discipline with well over two centuries' worth of serious intellectual capital, is a product or service of great potential value to managers—*provided that knowledge can be conveyed in a language and framework that is understandable and relevant to their experience and needs.* It is stimulated by the incredible, rapid changes sweeping over the world, as nations once guided by blind adherence to central planning and Marxist doctrine switch to business-driven, free-enterprise market systems and bureaucrats yield power to entrepreneurs.

During the past three decades, management became "discipline-based." Managers sought expertise in one particular area—accounting, law, marketing, finance, production—and rose to top jobs as their companies perceived that particular expertise crucial. Four of every 10 top executives rose to the top of their companies either through finance and accounting, or marketing—roughly equally divided between the two disciplines.[4]

To some degree, this trend continues. High-technology companies like IBM and Westinghouse have recently wooed and appointed to top posts managers with backgrounds and skill in *marketing* (from, for instance, RJR Nabisco, a food company, and Pepsi-Cola). They did this because they believe that this particular skill is of crucial importance for the health of their business.

Today, however, there is an increasing need for managers who have a broad range of skills and who understand their company's technology and R&D operations as well as its production, finance, marketing, and human resources. Only the *general manager* can see the enterprise as a whole and imbue it with its own unique culture and set of values, appropriate for the times and for its competitive situation. As management expert Peter Drucker has phrased it, a manager's *discipline* or professional training has become far less important than their *competencies,* such as dealing with pressure, handling information, communicating with others. It is managers' performance, not credentials, that matter more now, in information-based organizations.[5] (The same applies to organizations themselves. With increased global competition spurring rapid change in products and services, companies' "core competencies"—what they *know* well and *do* well—become far more important than what they currently *make* well, because those abilities enable companies to change their products quickly in response to market conditions.)

Take General Electric, one of America's most consistently profitable and well-managed companies, fifth-largest industrial company in the U.S., with a market value of $90 billion as of March 1994. GE has shown the ability to make money from such diverse businesses as jet engines, financial services, and a TV network (NBC) on a global basis. Part of that success is due to their cadre of good general managers, assiduously trained and cultivated, able to move between GE's widely differing businesses because of strong management competencies that cut across many different disciplines.

The new breed of general manager is far different from the ones that ran the old-style patchwork firms. The new-style manager is comfortable with diversity. He or she is able to assemble a well-defined company culture out of seemingly incompatible pieces. No longer is the CEO the only person expected to understand the company as a whole. No longer do functional vice-presidents meet and communicate only when the CEO calls them together. Increasingly, middle managers, too, need to have a broad view of their company, even if their responsibilities lie mainly in finance or marketing, or a single business or product area. Decisions are now often made by teams and team members, who need to know far more about each other's problems and expertise than in the past, because they cut across narrow functional partitions and product lines.

New corporate structures are forming with "fuzzy boundaries" that create many horizontal links among departments and divisions. Such links are facilitated by new technology like computer networks and information technology that enable managers to easily communicate with colleagues, subordinates, and suppliers across long distances. Once, top management found it costly and time-consuming to acquire information about a company's operations. Today, an unending stream of information is available at the touch of a modem button. General managers need to know how to tap that stream and how to sip from it judiciously.

The rise of the general manager poses new challenges for American companies. Companies with cadres of managers who read blueprints as easily as they decipher balance sheets, who can cooperate with competitors in R&D as fiercely as they compete with them in markets, and who know a lot of things about a lot of businesses, will win an enduring advantage over their rivals in the struggle to create new wealth and profits from new and existing assets.[6]

In this new and different business world, competency counts, not credentials. As a result, it will no longer be sufficient for managers to *employ* economists. To some degree, they will have to *become* economists. That will require a fundamental understanding of the language and logic that underlies the economic approach to decisions.

To manage is to choose. Economic logic, employed properly, can be a tool of great parsimony and power for the new general manager, as he or she makes hard choices across a broad spectrum of business issues including technology, human resources, markets, production, finance, marketing, and social and ethical responsibilities.

The job of managers is to build and run businesses by selling goods and services that provide value at a reasonable price for their customers at an acceptable cost to the business. If managers create more value at lower cost than their competitors their businesses prosper and profit. This is the nub. Everything else is embroidery.

The health and wealth of a large number of individual businesses—small, medium and large—determine the economic health and wealth of a nation. When they succeed, managers create wealth, income, and jobs for large numbers of people. When they fail, working people and their families suffer. It is *businesses* that create wealth, not countries or governments. It is individual businesses that are either competitive in world markets or are unable to sell in them. It is businesses that decide how well or how poorly off we are. And in the end, it is the consistent quality of managers' decisions, along with how well they are implemented by the people who work for them, that decide how competitive businesses are and will become.

Business decisions are built on three pillars—cost, value, and price (see figure 1.1). Cost is what businesses pay out to their workers and suppliers in order to make and market goods and services. Value is the degree to which buyers think those goods and services make them better off, than if they did without. And price is what buyers pay. Those are the three essential elements in the day-to-day choices managers make. Juggling those three elements is what managers are paid for.

Managers who know what their products cost and what they are worth to customers—and who also know the costs, values, and prices of competing products—will build good businesses, because their decisions will rest on sound foundations. Businesses

FIGURE 1.1
Three Pillars of Profit: Cost, Value, Price

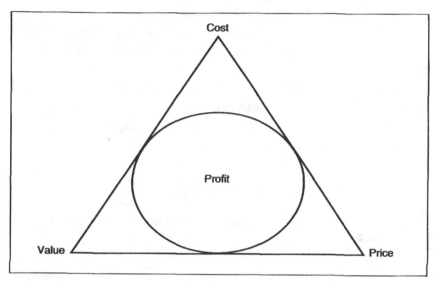

run by managers who have only fuzzy knowledge of one of those three pillars will eventually stumble. It is deceptively difficult to build them, precisely because they *have* to be built—the information required is often incomplete or not readily at hand.

Knowledge of the three pillars is necessary, but not sufficient, for smart decisions. Success also requires wisdom, experience, good humor, humility and courage, and luck. But other things equal, managers who truly understand costs, values, and prices and how they interact will do much better in the long run than those who do not.

This book provides a series of economic tools to help decision makers stay focused on building accurate perceptions of their companies' costs, prices, and values, and the links among them.

Regrettably, there is a large gap between what managers know about economic decision tools and what they *need* to know, one that needs to be closed. The eminent British scientist Lord Kelvin once said that "theory begins with measurement." His precise measurements formed the basis for what came to be known as Kelvin's Law. Many scientists would disagree with Kelvin. They would argue that theory begins with ... theory. Few people would dispute, however, that *management* begins with measurement. What you cannot measure, you cannot effectively understand, control, or alter. Without an adequate understanding of the ten economic tools explained in this book, decision makers are more likely to miss, for example, important but hidden costs that should be taken into account, or regard as important sunk costs that deserve to be completely ignored. A major benefit of cost-price-value economics is that it forces decision makers to scrape together—or have someone do it for them—the basic data on performance without which good decisions cannot be made.

WHAT ARE MANAGERS WORTH?

Are managers really worth their pay? If cost-value logic is useful, then it should be be possible to use it to measure the value of managers, compared to their cost. This is an especially controversial topic these days, as the flagging performance of many American businesses contrasts sharply with the allegedly excessive salaries that their managers draw. According to a recent survey, American chief executives of companies with annual sales above $250 million earned five times more than their counterparts in Korea, and double or triple that in Austria, Germany, Canada, Argentina, Sweden, and Japan.[7]

Here is how cost-value economics can be used to determine whether or not a company's executives and managers are in fact earning their way, developed by business expert Paul Strassman.[8] Strassman's method shows that contrary to common belief, not all Japanese managers are the corporate equivalents of Babe Ruth. Even the legendary Sony Corp., regarded by many as one of the world's best-managed firms, with a long list of products that it innovated, may have much inefficiency among its top brass and line managers.

Strassman measures the value or contribution to the company by managers by what he terms "management value added"—literally, what managers themselves add to the firm's value.

Value added is a very important idea in economics that is frequently encountered. It means exactly what it says: how much *value*, for example, does the carpenter *add* to the wood he buys, when he turns it into a table? It is the difference between the cost of the wood to the carpenter and the value of the table when he sells it. For knowledge-based products, value added tends to be very high; the cost of the silicon and glue that comprise microprocessors is miniscule, compared to its value, and the cost of the eight or ten diskettes on which a software application is written is negligible compared to the price and value of that software.

Management value added is what managers add to the firm's value. It is the difference between what they cost the company (like the carpenter's wood), and what they bring in to the company (i.e., the value of the table).

Management value added is the part of overall business value added that is not attributable to a business's worker or shareholder capital. To calculate management value added, we must first compute total *"business value added."* This is equal to the firm's total revenues (what it earns from selling its products and services), minus all taxes and purchases (the cost of raw and finished materials, parts, energy and services, including interest payments). This is directly comparable to the difference between the value of the carpenter's table, when sold, less the value of the wood used to make it.

In 1989, Sony had sales of $9.5 billion. It bought materials (and paid taxes) of $8.5 billion. That means that it added $1 billion of value to the inputs it acquired—its business value added was $1 billion. (See table 1.1).

Not all business value added is created by managers. Much of it comes from the capital provided by shareholders. Hence, to isolate management value added, we need to deduct from business value added the value that the shareholders' capital has provided: "Shareholder value added."

Shareholder value added is equal to the total value of shareholder capital—known as "shareholder equity," an important concept discussed in a later chapter—multiplied by the going interest-rate cost of that capital (say, 8–9 percent). Shareholder equity is simply the value of Sony to those who own its stock and is equal to the difference between what Sony owes (its liabilities, or debts), and what it owns (its assets). In principle, this is what Sony shareholders would be left with if Sony sold all its assets and used the money to pay off any outstanding debts.

TABLE 1.1
Sony's Management Value Added in 1989
(billions of U.S. dollars)

	Sales	$ 9.5
−	Purchases and taxes	− 8.5
=	Business value added	$ 1.0
−	Shareholders value added	−$0.5
−	Operations costs	− 0.3
−	Management costs	− 0.4
=	Management value added	−$ 0.2

Shareholder value added is the interest that shareholders could earn on their money *in an alternate investment that has equal risk.* (The notion of hidden, or opportunity, cost is crucial in management decisions; it will be discussed at length in the next chapter.) For Sony, shareholder value added amounted to $0.5 billion—say, $5 billion in shareholders' capital, with each dollar of that capital earning about 10 percent a year, giving $5 billion × 10 percent = $0.5 billion. Deduct this sum from business value added.

To further isolate managers' contribution to value added, another component must be substracted: Operations costs. This includes payrolls and depreciation, the cost of "everything that is essential for getting today's goods and services produced and delivered to today's customers." Deduct as well management costs—payments to managers, including bonuses and fringe payments. (Note that this is not only what managers are *paid* directly, but also their additional costs to the firm, including health benefits, pension contributions by Sony, and so on.)

Sony's operations costs in 1989 amounted to $300 million. Its management costs were even greater: $400 million. (This may be somewhat misleading—Sony purchases a lot of its components from suppliers, so a large part of its costs appear not as wages but as purchases.) Deduct operations and management costs, and what remains is "management value added."

Using the cost-value decision framework: *What do managers cost? What are managers worth?* it is seen that for 1989, Sony's managers cost more than they contributed in added value. This does not mean that two-thirds of Sony's managers should be instantly fired. But it does mean that Sony needs to examine closely whether its spending on all levels of management might not be excessive.

Paul Strassman suggests looking carefully at the ratio of "management value-added" to "management costs," what he calls "Return on Management."[™] This is similar to the "Return on Investment" concept, where investors take the profit they make from their investments and express it as a percentage of the cost or value of that investment itself. "The high-purchase, capital-intensive and low Value-added Sony shows a negative value of R-O-M [return on management] which suggests that this firm has a productivity problem," Strassman concludes.

Strassman studied over 300 firms. *Of these, more than a fifth showed negative management value added.* Those firms clearly need *less* management (or better), not more. Executives of firms that do not use the value-cost decision framework on themselves and their managers may not be aware of this. Their company will do more poorly than it could or should. The average return on management for manufacturing firms is, he observed, 50 percent. If your company is making less than that consistently, over a period of years, you need to re-examine the quantity and quality of your management work force.

He provides a comparison of the return on management for the leading Japanese consumer electronics firms. They differ widely.[9] For Toshiba, for each dollar spent on management, about two-thirds of a dollar was *added* in value, over and above that dollar itself. This is the highest return on management of all the companies, and far above the rate of return that most companies or individuals earn on their capital investments, for instance.

An expert on information systems and computers, Strassman uses his "return on management" concept to examine whether and when firms should invest in more computing power—a good example of cost-value logic. His prescription, based on long experience and data: You get better value out of the high cost of investing in computers, when you *first* try to get better value out of your existing managers by trimming excess numbers of them. Since new computer systems often need *more* managers, if you *fail* to do this, you may end up with *both* unneeded computers and unnecessary managers—and will likely be unable to tell this is so, because the managers will look exceedingly busy and efficient with their new hardware. Computers are terrific at helping us do many tasks that may not need doing at all. Don't do fast and well, Strassman warns, what need not be done at all. This is confirmed in Peter Drucker's account of a conversation with an information manager at a large financial institution that invested $1.5 billion in information technology. Despite the massive spending, no one in his department had yet thought seriously about what information was needed—and what was not—in order to serve their customers.[10] The issue of what information is needed, or not needed, needed resolution well *before* the $1.5 billion in information technology was spent, not long after.

HOW SUCCESS BREEDS FAILURE

The American humorist and writer James Thurber once said, in a serious moment, that it is more important to know some of the questions than all of the answers. This is especially true in running businesses. Successful businesses pose no questions, because they *are* successful—yet to remain so, those who run them have to question themselves and their actions daily. And it is not easy to raise questions, and get organizations to deal with them in earnest, when no evident problem is in sight. Yet, there may be no sillier slogan in management than "if it ain't broke—don't fix it." If it "ain't broke," it probably soon will be, given the rapid pace of change in global markets and technology. And it is much tougher to cure the problems of a business while it tumbles downhill than to patch up one that is still at the summit, though starting to teeter.

Take, for instance, IBM. In 1972 and again in 1982, IBM was the world's largest company, measured by the market value of its stock. Indeed, in 1972, IBM shares alone were worth $46.9 billion, close to the value of the shares of its two closest rivals taken together, AT&T ($29.2 billion) and Eastman Kodak ($23.9 billion). At its peak in 1987, IBM stock sold for $176. By 1992, IBM was

not even among the top 20 most valuable firms. In 1993 its shares
sold for a quarter of their peak value. Much of IBM's rapid de-
scent occurred in a relatively brief period, since 1989–90.[11]

What happened? The answer lies in the cost-value-price triangle.

Costs: Like many big, profitable companies, IBM's problems grew
out of its success. Its profitable System/360 mainframe computers
gave IBM market leadership. But it also created a huge bureaucratic organization, one that led IBM's payroll to double in only three
years (1963–66), and ultimately peak at 407,000 in 1986, and
made its decision-making process cumbersome and sluggish (in
some cases, over a dozen executives needed to "sign" a decision in
order to implement it). When IBM's new CEO, Lou Gerstner,
took over in early 1993, he found that IBM was spending 42 percent of its sales on costs (including Research and Development
costs), compared with less than a third by its rivals. True, personnel costs were slashed sharply, by $3 billion, as IBM quickly shed
120,000 workers. But other expenses (such as the writing-off of
products in inventory that no longer could be sold, or could be
sold only at lower prices) rose by $7 billion. IBM's costs of pro-
cessing data amounted to one dollar out of every 14 sales dollars—three-and-a-half times the proportion of other American
firms, on average.

Perhaps worse than the excessive costs themselves was the fact
that it was hard to pin down why they were so high. In 1990, in an
effort to fix what was clearly broke already, IBM decentralized
into 13 operating units. This major organizational change apparently was not accompanied by a change in the way IBM collected
and analyzed its cost data. As a result, efforts to cut costs were
hampered by difficulty in pinning down where unnecessary expenses were being made.

Value: IBM once commanded premium prices for its products, as
the market recognized IBM products' market leadership and superior performance and quality. But while striving to preserve its
lead in mainframe computers, IBM was caught from behind by
ever-more-powerful personal computers, minicomputers, and
work stations. It failed to exploit a technology that made smaller

computers much more competitive with their larger cousins dominated by IBM, a technology IBM itself invented (known as RISC, reduced instruction-set computing) but failed to see its huge potential. It failed to take advantage of its own highly successful PC (launched in 1981) and let competitors and imitators grab the market, partly because its PC had no strong constituency within IBM itself, especially in its sales force. And it clung to its "no layoff" employment policy, long after that policy was no longer viable.

Price: As the market's perceived value of IBM products declined, so did its relative prices. The result of eroding prices and rising costs was that IBM's gross profit margin—once much higher than its rivals, at 55 percent—dropped to the industry average, around 40 percent. IBM wrote off $28 billion of its capital in the process of restructuring. The profit circle, at the center of the cost-price-value triangle, was badly squeezed.[12]

In 1992, IBM declared a loss of nearly $5 billion, a bit less that than of Ford Motor Co. ($7.4 billion loss) and a lot less than General Motors ($23.5 billion loss).[13] Indeed, there are similarities between IBM, GM, and Ford. All three scorned the early competition from small, cheap versions of their products—PCs and compact cars—and missed the threat those products implied, in the value they provided relative to their cost.[14]

Some of General Motors' current troubles can be traced well back in time to another type of cost-price-value problem—one involving a decision about a new technology called "front-wheel drive." The story is related by David Halberstam, in his book *The Reckoning:*

> In the spring of 1973, Pete Estes, a top General Motors executive, asked a car expert named David E. Davis to "go to Europe and take a look at the new front-wheel-drive cars that were just coming out there," like the Volkswagen Rabbit, that were "generating excitement as no small cars had done in years" among both customers and engineers.
>
> The new cars used less fuel, saved weight and did it without sacrificing performance. "Our people are telling us that it's going to be very expensive—a whole new engine, a whole new power train," Estes said. "They think it will cost us about eighty-five or ninety

dollars a car. So if we put it on our small cars, will we be able to charge extra and make it work?"—which Davis thought was precisely the wrong question. [Those who truly loved building cars, he likely thought, would ask: Will they be better cars? Will they give more value for their asking price?]

In a few weeks, he reported back to Estes. They *were* better cars, he said, better engineered and better built than those Detroit was making. Front-wheel drive was a breakthrough of immense significance. It was the state of the art.

But Estes just shook his head. In the end, GM, Ford and Chrysler were all stuck with rear-wheel drive. None wanted to take the lead and pioneer in (for them) a new, costly and untried technology.

Davis told Estes he was making a major mistake, and that eventually the customers would let him know. In a few months, when the OPEC oil embargo struck, the American auto industry was completely unready, and its products were suddenly very wrong for the marketplace.[15]

Pete Estes weighed cost, price, and value. The source of customer value of front-wheel drive was its elimination of the bulky drive shaft that transferred power from the engine to the rear wheels. Instead, power was sent directly to the *front* wheels, giving the car better traction and handling qualities, less weight and better gas mileage, and flattening the annoying camel-hump in the back seat.

The added *cost* of front-wheel drive was then estimated at a minimum of $95 per vehicle. Could front-wheel drive justify the high cost (and risk) of building plants and buying equipment to produce it? Whole new engines and drive trains would have to be built. Cars would have to be totally redesigned. Existing plants and equipment would become obsolete. Was it worth it? Could the massive investment be justified to General Motors' shareholders? And would buyers pay enough extra for front-wheel drive— was it worth enough extra to them—to let GM at least recover the $95?

Estes' decision was: No. The value (and higher price) of front-wheel drive could not justify its added cost.

It is easy to fault Estes' decision from today's vantage point, knowing as we do how the price of oil and gasoline soared, making the fuel-efficiency advantage of front-wheel drive more valuable to car owners. But with crude oil then at $3 a barrel, and gasoline at 25¢ a gallon, with no hint that its price would soar, a decision to invest billions in a new, mainly fuel-saving, technology might have then been perceived not as courageous but as foolhardy. Whatever the case, it was a decision that ultimately would cost GM dearly, as costs, price, and value combined to squeeze once-high profits into huge losses. Like IBM, General Motors was once one of the world's biggest firms, ranking fourth in the market value of its stock in 1972 and fifth in 1982—but like IBM, dropping out of sight in 1992.

One small but notable element in GM's woes was a major cost that for years was kept invisible. Labor contracts call for GM (and the other major car firms) to pay for the health benefits of its thousands of retired workers. Since those costs were to be incurred far in the future—and could only be guessed at—for years, accounting rules permitted them to be ignored. The result was billions of dollars in expenses that were not acknowledged in financial reports. Those costly chickens did ultimately came home to roost, as top managers at GM knew they would.

THE VALUE OF CREATING VALUE

Each of the three arms of the profit triangle—cost, value, price—is important to decision makers. But if pushed to the wall, managers might agree that the "value" arm is perhaps more weighty than the other two. How your business creates value probably takes precedence over how it incurs costs, because cost-cutting is pointless if the good or service that results is not valued by the market. Determining on an ongoing basis how well your business is creating value, and how you can innovate to create value in new and important ways, compared to your competitors, is a key question every business decision maker has to address. It is the decision area in which top managers have the greatest impact. Here are two examples: Diet Coke and the Sony Walkman.

In 1980, Roberto Goizueta was chosen to become Coca-Cola's CEO. In 1982, he decided to invest a large sum of capital in order to introduce Diet Coke, a product his predecessor had utterly banned. Many of his advisors told Goizueta this was folly, including his lawyers, who said he was endangering Coke's all-important copyright on its brand name. Goizueta insisted, and persisted. He felt the value in the product—the taste of Coke without its heavy content of sugar and calories—would generate large sales, at reasonable prices, that, matched against the costs, would create profit. He was right.

Diet Coke has been called "probably the most successful consumer product launch of the Eighties" and is now the world's third most popular beverage, after Classic Coke and Pepsi.[16] Partly spurred by Diet Coke, the market value of Coca-Cola stock soared from about $4 billion in 1980, when Goizueta became CEO, to $54.0 billion on March 4, 1994. Coca-Cola now has market share close to half of the global beverage market. Its Diet Coke product also has numerous imitators—the inevitable fate of a new product that creates value by innovating.

Peter Drucker once wrote that "if you see a successful business, then you know someone once made a courageous decision." Coca-Cola is today a highly successful business. Its annual 1993 sales of $14.0 billion grew by over 12 percent. It has net profit of $2.2 billion. Its stock price, as of June 30, 1993, was two-and-a-half times its level at the end of 1989.

Coca-Cola has been labelled "the world's best brand" by *Fortune* magazine. Warren Buffett—one of America's wisest and most successful corporate investors and head of Berkshire Hathaway, which owns 7 percent of Coke stock—explained why. "It sells for an extremely moderate price. It's universally liked," Buffett said.[17] And, he might have added—it doesn't cost a lot to make and distribute. Price, value, and cost became three pillars of profit for Coke.

Sony's Walkman is another example of a courageous cost-value-price decision, made in the face of experts' warning of disaster. The founder of Sony, Akio Morita, was instrumental in developing the Walkman. He was told by all his executives that the Walkman would be a costly, disastrous failure. Morita believed that while the Walkman "subtracted value"—took away features that full-scale recording and playback units had—it also *added* value, by making music fully and easily portable. The net balance of the Walkman, Morita thought, was a large value plus.

"I do not believe any amount of market research could have told us that the Sony Walkman would be successful," Morita wrote in his autobiography. And it *was* successful. Sony made more than 70 different models, and sold more than 20 million units.[18]

One of the lessons Morita draws from his own experience is the importance to Sony of having its own sales and distribution network, so that "we could get to know [our customers] personally and make them understand the value of our products and the uses to which they could be put." In some ways, knowing costs is easier than knowing values, because costs are objective and data-based, while values are highly subjective and not easy even for consumers themselves to express or define. Both Goizueta and Morita had deep insights into the perceived *value* of their products, and as a result were able to make courageous, fateful decisions. One way or another, decision makers have to find ways to plug directly into the perceptions and psychology of their customers. Even the most thorough market-research studies do not always achieve this insight, especially when new products are involved that consumers have no real experience with.[19]

WHAT BUSINESS AM I IN?

Harvard Business School Professor Theodore Levitt, an expert in marketing and former editor of the *Harvard Business Review,* once wrote a famous article titled "Marketing Myopia." In it, he explained why railroad companies and Hollywood film companies shared a common fate—gallons of red ink and for some, bankruptcy and extinction.

What did railroad executives and movie magnates both do wrong? Perhaps, Levitt wrote, they failed to ask themselves a key question, one that can never be asked too often or too fervently: *What business am I in?*

Movies and railroads skidded downhill rapidly, because the managers who ran them failed to ask, and answer correctly, Levitt's question.

Hollywood moguls thought they were in the movie business, instead of in the entertainment business. Television, a new form of entertainment—and later cable TV and videorecorders, nearly buried them, because in the industry of "entertainment value," television proved to be an inexpensive and convenient substitute for movies.

Railroad executives assumed complacently that they were in the railroad business. In fact, they were in the business of creating value by transporting people and goods. So were truckers and airlines. Their stiff competition, with some help from public policy, killed the railroads.

Paraphrased loosely, "what business am I in?" breaks down into several others:

- What are my customers' needs and how are they changing?
- How well does my product meet those needs, compared to its competitors?
- What price can my product command for its need-satisfying value?
- At what cost can I produce that value?

High-value products and services that command premium prices can compensate for excessive costs. But even bare-bones costs will not enable a company to survive, if its products fail to create adequate value for customers in the marketplace.

Oscar Wilde once defined a cynic as "someone who knows the price of everything and the value of nothing." Managers are no cynics. They need to know the value of their products, the cost of producing them, and the price those products can command in the marketplace, and to constantly challenge their perceptions by confronting them with new, direct evidence and accurate concise information. Good management is a perpetual juggling act in which cost, price, and value are kept in an appropriate balance, with a sharp eye focused on trends and change that might in the near and distant future alter that balance, for good or for ill.

Chapter Two

HIDDEN COSTS

Memo to managers: I do not know you, nor do I know what business you are in. But I do know one thing. *Some of your highest ongoing costs are for things you already bought and paid for.*

No one ever writes a check for these hidden costs. Nor do they appear in financial statements. Still, wise executives take them into account and treat them as if they were real—because they are. If you fail to do so, you are in major trouble.

If you own buildings, factories, a head office, you have hidden costs, even if you own all those assets outright and debt-free. If you use the capital of your shareholders, you also face hidden costs, because using that capital is costly, even if you never formally pay a cent for its current use. If you use your own time and the time of others, you incur hidden costs, because—trite but true—time is indeed money, and its use is often expensive though not explicitly paid for.

Take Coca-Cola as an example. In the 1980's, Coca-Cola's CEO Roberto Goizueta re-evaluated Coke's various businesses—concentrate, bottling, wine, foods, coffee, tea, industrial water treatment, and aquaculture. Goizueta examined the costs of each business and its value to Coca-Cola. He began by asking: What businesses *are* we in now?—his answer was: far too many unprofitable ones—and: What business *should* we be in?—his answer was: the beverage business. The subsequent strategy Coca-Cola adopted was focused on building Coca-Cola as a profitable, global beverage company.

Implementing that strategy—deciding which parts of Coke's business to sell and which to retain—made use of the economic definition of costs. It was that definition that revealed which of Coca-Cola's businesses or divisions should be sold or shut down, and which should be kept and expanded. It was an exercise in applied cost-value logic.

COST AS LOST OPPORTUNITY

Economists have a curious way of defining and measuring costs. Rather than ask: What does it cost me? or How much do I have to pay for it? economists insist on costing things by framing the question as, *What do I have to give up in order to get it?* This rather strange phrasing, it turns out, has great analytic power for those who make regular use of it. All true costs are lost opportunities of one sort or another, but not all lost opportunities show up on a check stub. Some costs are exceedingly good at hiding.

In order to distinguish between the more general, loose usage of the term "cost" and their own, more precise way of defining it, economics use the term "opportunity cost"—the cost of lost opportunities. Opportunity cost—what you have to give up in order to get something else—is a very important notion in financial markets and investing. As business writer Susan Lee explains:

> At first blush, the concept of opportunity cost appears silly. Obviously, when one invests $1,000 in stock A, one cannot then turn around and invest the same $1,000 in stock B. Nonetheless, if the act of giving up B in favor of A is not a matter of whim, then there must be some basis on which investors decide between the two alternatives. There is. It's called opportunity cost.
>
> Take the earnings of a firm. Management can either pay it out to shareholders in the form of dividends or keep it to reinvest in the company. Presumably, management decides what to do by figuring out

the opportunity cost of reinvesting the earnings. If the company can use the money for projects which will earn 10 percent while the best return its stockholders can earn investing in projects with similar risk is 8 percent, then management will be doing stockholders a financial favor by retaining the earnings. If not, of course, management should pay the earnings in dividends so the shareholders can earn a higher return investing in other things.[1]

The same logic that assigns an opportunity cost to money also puts a cost on space. Suppose a dozen square yards of floor space in a factory can produce an item, X, that generates $100 in profit. Suppose also you are using that space to make a different product, Y. That $100 in foregone profit is a hidden cost in making Y, because it is profit that is foregone. It is hidden because no one writes a check for it, nor do accounting principles require one to list it in profit-and-loss statements. In fact, accountants in general are rightly allergic to imaginary "what if" calculations. Their job is to measure reality. But managers, in their decision making, need to reveal what accountants may unwittingly conceal.

Like so many economic tools, the notion of opportunity cost seems much too simple-minded to be useful or meaningful. But often it is the simplest ideas that are overlooked. To see this, ask yourself, Would anyone operate businesses that earn, say, 8 or 10 percent on invested capital, if that same capital could earn, for instance, 16 percent in another business with comparable risk?

Coca-Cola apparently did, unaware its capital cost more than it earned. Coca-Cola prided itself on a balance sheet that was nearly debt-free. As a result, Coke paid virtually no interest on money it had borrowed from banks. It got its capital from its shareholders, so-called "equity" capital, meaning capital that entails ownership, rather than debt. But Coke's shareholders were not obligated to leave their money in Coke. If their investment was not profitable, they could take their money and invest it elsewhere. One of Goizueta's changes was to emphasize the crucial importance of building profits for Coke's shareholders. He calculated that the opportunity cost of shareholder equity capital was a 16 percent rate of return. This is what the capital invested in Coke could have earned in other investments. But, he was surprised to learn, "all its businesses except soft drinks and juices returned only 8 percent to 10 percent a year."

"We were liquidating our business," he commented, "borrowing money at 16 and investing it at eight. You can't do that forever."[2]

Borrowing money? From whom? Apparently, from shareholders—even though that money was not in strict terms a loan. Shareholders had an alternative. They could put their money elsewhere at an estimated 16 percent return. The treasurer of Coke did not write an annual check amounting to 16 percent of its equity capital, but the cost was nonetheless as real as if he did. A quick calculation reveals that if Coca-Cola's shareholder capital costs 16 percent a year, but earns only 8 percent, that capital shrinks by one-third in five years and by one-half in eight years.

Why is it often so hard to tell that capital is shrinking? In part, because it is not really contracting, simply growing much more slowly than it should. Capital that earns 8 percent a year, with profits reinvested, doubles itself every 9 years or so. Capital that earns 16 percent doubles itself roughly twice as fast, about every 4.5 years.[3] Hence, Coke's capital was doubling itself only once every 9 years, instead of twice. It was losing a full doubling, hence was half of what it could and should have been.

In this sense, Goizueta was right—Coca-Cola was liquidating its business, by liquidating its capital. His solution was first, to sell off those businesses whose capital made a lower return—i.e. less than 16 per cent—than it cost, and second, introduce a system of accounting in which every operating division of Coca-Cola knew precisely its *economic profit*. What he meant by economic profit was sales revenues minus operating costs, including an opportunity-cost charge for capital. Those divisions earning a 16 percent return on their shareholder's capital were told that their *economic* profit was zero. And each division's operations were judged solely on the basis of the *economic* profit it earned.

That economic profit, as division heads learned to their chagrin, is often decidedly different from accounting profit. Accounting profit depreciates capital based on formulas from the tax laws. There may be little relation between the true cost of capital for a company and the costs that tax laws permit it to charge itself. A financial system that forced managers to charge themselves for the true costs of capital was what Goizueta eventually put in place.

While tax law makes companies compute their accounting profits based on depreciation formulas, no law forces managers to use this sometimes misleading measure as a decision tool, nor forbids them from looking closely at economic profit and exhorting their subordinates to do the same. The results of doing so at Coca-Cola were not slow in coming. "When you start charging people for their capital," Goizueta said, "all sorts of things happen. All of a sudden inventories get under control. You don't have three months' concentrate sitting around for an emergency. Or you figure out that you can save a lot of money by replacing stainless-steel containers with cardboard and plastic."

Goizueta's approach was not to try to *make* all decisions about the use of capital, but to structure the decision-making process of others to achieve the right result. Increasingly, in the new era of "looser" corporations, with flexible or nonexistent hierarchies and less rigid control systems, it is up to managers to create incentives that help *others* to choose well, rather than focus solely on the quality of their own choices.

As will be shown throughout this book, when cost-value logic is applied, and when proper numbers are attached to costs, incentives are created to economize on valuable resource—in Coca-Cola's case, capital. This is not qualitatively different, incidentally, from the abuse of our land, air and water, whose use is seemingly free but whose hidden opportunity costs—imposed on future generations—are very large.

HOW LOCKHEED LOOKED...AND LEAPED

The two functions of managers, Peter Drucker once wrote, are marketing and innovation—selling existing products and developing new ones. Not only current operations—marketing—face opportunity costs of capital. So do decisions about large, chancy future-oriented investments—innovation. Few business decisions are as difficult, as risky and as crucial as the decision to spend large sums of money to do basic and applied research and then to proceed to launch a product or process based on the fruits of that research. The vast majority of new products fail to return a profit.

Many companies pay for Research and Development with their own, internal funds, known as retained earnings, or profits that are retained in the company rather than distributed to shareholders.[4]

In the United States, in normal times about 85 percent of corporate investment is paid for out of undistributed profits and only 15 percent from borrowing. Such internal funds involve no payment of interest or dividends, to banks or other lenders. No checks are written to pay for the use of this capital. But opportunity-cost reasoning requires managers to ask, what *could* have been earned with this money in alternate uses, if it were *not* put into this or that project.

A billion-dollar decision of this sort faced Roy Anderson, then chairman of Lockheed Corp., a large aircraft, aerospace, and defense manufacturer, in 1967. Anderson had to decide whether to invest a billion dollars of Lockheed's money, a good part it from retained earnings, to carry out research, development, testing, and evaluation of a new widebody civilian aircraft, to be known as the L-1011 Tristar.

Long before something as complex as a modern jetliner can be built, huge resources must be invested to design it and test a prototype. When Lockheed decided in 1967–68 to go ahead with the L-1011 Tristar project, the first widebody airliner, the cost of R&D was estimated at about $1 billion. It was to be spent at a rate of about $200 million a year during the approximately four-and-one-half years needed to complete all the preparatory stages prior to making the first production model.

Had Lockheed paid for the L-1011 R&D *entirely* from its retained earnings (which it didn't; part was borrowed) would the funds have cost Lockheed nothing? No. If Lockheed had invested the $1 billion in risk-free assets, like 10-year Treasury bonds, it could have made 6.67 percent interest in 1969 or about $67 million a year.[5] That profit had to be weighed against, and compared with, the potential profit from designing, manufacturing, and selling aircraft. By borrowing its own money, Lockheed lost the opportunity to lend it to others and earn interest. The interest foregone, while not an out-of-pocket cost, is a hidden but real opportunity cost and must be taken into account when judging how retained earnings should be used.

It is sometimes claimed that high interest rates do not discourage corporate investment, because most such investment is financed through the firm's own profits on which no interest is paid. However, companies that use the right cost-value choice framework know that higher interest rates mean bigger "foregone-income" costs for using their own funds. To be worthwhile, therefore, investment projects have to be more profitable. Like a high-jump competition, as the interest-rate bar is raised higher and higher, more and more contestants fail to leap it and fewer and fewer projects are profitable enough to vault the hurdle that higher interest rates create. In 1981–82, when U.S. interest rates reached record highs, almost no long-range investment projects at all could justify the high opportunity cost of the funds they required. It was much safer and easier to sink the money into the capital market and pocket a secure, high return.

When alternate financial returns are high and tempting, in comparison with operating profits, companies seek executive expertise and talent in manipulating money, rather than in making and marketing new products and in improving existing ones, because profits from financial investments come to dominate those from R&D and manufacturing. And as fewer and fewer executives with engineering and manufacturing expertise hold top positions, more and more decisions about complex technologies and products come to be made by managers unfamiliar with them. Some writers have laid the blame for the decline in America's manufacturing competitiveness precisely at the doorstep of this process. Between the early 1950s and mid-to-late 1960s, the number of corporate presidents whose origins were in financial and legal professions grew by about half, faster than any other functional expertise.[6] Even today, finance and accounting remain the surest route to the CEO's chair—21 percent of America's top 1,000 CEOs chose it.[7] Ultimately, companies come to be run by persons who are unfamiliar with its core technology, and hence are leery about making risky decisions to develop or acquire expensive new technologies. A bias develops against innovation, especially in production processes, that can make businesses overly conservative and old-fashioned.

The solution, however, is not to foster a new ignorance of finance! Instead, innovation requires at least two things: low interest rates, and skill at sensing and creating new value-creating products. Managers are correct to compute opportunity costs and to avoid innovation when its risks and costs far outweigh the benefits.

Sometimes, *hidden* opportunity costs become costly *overt* ones, as owners of "property rights" discover their value and charge for them. This can happen when, for instance, people who live near baseball parks charge people for parking on their lawn, or when a supermarket manager charges companies for the opportunity of occupying shelf space in his store with their products. This happened to Caroline and her chocolate chip cookies.

CAROLINE'S COOKIES VS. A&P

Like many other mothers, Caroline baked excellent chocolate-chip cookies. "You ought to make these for sale," her family told her. "You could make a fortune." Unlike many mothers who were told the same thing, Caroline took up the challenge. She turned her chocolate-chip cookies into a successful business—Cookies by Caroline—baking, packaging, and distributing them to specialty food shops mainly in the Midwestern United States. Her cookies gave good value at modest cost and price.

In Caroline's marketing plan, the next stage was to get her cookies onto the shelves in major supermarkets. She knew that of the more than $300 billion worth of food sold every year in the United States, all but 6 percent of it was sold in supermarkets.

But Caroline ran into an obstacle, a practice known as "slotting." She found that supermarkets charged a stiff fee for giving some new products slots on their shelves. Shnicks in St. Louis wanted $3,000 for each new item they put on display. Lucky wanted $7,000 - $10,000. A&P in New York City wanted $25,000. To make the "slotting" pill even harder to swallow, some stores charged "failure fees"—companies had to buy back unsold items at their retail price. On national television—*60 Minutes*—Caroline screamed "foul!" She couldn't afford the fees, she said, and they severely limited the ability of smaller companies like hers to compete nationally with bigger, established firms.

Is "slotting" a justifiable practice? Should supermarkets be allowed to charge slotting fees? Generally, viewer sympathies lay with Caroline, the small underdog grappling with large supermarket chains. But here is how a supermarket manager might frame his or her response to Caroline's anger:

> I run a good store. Each yard of shelf space in my store generates about $10,000 in sales every week! If I put a new product on a yard's worth of shelf space, and if it fails to sell well, I lose those $10,000 in sales. That is a real cost to me, just as if I had taken the money out of the safe or written a check. It is still a cost even if I get the new product for nothing, or sell it on consignment (payment for it made only after it is sold). It is a cost, because sales are *foregone* or lost— the opportunity to sell $10,000 worth of goods—when I put, for example, Caroline's cookies on the shelf instead of some other, more familiar brand. So in asking for that $10,000, all I am doing is trying to cover my own real (though not out-of-pocket) costs. This is not playing Monopoly!

Caroline learned that hidden costs sometimes become very costly, prominent, and real ones. The supermarkets' charging for shelf space was as if Coca-Cola's shareholders had all voted to sell their shares and put their money elsewhere, if Coke did not get rid of divisions that failed to reach a 16 percent rate of return on shareholder's capital. Taking hidden, opportunity costs into account in decision making makes better businesses—despite *60 Minutes'* emotional account of Caroline's shelfless cookies.

To measure true costs, you have to be good at "what-if" thinking, by always imagining and calculating what *could* have been. Managers must ask, if I *do* undertake Project A, or if I do put Caroline's Cookies on the shelf, what am I giving up? What *could* have been had I chosen Project B? What *could* have been had I kept Plain Old Chocolate-Chip Cookies on the shelf? Imaginary scenarios are sometimes anathema to cost accountants, whose job is to measure the actual costs represented by money paid out, in the most objective and accurate manner possible. But to economists, they are very real, and they should be to managers as well.

In a profession as hardheaded and number-crunching as management, playing "what-could-have-been" games seems more appropriate for, say, Peter Pan than for Peter Drucker. Yet expertise in this approach to measuring true costs is one of the acid tests of economic thinking. The constant weighing of opportunities, especially lost ones, is a litmus test of logical cost-value decision making.

One of the most prominent sources of hidden costs is buildings that companies own rather than rent. For the average company in America, the next-to-largest cost of doing business is so-called "occupancy costs"—the cost of occupying the office space, warehouses, and factories they use. (The largest single cost item is usually labor and other direct production costs.) If the company *rents* its space, those costs appear explicitly in cost statements. But suppose the company *owns* all its buildings. If so, it does not have to pay rent at all. Does that mean it has no occupancy costs?

Applying the idea of "foregone income"—what *could* have been—supplies the right answer: Not at all! If the company were to rent out its buildings, it could earn income. By using the buildings for itself, it *foregoes* that income. That makes owner-occupied buildings as true and substantive a cost as if the company were to pay that amount outright in rent.

Many companies do not properly manage their property assets. One reason is that the cost of occupying them is hidden. Managers should carefully consider whether the asset value of company-owned buildings could be better used in alternate ways—say, by selling the buildings, renting similar space, and using the proceeds from the sale for new equipment or Research and Development. When capital is scarce and hard to get, it is hard to justify locking it up in a building, whose contribution to company revenues is often very indirect.

Some well-managed companies—Reebok, a shoe manufacturer, is one—are built on the strategy of not tying up their capital in relatively unproductive fixed assets like factories. Reebok found they could contract with plants to make their shoes, picking and choosing among the highest-quality, lowest-cost producers in a dozen or more countries. They are so-called "agile manufacturers." Their capital is put to best use in such areas as shoe design and marketing. Such firms treat capital as far too precious to sink into the ground—and, indeed, it often is.

Of course, there are tax advantages in renting rather than owning. Rent, an explicit cost, is a business expense deductible from revenue in computing corporate tax, but "implicit" rent, or foregone income, is generally not. This should not be ignored. The leasing industry has mushroomed in part because of similar tax advantages.

Just as businesses should charge themselves the opportunity cost of using their own buildings, so should individual households who own their own homes. If a home-owning family were to sell its home and instead pay rent, the monthly payment—often, a quarter or more of household income—would be an obvious, apparent cost of living. Owning a home does not *eliminate* housing costs but simply alters their nature— they now arise through rent payments that *could be* earned if the house were rented to another family instead of owner-occupied. Perhaps, instead of owning your home outright, you should sell it, invest the proceeds, and rent another house. If your investment pays your rent with money to spare, you may be better off renting than buying. The government understands this calculation—the accounting system that adds up the nation's total output of goods and services takes into account the "imputed value of rents for owner-occupied homes." "Spending" on rent by those who own their own dwellings is over 10 percent of total consumption spending for the United States.

About 60 percent of American families own their own home or apartment—a higher percentage than in almost any other country. One reason, a good one, is that owning a home has traditionally been one of the best investments—housing prices rose rapidly for two or three decades before collapsing in the mid-to-late 1980s. But another reason, equally valid, is simply that American families, not unlike American corporations, like the security, comfort, and prestige of owning their own place, instead of renting. But even when the "intangible" benefits of home ownership tip the scale in favor of buying a house, the hidden costs have to be carefully considered, too.

"Rent" has a different meaning to economists than its use in everyday language. " Rent," in common speech, is what we pay every month for the right to occupy a house, apartment, or office space. But for economists, *economic rent* is an opportunity cost, a *what-could-have-been* calculation. It is the difference between what labor or capital are *actually* earning and the most they could earn when used in some other place or company or investment.

Economic rents arise only if labor or capital creates some added value in its current use *beyond what it could create elsewhere.* For example, a large part of a free agent baseball player's salary, $2 or $3 million a year, may be rent, stemming from the player's particular skills that draw crowds and TV viewers; what the player could earn as, say, a sales manager or rancher, is likely much less.

The price of a company's shares is not unlike the salary-rent of Boston Red Sox pitcher Roger Clemens—the larger the rents the company's executives generate, by smart management, the higher the price of the stock, just as the greater Clemens's value (as an outstanding crowd-drawing pitcher) the higher his salary. Buyers seek to purchase the stock (instead of other company's stock) and its price rises, because the stock earns returns beyond what capital is able to earn elsewhere. If indeed the job of managers is to make decisions that create the highest possible price for the company's stock in the long run, then economic rents may be the correct way to measure how profitable a company really is.

How can a company's economic rents be measured? In essence, that is what Goizueta implemented at Coca-Cola, by asking divisions to charge themselves for the company's capital at the opportunity-cost rate. A similar method proposed by Evan Davis and John Kay (in *Business Strategy Review,* Summer 1990) can be used to better measure economic performance.

Their study uses as an example the British supermarket chain Sainsbury. The company's operating assets—its buildings, trucks, etc.—could have been sold for £ 2,624 million in 1988–89. On these assets, it made operating profits of £ 369 million for that year.

If it had sold its assets and invested the proceeds, Sainsbury could have earned interest. Using 10.8 percent as the interest rate (in 1988–89 that was the yield on long-term U.K. government bonds), the opportunity cost of *using* (rather than selling and investing) its assets amounted to £ 283 million:

$$10.8 \text{ percent} \times £ 2,624 \text{ m.} = £ 283 \text{ m.}$$

Therefore, the economic rent earned by Sainsbury was the

difference between the opportunity cost of its assets and the profit they actually earned:

$$\text{Operating Profit} - \text{Opportunity Cost} = \text{Economic Rent}$$
$$£ 369m. - £ 283m. = £ 86m.$$

Sainsbury therefore earned an economic rent of £ 86 million. It spent £ 889 m. on payments to its labor and capital. Measured as a percentage, or rate of return, Sainsbury's economic rents came to nearly 10 percent of its input costs:

$$£ 86 m. / £ 889 = 9.7 \text{ percent}$$

Using standard measures of profitability—say, operating profit as a percent of assets—Sainsbury was no more profitable than its competitor, Gateway. Both earned a 21 percent rate of return. But Gateway *used* its assets less well. Its economic rents, as a percent of spending on labor and capital, came to only 4 percent, compared to Sainsbury's 9.7 percent. One supermarket chain, Asda, had negative economic rents—implying it could have made more money by selling and investing its assets than by using them to retail food. Using this calculation is another yardstick for measuring managers' performance, in addition to the return on management one outlined in chapter 1. Using it, it is clear that Sainsbury's managers made decisions that utilized the company's labor and capital assets better than its competitors. Standard rate-of-return measures would not have revealed this.

If a business wants to sell or shrink divisions, *it should select the one that makes the lowest contribution to company rents,* Davis and Kay argue. (This is precisely what Goizueta did at Coca-Cola). To compare its performance with that of its competitors, a company should look at rents per dollar of spending on labor and capital. If incentive systems are to be implemented, linking pay to performance, then it should be linked to rents, not accounting profits or returns on assets or sales.

TIME IS MONEY

Hidden-cost thinking applies not only to money expenditures but also to how we spend our time. For a harried executive, time is often a scarcer resource than money, and allocating it properly can be crucially important. When considering whether or not to acquire another company, executives take into account not only the outright purchase price and what the acquired company will add to sales and profits, but also the managerial time required to fully integrate the new company with the old one—time that comes at the expense of other pressing matters.

The slogan "time is money" originated with Benjamin Franklin. It is sometimes linked closely with American culture and life-style. Americans—in the eyes of foreigners at least—have a taste for haste, both at work and at play. At work, large amounts of resources can be squandered, simply because they are spent as wasted time rather than as wasted money. A good example is the corporate meeting. Just how costly meetings can be is shown by the following cost–value computation. Paul Strassman estimates that a typical corporate staff meeting involves a dozen persons. The time invested by the meeting's initiator can easily cost $4,000. The time-cost of organizing the meeting runs around $1,000. Participants' time is worth $7,000. Total cost is thus $13,000, or, for an hour-long meeting, $55 a minute. "A manufacturing firm would have to earn incremental revenues of at least $150,000 to generate sufficient gross margin to cover these costs," Strassman claims.[8] How many meetings generate added-value equal to $150,000 more in revenues?

He describes software known as the Meeting Meter that registers the cost per hour of a meeting, as well as its elapsed minutes and total cost. His own all-time Meeting Meter record was an address he gave to 2,300 partners at the world's largest auditing and consulting firm. Each partner's time was worth $300 per hour, plus 20 percent for expenses—a total of $13,800 per minute for the entire audience. It was difficult, Strassman wrote, to be worth that. Assuming that he spoke at a rate of 120 words a minute, each word cost $115.

Meetings are not the only source of hugely expensive time. Consider higher education.

Many students and their parents struggle under the high cost of college tuition and related expenses. These costs are highly visible, being "out-of-pocket" ones that diminish our bank balances. Yet the biggest investment in college, for both individuals and society, is *not* the "out-of-pocket" tuition and living expenses they incur, but in fact the foregone income—wages that could be earned but are not, because of attending college full-time or part-time.

Some $100 billion is spent annually *out of pocket* on higher education in the United States, but the foregone-earnings cost for some 13 million college students is at least double that amount. (See table 2.1.) This is true even if we assume that college-eligible 18–22-year-olds without college experience would earn as little as $20,000 a year, or $12,500 for part-time jobs.

That $213 billion cost represents income and output that *could be* produced, but isn't, and it is a net loss both for the individual and for society. Students are of course keenly aware of this cost. Yet it does not appear explicitly in any budget or in any official reckoning of national investment.⁹

Does the resulting $213 billion opportunity cost of higher education mean that college is three times more expensive than we realized? Yes. Does it mean that we should close our colleges? Obviously not. It just means that students should—and generally do—compute what they can earn with and without degrees and consider all the costs, including foregone income, before they decide how much schooling to pursue.

Is the cost of colleges to society worth it? The value of investing in higher education is, for the individual, partly the higher income it will bring in future years; and for society, partly the higher output that higher education makes possible, in the future. University of Chicago Professor Gary Becker, a Nobel Laureate, has pioneered the concept of "investment in human capital." He and his colleagues have shown that such investment, including the cost of foregone income, usually pays a high social rate of return.

The cost of tuition at top private universities now exceeds $20,000 per annum. According to Peter Drucker, if "financial aid" is taken into account (a fancy word for price discounts, Drucker notes), true tuition is about $11,000. While that is a large sum for most students, it is substantially less than the opportunity cost of foregone income—what the student could earn if he or she went to work rather than study for that year. College is expensive not just because of tuition, but principally because it requires a major

TABLE 2.1
Opportunity Costs of Higher Education

7.2 million full-time students times foregone earnings per student (about $20,000/yr)......................................$144 billion
5.5 million part-time students times foregone earnings per student (about $12,500/yr)....................................<u>$ 69 billion</u>
Total: ....$213 billion

investment of time—and time is indeed money, the money foregone because human capital is being produced rather than goods and services.

Many decision makers fail to take opportunity costs into account. As a result, good projects are sometimes turned down wrongly; and bad projects get continual funding, when they deserve prompt euthanasia. According to business columnist Michael Schrage, "as top management will confirm, the only task more difficult and expensive than launching an innovation in a Fortune 500 company is killing one in its tracks."

"Killing projects?" snorts former Colgate-Palmolive Co. research chief Jules Blake. "It's easier to kill the chemist." Wishful thinking? Harold Geneen, the iron-fisted conglomerateur who ran ITT Corp. actually hired globe-trotting engineers to visit the company's labs with the express mission to snuff out any and all research activity in computers. Geneen didn't want to take the chance that some brilliant technologist would figure out a way to drag ITT into direct competition with International Business Machines Corp. Geneen intuitively understood that the research you avoid can be more important than the research you do....The smartest thing that most corporations could do today to take up their R&D people would be to institute a rule that people can't launch a research effort without eliminating an existing one....The point is to force people to set priorities not just on their budgets but also on their time. ..."At the margin, everyone wins if a project is funded," says McKinsey & Co.'s Lawrence H. Linden, co-leader of the consulting firm's technology management practice. "So people take the easy way out....That process runs amok and too many projects get funded.

... If you're really good in research or development, you can always get tantalizing data. *Building in mechanisms that force people to justify their tradeoffs* is the best way to get people to face up to the fact that tantalizing data may whet their personal curiosity, but they don't generate tangible results."[10]

There are two major sins linked to hidden costs. Both are serious and if they persist and are large in magnitude, can be murderous to the health of a business. One sin is that of ignoring hidden costs when they are real. A second sin is the opposite—treating costs as if they were real and large when in fact they are zero. The business application of cost-value logic demands that neither sin be committed. If bad decisions are made in ignoring hidden costs, perhaps as many are made in treating nonexistent costs—money already spent—as if they were still real and significant.

One reason bad projects die a hard death is because of the pervasive influence of sunk costs. Sunk costs measure money that has already been spent, but rather than treating it as water under the bridge, executives often pretend that they can and will recover revenues from them. They refuse to let go, becoming captives of spent money which is only a part of history and of no relevance in the present and future. Sunk costs are utterly without relevance for forward-looking decisions that ask, as they should: What will the project cost *from now to completion* and what will it be worth *from now to completion?* The same logic that demands that we take into account lost opportunities, insists that we ignore resources whose opportunities are all dead and buried. Sunk costs are the business equivalent of guilt—one ought to be aware of the past, but its influence on future decisions should be carefully limited.

Many executives endure the pain of both these contradictory ailments. They are blithely unaware of large hidden opportunity costs, yet at the same time are powerfully influenced by the magnitude of sunk costs. Why is this so?

Consider this example. Your company has spent millions on an R&D project to develop a tasty, high-protein meat substitute. But the resulting product is dubious. Market research suggests it is a loser. Nonetheless you decide to produce it and try to sell it. Faced with similar choices, many managers would do the same. To do otherwise would be to admit a bad decision or to admit the investment was a total loss. That hurts.

But throwing good money after bad in continuing a risky project long after it is demonstrably a failure is a compound problem. To do so is to ignore the opportunities lost for the good money, on top of refusing to admit the bad money's loss, in tossing even more money after it. This is a special case of a psychological phenomenon common in capital markets—investors are willing to accept large, unjustified risks in order to avoid losses, when those same investors are loathe to take risks in order to pile up large gains. For instance, many investors sell far too long after it is clear than an investment in stocks has not paid off and should be sold off. Such a sale involves admission of error and loss, with attendant psychic pain.

SUNK COSTS AND TENNIS ELBOW

Cornell University economist Richard Thaler has a persuasive explanation why sunk costs, which logically and rationally are irrelevant, play so large a role in many business decisions. Consider the person who develops a tennis elbow soon after paying a stiff nonrefundable membership fee to an exclusive tennis club. Chances are, Thaler argues, he will continue to play despite the agony. Were it not for having paid the high fee, he would gladly choose not to play and avoid the pain. Where, then, is the gain in playing? Thaler believes that playing and suffering pain avoids the admission that the membership fee is a total loss. The agony of accepting loss may be much worse than the ache of the elbow. Sunk costs are the business equivalent of the high membership fee.[11] If you paid, then you play, even with pain.

Decisions about aircraft seem particularly susceptible to this variety of corporate tennis elbow. Aided by a $250-million loan guarantee narrowly approved by Congress, Lockheed decided in 1971–72 to take the plunge and put the L-1011 Tristar into production, despite fairly strong evidence that the plane would never make money. The plane was technically first-rate, but had little chance of breaking even in a fierce struggle for a limited market against two similar competing planes—the DC-10 and Airbus

A300. The $1 billion entry fee Lockheed paid during 42 months of Research and Development became a powerful argument for going ahead with the project, even though it was a sunk cost, incurred in the past, and not relevant for the appropriate cost-value decision that asked: How much will it cost us to produce Tristars in the future, and how many will we sell? The stock market saw the dilemma accurately. Lockheed's stock plummeted from about $70 in 1967 to less than $10 in mid-1970.[12]

One solution to the destructive effective of sunk costs on decision making is what has been called by Barry Staw and Jerry Ross, the "experimenting organization," in which "managers...consider all ventures imperfect and subject to question....Every program should be subject to regular reconsideration (a la zero-based budgeting) and every line of business should be up for sale at the right price... when a market or a technology changes, the experimenting organization would not simply try to patch up the old product or plant but would be quick to see when it is best to pull the plug and start anew."

The movie business is an extreme example of the dominance of sunk costs. It takes about two years to make a movie, from the initial script to its first showing. The average U.S. production cost is $20 million. It takes another $7 million to market and distribute the film in the United States, and about another $3 million to cover the movie studio's overhead costs. All of that $30 million is a sunk cost—money paid out before the first viewer buys the first ticket. It does not change whether the movie in future earns $1 million, $10 million, or $100 million.

Only one movie in five earns back its sunk cost through box office sales; additional revenue trickles in from television, cable TV, and ancillary revenues like video sales. Generally exhibitors (movie theatre owners) keep half of a movie's average $30 million in ticket sales, and movie studios get $13 million, of which more than half goes to marketing costs. Only two movies in every five make a profit. Rarely, movies earn huge profits. *Batman* cost $75 million and earned $1 billion in total revenue.[13]

Should movies with huge sunk costs be promoted and advertised more heavily than cheaper ones? Not at all. What matters is the future prospects of the movie in generating revenue and the ability to enhance those revenues through heavy promotion. This need not be related to what was spent in the past on making the movie.

Often, companies themselves unwittingly enhance the importance of sunk costs by stiffly penalizing failure. The result often is a " decision to persevere, [when] good management consists of knowing when to pull the plug."

"... Because a strong fear of failure can cause overcommitment (to losing projects), management is better off setting only a moderate cost for failure," Staw and Ross note, "something to avoid but not to fear intensely." Otherwise, losing projects—or movies— may draw excessive continuing investments. They describe a large computer company that puts erring managers into a "penalty box" for up to a year, where they are ineligible for major new assignments. After their penalty expires, they are restored to full status.[14]

Managers need two kinds of wisdom. They need the perceptiveness to take into account hidden costs when they exist, especially for resources already bought and paid for. They need the courage and honesty to write off visible sunk costs, and henceforth totally ignore them, when they exist, again especially for resources or products long ago bought and paid for, often at high cost.

And they need the common sense to know the difference.

Chapter Three

TRADEOFFS

Pain versus Gain

"There is no gain without pain."
— Adlai Stevenson

Tradeoffs—giving up something in order to get something else—
are the mother of all opportunity costs. They lie at the heart of the
executive's job. And they are something of a paradox. The more
successful you are, the greater the opportunity costs you face. In
fact, success is measured by how well executives *create* this very
thing that haunts and torments them.

Every executive faces two tasks. First: to work with courage,
skill, perseverance, and creativity to *create* tradeoffs where none
presently exist. If you face no tradeoffs, your company is poorly
managed. If you don't have to settle for less of one thing, to get
more of another, then it follows you could have more of everything if you just managed or organized affairs better. That, in turn,
means there is much fat and slack in the system, which need to be
eliminated. Second: to manage those tradeoffs in the best possible
way, balancing gain and pain in a manner that leaves your business
best off, with the most gain for the least pain.

The textbook cliché for tradeoffs is "guns... or butter." "Fewer
guns could mean a whole lot more butter," a *BusinessWeek* article

headline stated, in mid-1989. "By eliminating missiles and demobilizing troops, America could reap a sizeable peace dividend by the year 2000."[1] President Ronald Reagan had earlier promised to increase defense spending to match the USSR's $300 billion defense budget. And he had kept his word. America's 1981–85 military buildup created over 7 million defense-related jobs. The United States reached parity in defense spending with the USSR in about 1987. Slight reductions in domestic spending and a lot higher arms spending caused a growing deficit.

Tradeoffs have a time dimension attached to them. Now that the arms race has ended, defense spending is being cut sharply in America. Shifting workers from defense-related plants to civilian ones—butter factories?—takes a long time. Meanwhile, as some economists have noted, the main peace dividend—not only in America—has so far been unemployment.

Managing tradeoffs can involve painful decisions about other people's lives, and can require rapid changes in perspectives and ways of thinking. Consider, as an example, the once-vaunted Japanese efficiency. As a matter of management policy Japanese firms have been reluctant to lay off workers during hard times. They have traded the inflexibility of "lifetime" employment for the greater loyalty and motivation it creates. As a result, by one estimate Japanese companies currently harbor a million hidden unemployed—workers who add nothing to company output but nonetheless draw pay. Many of those million workers are in Japan's least efficient sectors—banking, finance, and real estate.[2] Some are in management jobs and are called "madogiwa-zoku"—those who stare out the window. (They have counterparts in every country; were it not for ignominy, they could form perhaps the world's largest trade union.)

Japan's official unemployment rate was 2.9 percent of its labor force in Dec. 1993, up from 2.4 percent a year earlier. Adding the "hidden unemployed" to the jobless rolls would raise that rate to 4 percent or more. Some Japanese firms have found it worthwhile to pay workers 90 percent of their regular salaries—in return for *not* coming to work—just to prevent the demoralizing effect of having on-the-job unemployed, staring out windows around the office or the factory. Their presence in a company implies that, for instance, expanding one profitable product line need not necessarily come at the expense of reducing another product line—there are more than enough workers to do both. This absence of tradeoffs may sound attractive to managers, but it isn't and ought not to be. When there are no painful tradeoffs to consider, then there are idle, wasted resources, those that yield no value in return for what they cost.

THE ECONOMIC NOTION OF EFFICIENCY

The task of creating tradeoffs and *managing* them are both related to the economic notion of efficiency. Each task involves a different concept of efficiency, focusing on a different sort of management skill. In the first case, managers get rid of waste. In the second case, they make tradeoff choices. After explaining the relationship of each task to the economics of efficiency, we will concentrate on the tough job of making tradeoff decisions.

For economists, efficiency is the ratio of what an organization—which could be a group of workers, a production line, a factory, a company division, or a whole firm—*actually* produces, and what it *could feasibly* produce with its existing resources, knowledge, and ability.

There are two reasons for *in*efficiency—when actual output may fall short of full potential output. One is simply waste. Resources are wasted—as good as thrown away—when more of something can be produced without making less of anything else. Economists sometimes call this technical inefficiency, or more often, "X-inefficiency." The originator of the term "X-inefficiency" is the late Harvard professor Harvey Leibenstein. He wrote a classic article in 1966 in which he made a key observation.[3] Many developing countries, he noted, hired management consultants at high cost to help them perform better. Most of those consultants' reports gathered dust in a drawer and their recommendations were never implemented. If even some of those reports could have improved performance, and were unused, that must mean that those countries who failed to use them were not employing their resources as well as they could. He called this "X-inefficiency"—"X" for unknown, as in algebra—because it was not entirely clear what the precise sources of this type of waste were. A generation later, it is apparent that there are a great many causes of X-inefficiency, some of them related to shortcomings in decisions executives make.

Leibenstein believed that the average rate of X-inefficiency in American business was 20 percent, meaning businesses could on average produce 20 percent more with the same amount of labor, capital, and materials. I often ask managers, in and out of classroom settings, whether they could increase the output of their firm, division, or team, by 10 percent, without needing any more resources. The answer is invariably positive.

A business that has attained zero waste, eliminating X-inefficiency, finally attains the mixed blessing of necessarily facing tradeoffs. But so does a business that for some reason is unable to wipe out or reduce waste. The inability to squeeze more output from given resources means that managers have bumped up against their production ceiling. Future gain—more of one thing—will involve future pain—giving up something desirable or useful.

Failing to make the most appropriate tradeoff choice leads to the second type of inefficiency, "economic" or "allocative inefficiency." This type of inefficiency occurs when resources—labor, machines, financial capital, information, even the time of executives—are allocated in an inappropriate manner among various types of endeavours, so that either too little or too much is given up, to gain something else. It is cost-value logic put to work. Finding just the right balance between pain and gain, by managing tradeoffs, is known as "allocative efficiency." In other words, to squeeze the most they can out of their organizations, executives need to structure their businesses so that the full potential of their resources are realized; they do this by reaching their production frontier—where their labor, machines, financial resources, materials, and time all work to their full potential, in the right combinations and in their appropriate slots.

For example, when Coca-Cola CEO Roberto Goizueta discovered that Coke's wine and concentrated juice business was less profitable than, say, the beverage unit, he reallocated Coke's resources away from wine and juice and eventually sold those operations, directing resources to more profitable uses. He found that those unprofitable divisions were using capital that could better be allocated to other markets and products. Goizueta got Coke's top job after climbing its corporate ladder. Increasingly, companies are choosing to fill CEO positions with executives hired from other firms, believing that an outsider's perspective makes such decisions more evident.

A vivid comparison between eliminating waste (X-efficiency) versus making tradeoff choices (economic efficiency) is provided by the USSR and United States in World War II. At the outbreak of war in 1939–40, the United States was mired in a deep Depression that had lasted over a decade. With great waste built into the system, the United States did not face a tough "guns or butter" trade-off; it was "guns *and* butter." In 1939, after more than nine years of Depression, one out of every six workers was still unemployed. A rapid and huge increase in government defense spending quickly absorbed the unemployed. By 1944, the United States had nearly doubled its Gross National Product, from $850 billion (in constant 1987 dollars) to 1,637 billion; that year, unemployment was only 1.2 percent, having fallen by nearly half in 1941, and again by half in 1942. The economic pain was quite minimal—in fact, there was a net gain—though of course the human toll (823,483 dead and wounded American soldiers) was enormous.

In contrast, the USSR entered World War II without significant unemployment. Its leader, Josef Stalin, had chosen to isolate his country from the world economy, and it was unaffected by the Depression. The consequence was that Stalin and the Russians *did* face a guns-or-butter tradeoff during World War II, as Russians gave up large amounts of civilian goods in order to produce the materials of war. Russia not only suffered heavy casualties—by their account, some 20 million dead and wounded—but also severe economic deprivation. Later, during the arms race of the cold war, the same bitter tradeoff between weapons and widgets continued. Survival dictated the choices of "guns" over "butter." There was far less "butter," or any civilian goods for that matter, in Russia, beginning in 1941, to enable production of far more guns.[4]

The way to distinguish "X-inefficiency" and "economic inefficiency" is to look for pain. Where there is none, managers' decisions concern X-inefficiency and the elimination of waste. Where pain exists, managers face economic inefficiency—making choices so that just the right amount of one thing is given up, in return for another. In deciding whether to run for President in 1952, Adlai Stevenson clearly thought hard about the particular tradeoff he faced—"gains" and "pains." In choosing to run, he believed the gain—for himself, the Democratic Party, and for the country—outweighed the pain. As with most decisions, much uncertainty shrouded the "pains" and the "gains." Tradeoff decisions are only as good as the tradeoff data on which they are based. Stevenson probably estimated accurately the "pains" caused by the rigor of a political campaign. (As president of the University of Chicago, Stevenson was once asked why he chose to run for governor. "I got tired of politics," he replied). He was not becoming "X-inefficient." But he clearly had difficulty estimating the "gains"—the likelihood of defeating a popular military hero, Dwight D. Eisenhower, who twice trounced him.

———

The way economists model business decision making asks executives to define and state their goals (perhaps, making the long-run value of shareholders' capital as large as possible), list their options (the various choices open to them, for example, regarding new and existing products and services), and then choose the options that get them closest to their goals.

Picking wisely from a wide array of options —that is, managing gain-pain tradeoffs—requires decision makers to employ two-question cost-value logic. They must ask:

• What am I giving up?
• Is it worth more or less than what I am gaining?

A good tradeoff choice depends on matching costs—what you give up—with the value of what you gain. It requires executives to evaluate each feasible option by comparing its value—what it contributes toward achieving the objective—and its cost—what must be sacrificed in order to attain it. *The perpetual tension between cost and value is the essence of nearly all business decisions.* The full and accurate measurement of costs and benefits is the basis of nearly all wise ones. Sometimes, economists' cost-value logic is mocked and berated, because of an inherent bias: while costs are generally visible and concrete (though not always, as the previous chapter on hidden costs argued), values or benefits may be far more ephemeral, subjective, and difficult to quantify. This leads economic choices to reject options that are of redeeming value. The problem, of course, lies not with the decision logic but with the ability of the decision maker to properly take into account gain as well as pain.

Take, for instance, the perennial issue of people versus machines—is investment in expensive labor-saving machinery worthwhile? The gain of machines— more output, lower labor costs— comes at a cost of using up scarce financial capital. Is the tradeoff worth it?[5]

That depends. Ten years ago, the cost of replacing an assembly-line worker in Japan with a sophisticated industrial robot was between 5 and 10 million yen—at that time, between $20,000 and $40,000. The gain seemed well worth the pain (i.e., the cost) and many Japanese firms automated their plants. This created new hosts of window-starers, and new opportunities for Japanese unions, who demanded that robots be included in their membership rolls. However, tradeoffs are often moving targets, shifting and changing with great speed. In Japan, capital was relatively cheap at that time, with interest rates much lower than in the United States. The tradeoff between employing more labor, or employing more capital (e.g., assembly robots), was strongly biased in favor of machines. But this is no longer the case. Now, because the cost of capital is higher in Japan than it was in the past, and even higher than in the relatively unthrifty United States, the cost of replacing a line worker with a robot has doubled. At that rate, the tradeoff has tilted in favor of hiring more labor, or at least retaining the existing laborers and not dumping them in favor of machines.[6]

In general, the lesson for managers is that tradeoff choices demand constant testing and reconsideration. This is not always the case. Some types of tradeoffs are based on the unbending principles of physics, and on precise formulae. In his book *Economic Analysis of Product Innovation: The Case of CT [Computer Tomography] Scanners*, Manuel Trajtenberg describes the difficult tradeoff arising in the costly, and often lifesaving, machines, that send X-ray beams through the body from various angles, then use computers to construct detailed three-dimensional images based on how the body affects those X-rays. CT scanners have two key properties. One is "resolution—the ability to record detail—that is, to distinguish (or resolve) objects having different densities." One way to measure resolution is "the size of the smallest object that can still be visualized." CT scanners used to search for cancerous tumors require a high degree of resolution. A second key property is "contrast" or detectability, defined as "the ability to discern between the object itself and the background. There is a tradeoff between the two, because the greater the degree of resolution, the smaller the degree of contrast—a tradeoff dictated by the properties of X-rays and the electronic equipment that turns them into images. This tradeoff can be calculated by a single formula based on the laws of physics that do not change.[7]

Business decisions, unfortunately, are usually not so easily quantified. Organizations that face shrinking resources—such as government bureaucracies facing budget cuts, or universities—have to manage difficult tradeoff decisions under conditions of uncertainty. Recently, the 20 campuses of California State University faced a cut of 8 percent in state funds for each, on top of a 15 percent slash in funding the previous year. The state university campuses rely on state funding for 80 percent of their budget, so the cuts were very serious.

How were the campuses to measure the pains and gains? No precise formula was at hand. Presidents of each of the 20 university campuses dealt with the crises in different ways. Some of them apportioned the budget cuts equally among all departments. This tradeoff decision, while it seems fair, may not always be economically logical, when the value of resources in some departments may exceed those in other departments. San Diego State president Thomas Day made another decision. He chose to ax whole departments, eliminating anthropology, German, Russian, religious studies, aerospace engineering, health sciences, family studies, industrial technology, natural sciences, and recreation, parks, and tourism.

"If you don't do it this way, everybody gets chopped off one toe at a time, until you find you can't stand up," Day said. His decision understandably aroused great controversy and opposition.[8]

Executives find it far easier to impose proportional across-the-board cost and spending cuts, than to shut down whole divisions, or departments—but what is easy is not always what is most efficient or desirable.

Increasing numbers of Americans are facing tradeoffs in the area of health care, as a kind of unhappy "good news, bad news" joke—a common way tradeoffs confront us. The good news is that Americans are living longer, *New York Times* reporter Daniel Goelman wrote. The bad news is that, as a result, they are on average older, and hence sick longer.[9]

The general type of tradeoff that faces America in its struggle with health-care policy illustrates another difficulty inherent in many business decisions, for it is a three-legged stool—not a straight "this or that" choice—with "quality of care," "cost of care," and "accessibility" as the legs. Strengthen one and you may weaken the other two. Grant access to greater numbers of people, and you may lose quality or raise costs or both. This three-way tradeoff is complicated by what appears to be substantial waste in the system—America spends nearly twice the fraction of its national output on health care than other leading industrial nations do, and far more proportionately on administration costs.[10] The lesson here is that tradeoffs can be devilishly complicated—yet you ignore them at your peril.

Management faces a broad range of challenges in its tradeoff choices. These include: measuring costs and benefits, judging customer psychology, false choices, and problems related to time. We will examine each of these in turn.

Measurement Problems

Harvard law professor Alan Dershowitz, a famed courtroom defense lawyer, describes one such tradeoff he often faces: better courtroom *tactics*, achieved at a cost of lower courtroom *ethics*.

At this second-to-last meeting of his third-year course in legal tactics and ethics, [Alan Dershowitz] sketches the simple diagram that captures the essence of this course. Moving to the blackboard, he draws two vertical lines in chalk, marking the left one "E," for ethics, and the right one "T," for tactics. The left-hand line represents the scale of a lawyer's possible ethical standards, from 1 to 5 (1 being least ethical, 5 being most); the right-hand line stands for the possible range for tactics, up to the hardball maneuvers—say, badgering a rape victim about her sexual history—represented by "T-5." Tactics and ethics form, in his view, *the pivotal trade-off* facing any criminal lawyer, and therefore any client in search of a lawyer.[11]

"Very often," Dershowitz tells his students, "if you want a T-5 you're going to have to go to an E-3. If you want an E-4, sometimes you're going to have to settle for a T-2." Alan Dershowitz is proud to say he is an E-1, at least in any case where that is the price of achieving T-5.

In order to make hard decisions about courtroom strategy, based on his experience and knowledge, Dershowitz must put actual numbers on the Tactics bar and the Ethics bar—actually, *pairs* of numbers, showing what feasible or attainable Ethics score goes with what feasible or attainable Tactics score.

We can deduce that Dershowitz has assigned the following tradeoff values:

TABLE 3.1

Tactics (points)	1	2	3	4	5
Ethics (points)	5	4	3	2	1

That is, he believes that each increase in tactical value brings a decrease in ethical value by his own standards. When, then, is he proud to be a T-5/E-1? For him, that should be no different than a T-3/E-3; both choices produce a total of 6 points. That answer, for him, rests with his *clients'* values. For them, tactics are worth more than ethics. They want to win more than uphold a standard of conduct. Dershowitz is proud to place their interest over his own.

The measurement problem, however, remains. Dershowitz's measure of the value of ethics may differ from his client's. The difference endures, for it is subjective.

Two-question logic can successfully be applied even to areas where values are tough to measure, such as: How much is saving the bald eagle in Wisconsin worth? Or, one less day of coughing in Los Angeles? Or preserving the whooping crane in Texas? Using techniques drawn from psychology and market research, some economists have tried to place values on these esoteric "products." Here are some of the results:

TABLE 3.2

	Annual Value per Household	Total Annual Value ($ m.)
1. Fishing trips on the Eagle River, CO	$73	$0.5
2. Preserving the bald eagle in WI	$10	$30
3. One less day of coughing in L.A.	$10	$60
4. Preserving clear visibility of Gt. Smoky Mts. National Park	$6	$60
5. Preserving Texas whooping crane	$15	$109
6. One less asthma attack per yr. in U.S.	$25	$175
7. Preserving Mono Lake, CA	$25	$250

Source: BusinessWeek, Aug. 21, 1989, p. 30.

How were these numbers derived? One technique is to survey people and ask them directly what they would pay for each of these outcomes. But it is one thing to ask hypothetical questions about people's values, and quite another for them to put real money on the table. As a result, not everyone is willing to accept these numbers. As *BusinessWeek* notes: "The oil industry is not ready to write a check for someone's sense of moral outrage watching otters die on T.V." The language of economics insists that when choices are made, the *value* of options must be weighed against their price or cost. No decision can be made, unless our knowledge of values is at least as extensive and accurate as our understanding of prices. The subjective nature of values is no excuse for not trying to estimate their magnitudes.

What people perceive and think is as important a part of reality as the physical quantities we regard as eminently real. With some effort, these perceptions, too, can be brought into relation with numbers. Good decisions depend on doing so. This is an area where the experience and intuition of the decision maker play a major role, qualities that sometimes have no reasonable substitute.

Customer Psychology

"What is it worth?" "What do I have to give up to get it?" arose in the design of the United States Air Force's new Advanced Tactical Fighter. Tens of billions of dollars in sales—the estimated value of the contract to build the plane—were at stake. The tradeoff was not between ethics and tactics, but between two key attributes of a new tactical jet fighter—agility and stealth. The nature of the tradeoff was known to decision makers—but the preferences of the ultimate consumer, the Air Force, found expression only at the end of the process.

In what was called the competition of the millennium, the United States Department of Defense opened a competition between two groups of companies—one led by Lockheed, the second led by Northrop—to build the ATF (Advanced Tactical Fighter) for the U.S. Air Force. Lockheed's plane was dubbed YF-22 Lightning 2, Northrop's was called YF-23 Gray Ghost.

The competition was "winner-take-all"—meaning that the design and aircraft judged best would be awarded a contract worth, over its lifetime, about $75 billion.

The Pentagon set out basic requirements for the plane it wanted. But within those requirements, the two competing groups of companies had a good deal of freedom. As the *Wall Street Journal* described it:

> For all the planes' similarities, the two teams took sharply different tacks in their designs. Because the Pentagon didn't spell out down-to-the-millimeter specifications, the companies were left to decide on any

tradeoffs beyond meeting the basics. Making the aircraft spryer, for example, likely meant sacrificing stealth [invisibility to radar]. Added speed probably compromised maneuverability. That's one reason the two planes, designed for the same mission of controlling air space, look quite different.

Northrop's approach is that the ATF's ability to see enemies while remaining unseen will reduce close-in combat over the battlefields of the future. Lockheed, though, believes that after hitting an initial flock of enemy planes with missiles, "you're going to be in there eyeball to eyeball" with other hostile jets, explains Dave Ferguson, the (YF-22) test pilot.

In the stealth versus agility tradeoff, one plane (the YF-23 Gray Ghost) opted for more stealth, sacrificing agility. Another (the YF-22 Lightning 2) opted for more agility, presumably sacrificing some stealth. The *Wall Street Journal* continues: "Thus, during three months of flight tests last year the Lockheed YF-22 set out to demonstrate unparalleled agility. It uses "thrust vectoring," moving the engine nozzles up and down to help control pitch. This frees the horizontal stabilizers to raise the rate at which the plane can roll."

Apparently, Lockheed guessed right. The Pentagon felt the gain of more agility was worth the pain of decreased stealth. In May 1991, the secretary of defense announced that the YF-22 Lightning 2 was the winner. In this decision, the two competing design teams did their best to attain the highest possible levels of both stealth and agility, by moving to the frontiers that aerospace engineering would permit, within the limits of time, cost, and manpower. This was "X-efficiency." They then faced the tough tradeoff of increasing one characteristic of the aircraft, at the cost of reducing the other. This decision involved allocative efficiency.

Was more agility worth somewhat less stealth? The answer depended on "value"—not the designers' own values but those of the air force and Department of Defense, in whose hands the final decision rested. Much guesswork was involved.

Business dilemmas of this sort are common. They are very difficult ones, because when producers make products for consumers, it is the *consumers'* values that count. The producer must weigh tradeoffs (what do I have to give up to get it?) and ask, what is it worth *to my buyers?* While tradeoffs themselves are generally objective in their nature and rely on concrete economic and engineering data, values are subjective, depending on the whims, tastes, and preferences of customers.

To make effective tradeoff decisions, the decision maker needs to know both the underlying *technology*—in the tactical fighter case, the relation between agility and stealth, and the gain in one that a drop in the other permits—and the appropriate *psychology*—the relative values of agility and stealth, on the part of the ultimate consumer (in this case, the Secretary of Defense and his advisors).

The two-bladed nature of business decisions, with the technical, engineering blade scissoring against the subjective, psychological blade, is typical. It requires that decision-making executives be capable of blending hard-headed technical knowledge with sensitive understanding of how people feel and think. This, too, appears to be a tradeoff—skill in one type of knowledge can come at the expense of the other. Executives need to be aware of their own strengths, and cultivate the area of decision making in which they may be weak. And above all, they must never lose touch with their customers."[12]

False Choices

Sometimes, tradeoffs can seem like all-or-nothing choices, when in fact compromise is possible and probably wise. A critical type of tradeoff decision dilemma emerged in the early planning stages of America's space shuttle project, the program aimed at building a vehicle for launching satellites and conducting research in space. Engineers and other experts grappled with a tough tradeoff between two features: Nonrecurring costs incurred building the space vehicle, versus recurring costs incurred each time the vehicle was launched. A very expensive system could be built that could be reused again and again. High initial nonrecurring costs would lead to lower operating costs in future. In this way, money could be spent now that would save money later.

Alternately, a relatively cheap system could be built—rockets that were discarded every time they were used—that would lead to high costs for each launch. This would save money now, in building the system—such a system could be made largely off-the-shelf, with existing components—but it would lead to much higher costs later, each time the vehicle was launched.

The choice actually made (based on the recommendation of a Princeton, N.J., consulting firm known as Mathematica) was a moderate compromise. The two-stage rocket that launches the shuttle has external hydrogen and oxygen tanks that are expendable (and therefore relatively costly for each launch). However the space shuttle itself is designed to return to earth and can be reused for many launches.

Making the *entire* system reusable was not considered the best pain-gain choice, because the saving in per-launch costs was not enough to justify the very high cost of building the system. But making the entire system expendable, thrown away for each launch, was also not worthwhile, because the saving in construction costs was not enough to justify the addition to per-launch costs. The actual space shuttle chosen—the chubby crafts we now know as Atlantis, Columbia, and Discovery—was a compromise, a tradeoff between saving money now and saving money later.

Choice Over Time

The tradeoff dilemma faced by the space shuttle designers is an example of the most important and difficult of all tradeoff choices facing executives— sacrificing some present gain for an even larger one in the future.

It has been argued that American managers suffer from myopia or "short-termitis"—under the gun of quarterly income statements, scrutinized closely by shareholders and Wall Street, executives tend to make choices that offer present gain, even at the cost of considerable (and perhaps, enormous) future pain to the company. Finding the right balance between present and future is central to many key executive decisions. As Peter Drucker has noted, "a management problem is not solved if immediate profits are purchased by endangering the long-range health, even survival, of the company. A management decision is irresponsible if it risks disaster this year for the sake of a grandiose future."

Management—almost alone—Drucker notes, has to live always in both present and future.[13] The hard choice between building a business's strength today and investing to augment its strength tomorrow, or next year, is rarely as simple a tradeoff as it is portrayed—when faced with gains in the present or the future, always choose the future. "We know how to establish and maintain this balance," Drucker has written—have two operating budgets: one, short-term, for on-going operations, a second, amounting to 10–12% of spending, covering the next 3–5 years, needed to maintain and build the company's wealth-producing capacity. This budget should not be cut in bad years nor increased in good ones.[14]

While managers juggle tradeoff choices and struggle to make their organizations efficient, they must simultaneously operate in another dimension—pushing out the existing frontiers that delimit their organizations' abilities. Peter Drucker calls the ability to expand an organizations' limits "effectiveness." It differs sharply from efficiency, which deals with using existing resources in an optimal way. Effectiveness—"the opportunities to produce revenue, to create markets, and to change the economic characteristics of existing products and markets"[15] is the foundation of success, Drucker claims, while efficiency is a minimum condition for survival after success has been achieved. In some ways, the contrast between effectiveness and efficiency is parallel to that between entrepreneurial ability and executive ability. Entrepreneurs are effective in creating new customers. Executives need to be good at keeping existing ones. Just as every executive needs to have some entrepreneurial qualities—including a clear vision of future goals and directions—every entrepreneur at some stage needs the present-oriented qualities of an executive. Vision and practicality rarely exist in optimal proportions within the same person. Perhaps this is why new knowledge-based companies with three founders, combining managerial ability and entrepreneurial vision, have a better chance to survive than ones founded by a single person.[16]

The worst way to deal with tradeoffs is to fail to acknowledge they exist. In Woody Allen's movie *Zelig*, the main character shows an extraordinary ability to transform himself, chameleon-like, to resemble his surroundings. Dining in a Chinese restaurant, Zelig becomes a slant-eyed expert on Chinese cuisine; at his psychotherapist, he becomes a close, valued associate of Freud; at a football game, he joins one of the teams and slashes through opposing lines as a brilliant broken-field runner. Zelig refuses to choose, to acknowledge tradeoffs—and the results are comical, and in the end tragic.

The Zelig syndrome—recognizing only value, never costs or tradeoffs—is not uncommon, especially to political systems where such choices are painful and may alienate supporters, voters, or interest groups. Some legislators have urged that legislation involving new spending should be required to state which other programs will be cut—forcing a difficult and un-Zelig-like choice.

An opposite criticism of the "tradeoff" model of decision making argues that costs are not *under*emphasized—the Zelig syndrome—but in fact overstressed, because costs are more visible and easier to quantify than values. The fierce debate over free trade—for instance, the North American Free Trade Agreement, NAFTA—is an example. The costs of the agreement are clearly evident—freer trade with Mexico will cost America some 150,000 jobs between 1990 and 1996, mainly in labor-intensive industries that rely on relatively low-wage workers.[17] But the benefits—expansion of exports from the United States in automotive parts, cars, household appliances, industrial machinery, and machine tools—while probable, are still only predictions, birds in distant bushes rather than in our immediate hands. One result is that American public opinion opposed NAFTA by about a two-to-one margin. Congress approved it nonetheless.

HOW TO MAKE THE HARD CHOICES: A GUIDE TO COMPARATIVE ADVANTAGE

The rest of this chapter is devoted to a single idea, a simple one but often ignored. It is the notion of comparative advantage, one that can be extremely helpful in guiding such hard tradeoff choices as how to assign tasks among members of a team. Comparative advantage argues that people—and countries—should specialize in endeavors that they do relatively less inefficiently.

One context in which comparative advantage finds use is the issue of trade among nations. The plan to create a free-trade area embracing Canada, the United States, and Mexico, in which most goods and services would be allowed to move freely across national boundaries, is now being actively implemented.

Two seemingly unrelated questions—one at the "micro micro" level, the other at the national, "macro" level—fall within the borders of the comparative advantage concept, and hence turn out to be closely linked. They are:

* How should a relatively unproductive worker, or plant, or division, be utilized (if at all)?
* How should countries build their trade strategies and policies, and why do a majority of economists favor free trade and oppose high tariffs?

Ignore countries, for a moment, and think about baseball. When Babe Ruth played for the Boston Red Sox, he was an outstanding pitcher with fine won-lost records (18-6 in 1915; 23-12 in 1916; and 23-13 in 1917). In the early 1920s, Ruth was traded to the feared and hated rival New York Yankees—a decision Bostonians never forgave, and whose lingering aura is said to still hover over Boston's Fenway Park stadium like a black cloud. Ruth was traded for a sum that in those days was thought large, based on the value of a very good pitcher who could also hit.

New York Yankee manager Miller Higgins chose to use Ruth as a hitter and outfielder, who played every day, rather than as a pitcher. Higgins reasoned that Ruth had an absolute advantage over most other players, both as a pitcher and as a hitter. But if used as a pitcher, he would play only every four or five days. If used as a hitter, he would get to hit every day, and his services as a pitcher woud be lost. He had a *comparative advantage* as a hitter—he was, say, twice as valuable to the team as a hitter than other hitters, but perhaps only 50 percent more valuable to the team as a pitcher, compared to other pitchers. So it was smarter to replace him with another pitcher, than replace him with another hitter. In the tradeoff between Babe-hitting and Babe-pitching, Babe-hitting won.[18]

Smart executives imitate Higgins's reasoning in allocating their human and material resources. So do smart countries. The link between, say, Babe Ruth and textile mills in the southern United

States facing competition from Mexico is not obvious. To see this link, let us work carefully through a rather lengthy example.

Suppose, as supervisor of an assembly-line team at an auto plant, you face a tough decision regarding two of your line workers, Ernie and Burt. Their job is to install car radios and radio antennas. You need to assign one of the two to radios, and the other to antennas.

Long experience has shown that Ernie is a better, faster, and more productive worker than Burt. He takes only 60 percent of the time Burt needs to install a car radio and only a third of the time Burt needs to install an antenna. (See table 3.3 for a summary.)

Labor contracts and a local shortage of skilled experienced workers do not give you the option of replacing all the Burts with someone more productive—Ernies. Besides, you realize that there will always be Ernie—relative to younger, more energetic workers, Ernie may become the equivalent of Burt. So one way or another, you need to face up to the tradeoff dilemma. Besides, if you dumped every worker who did not quite measure up to Ernie, for a while at least you would be left with just Ernie and a pile of rusting rivet guns.

To whom do you assign installing radios? The answer is: Burt, who takes two-thirds longer at it than does Ernie (50 hours, instead of 30) because his disadvantage in antennas is far bigger—for those he takes three times longer, 45 hours rather than Ernie's 15. As supervisor, you assign each worker the task he or she does relatively well, in comparison to the others. It is far more efficient to have Burt install radios than remain idle.

TABLE 3.3
Time It Takes Ernie and Burt to Install 1,000 Car Radios or 5,000 Antennas (hours)

	Ernie	Burt
Radio	30	50
Antenna	15	45

In fact, using Burt to install radios turns out to be very very expensive, if you measure "cost" the way economists preach, as what you give up (i.e., antennas). If Ernie installs 1,000 car radios (in 30 hours of work), he could have installed 10,000 antennas (at 15 hours per 5,000 antennas, or 10,000 in 30 hours). The cost of the radios Ernie installed was 10 antennas per radio. That is expensive indeed. The reason it is expensive is precisely because Ernie is so good at installing antennas—using him to do anything else entails a high cost in lost antennas.

Burt, in contrast, installs radios quite cheaply. In the time it takes Burt to install 1,000 radios—50 hours—Burt could have put in a bit more than 5,000 antennas (to be exact: 50/45 times 5,000, or 5,555). So Burt's opportunity cost for installing radios is about half that of Ernie's—again, because Burt is relatively better at antennas.

It turns out that the logic of the Burt-or-Ernie problem is quite similar to that of another issue with a far greater scale—the gains to a business and to a country of engaging in trade with other countries, by selling products to them in return for imports. In 1776, Adam Smith wrote, "If a foreign country can supply us with a commodity cheaper than we ourselves can make it, better buy it of them with some part of our own industry."[19] Two generations later, the British Parliament held a fierce debate on the imposition of high tariffs on French grain (or"corn," as the British called it). Speaking on the issue was David Ricardo, an economist. Ricardo argued eloquently that if French farmers were willing to feed the British for less than it would cost them to feed themselves, then the British should eat French food—and spend time doing something else, that they did comparatively better.

Suppose we translate our auto-plant example to the currently hot issue of trade between America and Mexico, simply by relabelling the products and people:

- Ernie becomes the United States, Burt becomes Mexico;
- radios become cars; and antennas become computers:

Reread the above passage, replacing Ernie and Burt with the United States and Mexico, radios and antennas with cars and computers. Like Ernie, the United States is more efficient in making both cars and computers. But it still pays for America to trade with Mexico, by specializing in what it does relatively well (computers), and leaving Mexico to buy United States computers with cars, which Mexico produces relatively well.

TABLE 3.4
Time It Takes the United States and Mexico to Make One Car or One Computer (hours)

	U.S.	Mexico	Ratio: U.S. to Mexico
Cars	30	50	0.6
Computers	15	45	0.33
Tradeoff Cost of 1 Car: (number of computers given up for 1 car)	2	1.11	

As table 3.4 shows, it costs the United States fewer hours to make both cars and computers. But like Ernie, the United States has a comparative advantage in computers, just as Babe Ruth did comparatively better as a hitter, and Ernie did comparatively better as an antenna assembler. *Because* the United States is so efficient at making computers, cars are comparatively expensive in the U.S.—the tradeoff cost is two computers (30 labor hours) per car (also 30 labor hours). In Mexico, the tradeoff cost is roughly 1.11 computers (45 hours of labor) per car (50 hours of labor). It pays America to have Mexico make the cars, and to "buy them from Mexico with parts of its own computer industry."

The above example can be applied not only to macroeconomic settings involving whole countries, but also to regions and even to divisions or branches of the same company. The United States of America is a huge free-trade area. California freely exports microchips and oranges to other parts of the country, in return for products it needs. This free trade is facilitated by the lack of economic borders between states and a single currency, the American dollar.

The benefits of organizing production in the United States along comparative advantage lines are immense. Seeing this, European countries are engaged in building a similar "single market" among them, trying to eliminate economic borders almost entirely.

Within a company, there are always workers and plants that are more efficient and productive in every endeavour they are assigned. What, then, should be done with the inefficient workers and plants, if in the short run they must be paid because of long-term contracts? They should be employed according to comparative advantage—What do they do *relatively* more efficiently than others? In the same way that both the United States and Mexico can gain from employing comparative advantage to guide their decisions, so can executives and companies.

A great deal of fog and misunderstanding shrouds the "free trade or tariffs" issue. By definition, goods bought from other countries represent a "leakage" of spending power and jobs, because if those goods were made locally, the jobs and money would be kept at home. So in times of unemployment, urgent calls are often heard to limit imports—and these are indeed times of unemployment, with the number of jobless in the two-dozen industrial nations of the West climbing above 35 million, or an 8.5 percent unemployment rate. While one country may gain by limiting imports, retaliation generally follows—and then all countries tend to lose as world trade shrinks and countries produce an increasing range of products that other nations are comparatively better at making. This happened in 1930, when the United States tried to fight its deepening Depression by a steep hike in tariffs—the Smoot-Hawley tariff. Other countries did the same, and world trade essentially disappeared. Nobody gained, everybody lost.

Many companies engage in "free trade" within the company. Project managers "purchase" R&D engineers, or marketing experts, or production workers, from functional vice-presidents. This is known as the "matrix method," because, like elements in a giant matrix, company workers owe allegiance both to a "row" (a project) and a "column" (a function or expertise). This sort of open-market trading can be very efficient.

Regions within countries engage in free trade; rural areas export food in return for the manufactured goods made in cities. Both intra-region and intra-company trade are built around tradeoffs and the idea of comparative advantage that Adam Smith and David Ricardo favored. The profitability of companies, and standard of living of whole countries, are built in part on it. It seems natural, therefore, to extend the notion to groups of countries engaging in open free trade. But the politics and emotions of nations pose major obstacles to tradeoff logic, however persuasive it may be.

Perhaps the two most important messages of the comparative advantage notion are these:

- Every country has a comparative advantage in at least *some* products or services. As the British writer Samuel Brittan put it, "competitiveness is a relative concept; and we cannot all be uncompetitive against each other."[20]
- From that notion, it follows that it is *companies*, not countries, that are competitive or uncompetitive in world markets. Though one can speak of countries with relatively high labor costs compared to labor productivity—the focus of chapter 5 on "people versus machines"—it makes little sense to speak of whole countries that are uncompetitive. Comparative advantage necessarily gives even a high-cost country competitiveness in *some*thing.

The task of those who run firms that compete in world markets is to create more value, at lower cost, than other firms. If they succeed, their *firm* is competitive and their country gains exports and jobs. Those who speak of a "competitive" country really mean that it has a significant number of such competitive firms.

He drew his trenchcoat tightly about him. The wind swirled and blew dust devils in the gutters. The sodium vapor street lamp gave his skin a greenish pallor.

"You want something, you have to give up something else, sweetheart," he said to the young woman facing him. Silent tears rolled down her face. Her blond hair was tied in a ponytail.

"Everything has a price. It's the way of the world. It's just a matter of finding out what it is, and figuring out whether it's worth it or not."

He turned and walked away quickly, the sound of his footsteps echoing against the curtain walls of the tall buildings. After a few steps, he stopped.

"Good-bye, baby," he said, without looking back at her. "You know where you can find me."

"Economist!" she shouted.

She climbed into her priceless antique Bugatti—one of only three in the world—and sped away.

Chapter Four

DO YOU KNOW WHERE YOUR COSTS ARE?

Costs are always higher than expected, even when they are expected to fall. They require scrupulous scrutiny and constant containment.

— Theodore Levitt, *Thinking about Management*

"It was the best of times, it was the worst of times..." That is how Charles Dickens began his stirring tale of Paris and London during the French Revolution. It could apply equally to the near-revolution executives are caught up in today.

Top executives of IBM, Digital Equipment, General Motors, Sears, Chrysler, Salomon Brothers, Westinghouse, Kodak, and American Express were all replaced by their boards of directors in the past few years. The reasons were very similar—usually, the need to increase sales revenues and reduce costs, as global markets became more and more competitive in the new world order.

With the death of the cold war, nations of the world have chosen to compete on the basis of market war: economic, rather than military, strength. The central organizing principle of this brave new world is the race for markets, not for arms, on the basis of innovation, cost, and value. Joining this competition are many newly industrialized nations who challenge the domination of the Great Powers. In fact, spending on weapons rather than on technology may have weakened the Great Powers and given other

65

countries who put their resources into productive investments a window of opportunity.[1] A small but clear symbol of this new and competitive world is the bright neon sign atop a tall building in Kuala Lumpur, Malaysia. The sign reads "2020"—the year that country hopes to catch up with its wealthier, less energetic rivals.

This revolutionary and constructive change in how the world runs its business is forcing countries and companies—including huge ones that not long ago enjoyed outstanding success and record profits—to undertake some painful adjustments. Executives are facing the need to look more closely than ever before at their costs. The watchword has become "restructuring"—cutting costs and excess labor and capital capacity. As costs become more crucial, so does an economic tool that helps measure them, the cost function: the empirical relationship between how much is produced and the total expenditure or cost incurred. This chapter focuses on this tool. It shows how top managers can use it as a key aid in such tough decisions as whether to continue operating a factory or shut it down.

CAN LESS BE MORE?

In 1955, the founder of Sony Corp., Akio Morita, brought the prototype of a small, practical transistor radio to America. Today Sony is one of the world's largest industrial firms, with $30 billion in annual sales. A generation ago, it was a fledgling startup, not much more than a gleam in Morita's eye. The transistor had been invented not long before by the American scientists William Shockley, John Bardeen, and Walter Brattain. Morita saw its great commercial potential.

"I saw the United States as a natural market," he said. It may have been the *only* real market. At the time America accounted for over half of all the world's output and income, and was nearly the only game in the globe.[2]

Morita took his little $29.95 radio to New York, which then had "more than twenty radio stations." He knew his market. America had large houses, Morita noted, big enough to let household members listen to their radios without disturbing others.

Morita showed the radio to Bulova, a large watch and appliance firm. "We want some of these, their purchasing officer said. We will take...100,000."

I was stunned, Morita wrote. It was an incredible order, worth several times the total capital of our company. There was one condition, the Bulova buyer said—we would have to put Bulova's name on the radio. Sony would be a so-called OEM (original equiment manufacturer) supplier. Morita refused. "Fifty years from now I promise you that our name will be just as famous as your company name is today." (Thirty-nine years later, that has come true). Morita continued on his rounds. Another American buyer, representing a chain of 150 stores, liked the radio too. He asked for price quotes on quantitites of 5,000, 10,000, 30,000, 50,000 and, like Bulova, 100,000 radios.

"We did not have the capacity to produce one hundred thousand transistor radios a year and also make the other things in our small product line," Morita noted.

Our capacity was less then than a thousand radios a month. If we got an order for one hundred thousand, we would have to hire and train new employees and expand our facilities even more. This would mean a major investment, a major expansion, and a gamble.

I sat down and drew a curve that looked something like a lopsided letter "U." The price for five thousand would be our regular price. That would be the beginning of the curve. For ten thousand there would be a discount, and that was at the bottom of the curve. For thirty thousand the price would begin to climb. For fifty thousand the price per unit would be higher than for five thousand, and for one hundred thousand units the price would have to be *much more* per unit than for the first five thousand. (See Figure 4.1).

"My reasoning," Morita explained, "was that if we had to double our production capacity to complete an order for one hundred thousand and if we could not get a repeat order the following year we would be in big trouble, perhaps bankrupt, because how could we employ all the added staff and pay for all the new and unused facilities in that case?"

FIGURE 4.1

Akio Morita's U-shaped average cost curve for early transistor radios

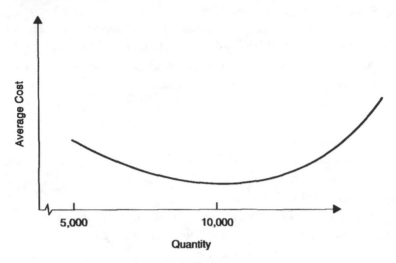

The average cost of making transistor radios starts at a fairly high level at 5,000 radios, then drops when 10,000 radios are made over the course of a year. At 10,000 average cost starts to rise, as making radios becomes more expensive— hiring new workers or paying existing ones overtime, crowded floor space, higher prices paid to suppliers to hurry their production, all take their toll on costs. So the average cost per radio when 30,000 or 100,000 radios are produced is much higher than the average cost for 10,000 radios.

After looking at Morita's U-shaped cost curve the buyer blinked and said to him: "You are the first person who has ever come in here and told me that the more I buy the higher the unit price will be. It's illogical!" But he listened to Morita's explanation and eventually bought 10,000 transistor radios—"right for him and for us," Morita concluded. For Sony and Morita, in this particular case selling fewer was better (and cheaper per unit) than selling more.

That fateful decision was an important milestone in the life of Sony Corp. With the wisdom of hindsight, it was the correct one. Had Morita succumbed to the temptation of a large order, his company might have stumbled by sacrificing quality, efficiency, or cost controls, in the haste of rapidly boosting production. The right decision was made because Morita had an intimate, if largely intuitive, knowledge of the shape of Sony's costs. Like many decisions, good common sense overlapped with good economics.

To manage costs and production, and to make smart decisions about how much to produce and what price to charge, executives must have detailed, accurate knowledge of how much it costs to make their goods or services at various levels of output. The previous chapter discussed tradeoffs. Clearly, it is impossible to make smart decisions about tradeoffs if the decision maker is utterly in the dark about what those tradeoffs look like. Put another way, the quality of tradeoff decisions is only as good as the quality of the tradeoff data on which they are based.

The scrap heap of management history is piled high with executives who scorned basic business intelligence about costs. An ironic, early example is Henry Ford. The man who pioneered one of the most significant cost-reduction plans in history—standardized parts and assembly-line production—"hated bookkeepers and accountants," whom he regarded as parasitical. His dislike of those whose job it is to gather data on costs got Ford Motor Co. into serious hot water.

Once, walking into a room, Henry Ford asked an aide what the white-collar workers in the room do. Told that they were accountants, he ordered, "I want them all fired. They're not productive, they don't do any real work." The result was chaos, as Arjay Miller (who later became president) discovered. Miller was asked to obtain a monthly estimate of Ford company profits. Doing so required estimates of revenues and costs. Sales projections were fairly straightforward. But Miller was amazed to learn that the Ford Motor Co. estimated its costs by dividing its bills into four piles (small, medium, large, extra-large), guessing at the average sum of the bills in each pile, *then measuring the height of each pile* and multiplying height in inches by average bill size. (It would have taken a roomful of accountants to make cost measurements accurately—and Henry Ford had fired them.) The system was not unlike that used 20 years earlier; when the piles of bills were not quite so unwieldy, the understaffed accountants had weighed them.[3] It is not surprising that Ford found itself in deep trouble very soon, with large profits, squeezed between steady prices of its cars and sharply rising costs, ultimately becoming transformed into large losses. Its costs got out of control, because what you do not know, you cannot manage.

Assume you do not share Henry Ford's allergy to accountants and recognize how important it is to have reliable up-to-date data on costs. Once you have cost numbers, what do you do with them?

Here is an imaginary conversation between an Executive and an Economist, whose purpose is to show how a minimal amount of cost data can provide a maximal amount of guidance for business decisions.

FIVE PAIRS ARE (ALMOST) A FULL HOUSE

Poker players know two pairs of cards are not a full house. But for executives, five pairs of cost numbers, showing the total dollar outlays required to achieve five different levels of production, *including zero,* can be a truly full house of information. It can lead the way to winning business strategies.

Our Exec and Econ are discussing a fateful decision—whether or not to shut down a plant that makes microprocessors (CPUs, or central processing units, which are the brains of personal computers). They know that the market for CPU's used to be large and profitable, with price per CPU at $45. But lately new competitors have invaded the market, drawn by the sales and profits. The consequent rise in supply has driven market prices down. Market price, it is predicted, will fall by a third to about $30 and will likely remain there for quite some time.

ECON: Here are five pairs of numbers. These are total costs for five different amounts of production, including zero.

TABLE 4.1

Number of units Produced ('000)	0	40	60	80	100
Total Cost ($'000)	500	1,400	1,848	2,480	3,500

EXEC: This looks like very sparse information to me. Are you sure we can make decisions on the basis of such thin data?

ECON: I think you'll find these data, sparse as they seem, can tell us a lot—provided you know how to read them.

EXEC: Why do we need to know costs for zero output?

ECON: We need the zero-output cost number because even if the plant does not make anything, you will still have to sign checks— for things like licenses, rent, upkeep, maintenance—to maintain it. These are "fixed costs" or "nonrecurring costs" that do not vary with the rate of production. One major kind of nonrecurring cost is the startup costs involved in building a production facility.

Those costs are independent of how many units of output are manufactured. They are defined as costs that do not grow larger as output grows. In contrast, recurring costs are those that are incurred for manufacturing and which vary as more units of output are produced.

Our plant has half a million dollars in fixed costs. We need to pay them no matter how many CPUs we make. If you subtract these fixed costs from our total costs, you get our total variable costs. That will tell us what our direct manufacturing costs are, or "variable costs" as they are known, in making our CPUs.

EXEC: Where did you get these numbers from anyway?

ECON: From our accountants and engineers. We calculated the cost of labor; the cost of our raw materials; and the cost of energy. Those are all items that the company treasurer writes checks for. They are "variable costs," because the more we produce, the more labor, materials, and energy we use, and so the higher those costs. Once you have total variable costs, you can calculate "average" or "per-unit" variable cost. (This is what Akio Morita computed with his U-shaped curve.) We do this by dividing "total variable cost" by the number of CPUs we make. For instance, it costs us 1.1 million to make 40,000 units, so each unit has an average cost of $1,100,000/40,000 or $27.50.

Now, run your finger along the average variable cost row. What is it telling us?

TABLE 4.2

Number of units Produced ('000)	0	40	60	80	100
Total Cost ($'000)	500	1,600	1,848	2,480	3,500
Total Variable Cost	0	1,100	1,348	1,980	3,000
Average Variable Cost		27.50	22.50	24.75	30.00

EXEC: This looks like Akio Morita's U-shaped cost curve. Production costs per unit fall at first, then start to rise. I think I know why. Like Morita, initially we get better and better at making our product. Labor costs fall, we get quantity discounts on our raw materials, and hence average costs fall. But at some point, our production line gets crowded, we start adding second and third shifts (which entail overtime pay), and our costs begin rising.

Our most efficient scale of operation—the amount of CPUs that give us minimum production costs per unit—is 60,000. That is an important piece of information. Right now, we are making 100,000, because of the relatively high price we are getting. But with prices dropping, we will need to scale back our production, or run the risk of piling up stocks of unsold CPUs.

Let us do this right away. Let us start producing 60,000 units. That will get our production costs down. We can make CPUs for $22.50 and sell them for $30. So we can make $7.50 on each one.

ECON: Of course, this does not take into account the half-million dollars in fixed costs.

EXEC: True. But *we would have those in any case.* They are a write-off. So what I want to know is, can we recover our *production* costs? If we can, then it pays to keep the plant operating, at least *for now.* In a moment we will have to take a closer look at those fixed costs and what they mean.

ECON: Or, in other words—anything you make and sell for a price above its cost of production brings in revenue that can be used to offset the fixed costs, *which you have to pay out whether you operate the plant or not.* By my calculation, if we make 60,000 CPUs, our total revenue will be 60,000 times $30 each, or $1.8 million. Our total variable costs come to $1.348 million. So the difference is $452,000.

EXEC: We are still losing money. We have an operating loss.

ECON: True. Our fixed costs are $500,000. So our *total* all-inclusive costs—variable plus fixed—are $1.348 million plus 0.5 million, or $1.848 million. We lose $48,000. We are in the red.

EXEC: But it could be worse. If we didn't operate the plant, shut it down tomorrow, our losses would be even larger. We would lose the whole amount of the fixed costs, or $500,000. So clearly it pays to keep the plant going. Our workers will be glad to get the news.

ECON: The news is not all good. We cannot operate at a loss forever. And as we have discussed many times on the jogging track and in the weight room, a major cost item has been left out, one that should never ever be ignored.

EXEC: I know. Opportunity cost. Our shareholders never let me forget for one moment that they have $8 million worth of capital invested in this little plant. That money could eventually be pulled out of here—by selling the buildings, land, and equipment—and invested elsewhere. It would take months or years do to that, of course. When done, the company, and its shareholders, could make about an 8 percent rate of return on their money, at about the same degree of risk. Risk is important here. In order to compare the profitability of the CPU plant with the best alternative, the alternative needs to have an equal degree of risk, otherwise you are comparing apples and aardvarks.

ECON: Exactly. How will you take that opportunity cost into account?

EXEC: In one of two ways. Either by adding my opportunity cost of capital as an explicit cost to the *other* costs—it *is* a cost, even though I sign no checks for it. Or by comparing the rate of return on my capital with that 8 percent benchmark level. If our capital is earning less than that 8 percent, we could do better in the long run by shifting it elsewhere, and we owe it to our shareholders to do just that.

ECON: Exactly. Now, 8 percent of $8 million is $640,000. We have to factor this cost in to our calculations, before making a decision about whether this plant is viable over the long haul. Let us do that:

TABLE 4.3

Number of units Produced ('000)	0	40	60	80	100
Total Cost ($'000)	500	1,600	1,848	2,480	3,500
Opportunity Cost of Capital	640	640	640	640	640
Total Cost (inc. Opp. Cost)	1,140	2,240	2,488	3,120	4,140
Average Fully Allocated Cost		$56	$41.47	$39	$41.40

EXEC: This puts matters in a different light. If I take into account *all* my costs of doing business, including the fixed costs and the opportunity cost of my company's capital invested here, the cheapest I can produce these CPUs is $39 each, at 80,000 units of output. I notice that over the long haul, my most efficient rate of production is in fact 80,000, rather than 60,000. I think I know why.

ECON: Spreading the overhead?

EXEC: Yes. In other words—the more CPUs I produce, the smaller are those overhead costs per CPU. I spread my fixed costs, $500,000, over a bigger number of CPUs, so that each CPU bears a smaller weight to fixed costs. I guess it is like holding up the weight of a big bridge—the more bridge piers there are on which the bridge's weight rests, the smaller the weight on each individual pier.

ECON: How do our costs look for the long haul, including the fixed costs and the opportunity cost of our capital?

EXEC: Our CPUs will cost on average $39. With current technology and methods, that is the best we can do. It is the bottom of our average cost curve. If the market price is below that, then I will not be earning a rate of return on the company's $8 million in capital that could be earned elsewhere. The profit rate would be less than 8 percent.

The current price of CPUs is around $30. If that state persists over a prolonged period of time, then my shareholders are losing out, and in fact their capital (for which I am responsible) is misallocated. It would serve them better, and probably the economy as a whole, if it were invested in some other more productive plant or industry.

It pays us to keep the plant operating in the short run. But we do that knowing we are not earning a fair rate of return on our capital. At some point, that will have to be remedied.

ECON: All of that is true. But let us not despair too fast. Some of our competitors are hurting, as we are, and may throw in the towel. If they do, that will cut supply and perhaps strengthen market prices. Let's try to squeeze the slack out of our plant—cut costs, get rid of needless overhead, press our suppliers to charge us less for materials, introduce incentive pay to raise productivity, and try to get our costs down by 20 percent. I think that can be done. If so, we can make CPUs for a little over $31. At that cost, I think we are viable in the long run. If we explain our predicament to our workers, hopefully they will do their part. And let's explain it to our shareholders, too. I hope they will take a long, patient view and overlook what may be a temporary weakness in our quarterly profit-and-loss statements.

While this conversation is imaginary, similar ones are taking place all across America and around the world. Some executives are veteran cost-cutters. For others, it is a relatively new—and very painful—experience.

THE FICKLENESS OF COST EFFICIENCY

The speed of change in costs is remarkably rapid—no executive can afford to rest on his or her laurels, even after a major and successful cost-cutting effort. Germany and her major industrial firms are good examples. In 1992 that country was still regarded as an industrial powerhouse. It had $425 billion in exports annually—second only to the United States, and well above Japan—of which 60 percent came from autos, machinery and machine tools, electrical engineering, and chemicals. But Germany's hourly manufacturing costs rose to become the highest in the world—$25.21 an hour, compared with $16 an hour in the U.S. or Japan—while productivity grew only 1 percent in 1992, and actually declined in 1993. Germany companies found themselves at a cost disadvantage relative to competitors from Asia and North America.

As a result, executives in Germany did what was once unthinkable. They began laying off workers, shedding a half-million manufacturing workers in a year. They began shifting production "offshore" to other countries with lower production costs. Even the vaunted BMW has announced plans to make cars in the United States and other German firms are looking to China and Eastern Europe for production sites. Mercedes-Benz was "shocked to discover that their production costs were 35% higher than Japan's," and took radical action to cut costs, including building plants in other countries.[4]

The speed of their change is not the only fickleness in costs. Oddly enough, costs are sometimes a far less tractable problem for *profitable* companies than for unprofitable ones. When losses pile up, it becomes obvious to all, including (or perhaps especially) the hourly or temporary workers on production lines, that drastic steps have to be taken. Cost-cutting plans are easier to implement when crisis threatens. But when companies are apparently profitable, it is far harder for top decision makers to cut costs, even when it is clear that competitors are catching up, and may even have achieved lower costs with equal or superior quality. Today's successes, it is said, often obscure the first signs of tomorrow's failure. That is why constant cost benchmarking—matching your costs against those of your competitors—is so crucial.

Why has cost-cutting now taken center stage in executive decision making? One reason is given by MIT professor Nam Suh.[5] He distinguishes between "innovative" industries—ones that introduce new products—and "mature" industries, that produce and sell old, familiar ones. Mass-market consumer products are with few exceptions familiar ones—cars, TVs, VCRs, even PCs. Their technologies are known and the ability to make these products is widely available. "The economy is driven by major new innovations," Suh argues. "Such inventions as the steam engine, telephone, railroad, power loom, airplane, plastics, lasers, transistor and computer have created new industries in their own times. Many of these industries matured in about 50 years, reaching their zenith in about 20 to 30 years.... During the 1960's, we [i.e., the United States] did not develop any new major innovative concepts that could fuel our economy in the 1990's."

As a result, the United States finds itself competing in mature markets on the basis of *cost*, rather than in innovative markets, on the basis of *technology*. Newly industrialized countries can acquire Western technology and productivity, with far lower levels of labor costs. Then, the basis of competition in markets for standard, everyday products becomes one of cost—which firm can produce it, while maintaining quality standards, at the lowest per-unit cost?

In the competitive race among firms in mature industries, executives who know the structure of their costs and the forces that drive their costs up or down, and are able to raise productivity and shave costs without sacrificing product value, are literally worth their weight in gold. At a gold price of $400 per ounce, even a heavy-set executive weighing 200 pounds is worth $1.28 million a year— a salary level topped by more than a handful of top managers. When cost-savvy executives are worth their weight annually in precious metal, cost functions, too, become gold-plated.[6]

HALL OF FAME COST CUTTING

Executives who find ways to produce their products at lower cost are not mere "bean-counters" or "cost-shavers"—they often create markets for products that, in the absence of cost-cutting, are far too expensive for ordinary people to buy.

Henry Ford created the modern mass market for automobiles, now about 50 million vehicles a year worldwide, a $600 billion market. When he began producing the Model T, in 1908–9, it took half a day—12 1/2 hours—to make one car. Ford's goal was to make one car a minute—not for the sake of speed itself, but because that would make the cars cheaper to make, hence cheaper to sell. He reached the car-a-minute pace in only 12 years. By 1925, Henry Ford's mass-production assembly line at River Rouge, Michigan, was making one Model T every 10 seconds. The price of his car was reduced to nearly one-tenth its starting level. As a result, 15,456,868 Model T cars were sold. Henry Ford's net worth in 1946 was estimated at $600 million.[7]

Many of the great cost-cutting achievements occurred under the pressure of wartime. A subsidiary of General Motors, Saginaw Steering, contracted with the U.S. Army to make machine guns. The external shell of the building where the guns were to be made was finished only in early 1941, and the first gun rolled off the assembly in March 1941. The contract called for a total of 281 guns to be made within a year, by March 1942. Within 12 months, Saginaw had made not 281 machine guns, but 28,728—a hundred times more than the contract. The cost of each gun fell dramatically as a result.

In 1940, the world's best anti-aircraft gun was a Swiss-designed Oerlikon. It was licensed by Britain and brought to America for mass production. Engineers at Pontiac, an automobile company, re-designed it to facilitate faster, cheaper production. One of the most complex parts of the gun was a mechanism to cushion the barrel of the gun against its strong recoil after firing. Making this mechanism required 290 separate machining and finishing operations. Pontiac engineers redesigned it, improving it while cutting out 150 of the separate operations. The cost savings were very large.

Two generations later, IBM engineers would perform a similar "miracle" with IBM's dot-matrix Proprinter. By redesigning the printer and sharply reducing the number of parts, assembly time fell from 30 minutes to just a few minutes. At the same time, quality increased—products that are simpler to assemble generally are better assembled, with fewer errors or faults.

A lesson many executives have learned, or relearned—one well known during the fever-pitch R&D, design, and production days of World War II—is that design teams must include production engineers. Cost savings should begin not after an assembly line is built, but while the product itself is being designed. "Does it create value?" goes hand in hand with, "Can we produce it cheaply enough?" Value for money, in the end, is a two-way relationship between what a product is worth to customers, and what it costs them.

A key example again goes back to World War II. America once enjoyed superiority in producing machines to make other machines—machine tools—and indeed this industry is still one in which American firms are highly competitive. A skilled machine toolmaker, Hank Krueger, was asked by the Springfield Arsenal (where huge numbers of rifles had to be manufactured to meet wartime needs) to help solve a bottleneck, the machine that made the cartridge chambers in rifle barrels. The existing, standard method using a skilled machinist took 12 to 15 minutes per chamber. This was far too costly. Krueger went to the Springfield plant and watched the machinists work. He then went back to his plant and began designing a machine tool to solve the problem. It became known as the Krueger Vertical Automatic Chambering Machine, and it was ready, start to finish, in only four months. Its first 10 chambers were made perfectly. The machine increased output per machinist by 10 times, hence lowered production time and costs to one-tenth the previous level.

THE BIGGER, THE BETTER ... AND THE CHEAPER?

Nobel Prize laureate Herbert Simon has vigorously assaulted the economic theory of the firm and the U-shaped cost curve associated with it. "Empirical studies show the firm's cost curves not to be U-shaped, but in fact to slope down to the right and then level off, without a clearly defined minimum point," Simon claimed.[8] According to Simon, "such a curve implies decreasing costs in all sizes, with no upper boundary on the size of the firm." He proposes the idea that "firms, on average, have an opportunity to grow that is about proportional to their existing size," through improved access to markets, money, credit, and information. (The notion that large-scale production creates cost-savings, an important one in economics, is explored in chapter 7). A recent study on "the computer revolution" states, as an article of faith, two key principles: "the company with the highest unit volume (of production) nearly always wins," and "the place to find unit volume is the bottom of the market, where low prices create new customers."[9]

Akio Morita, who would have earned a Nobel Prize if one were given in entrepreneurship, and Herbert Simon, who won a Nobel Prize for economics, do not necessarily disagree. Morita's U-shaped cost curve reflected *short-run* constraints—the fact that output could be expanded quickly only by incurring higher costs. But in the long run Simon prevails. The latest "Global 1,000" tallies of the world's most successful companies put Sony Corp. at twelfth in the world in Research and Development investment, with $29.4 billion in annual sales, $1.5 billion in profits, and $1.8 billion in yearly R&D spending. Over the long haul Sony has had great success in mass-producing products like its Walkman portable radio and cassette players. The Walkman sold 20 million units, by the time Morita wrote his biography. High volume—far higher than 10,000 units—generated lower costs and higher profits. However, companies thrive in the long run only when they survive in the short run. The phenomenal success of Sony, and the Walkman, can at least in part be placed at the doorstep of Morita's early, courageous decision—that in the short run, "more" can be costlier, on average, than "less," even if in the long run, "producing more" means "costing less."

Not all costs relate to the near or distance future. Some "costs" are history, representing money already spent. Knowing *which* costs are pertinent (those incurred in the present and future) and which are "sunk" (those incurred in the past), is sometimes as important as knowing how much costs are.

SUNK COSTS (ONCE AGAIN)

Earlier, it was noted that pulling the plug—cancelling an R&D project to develop a new product or process—is one of the hardest corporate decisions to make. Perhaps the second-hardest is determining whether the results of an R&D project justify a full production and marketing effort.

Money already spent is a "sunk cost," and it is (or ought to be) utterly irrelevant to decision making. The application of cost-value logic to decision making requires executives to ask:

What *will* it cost? What *will* it be worth?

The emphasis here is on future tense. What *did* it cost? What *was* it worth? is worthy of a historian, not decision maker. I may have purchased a costly computer and paid $4,000 for it. But in deciding whether to replace it, that information is quite irrelevant. What I need to know is: What will the new computer be worth to me, from the day I buy it? And what will it cost me, the day I buy it? The price I paid for the old computer is only relevant indirectly—for example, in determining what I could get for it if I sold it. But that too is future tense—it refers to what the old computer *will* be worth to me in future, when sold—not what it cost in the past. Much accounting data are listed at historical cost, and in times of changing prices and market conditions, bear little true relation to their real value.

Sunk costs provide another of the many paradoxes that face top management. Few things are as important to managers as a clear understanding of history—the processes that have over the years taken society and companies in particular to their present state. Yet few things are as important as knowing how to *ignore* the history of a project, especially the resources sunk in it in the past, when deciding about the project's future and its likelihood to create profit opportunities. When decision makers' track records are carefully recorded, and the profitability of their projects duly noted from their inception, it becomes extraordinarily difficult for them to kill projects, and highly tempting to flog the project onward for a few more weeks or months, hoping that it will turn itself around. As a result, losses mount needlessly.

Time is not a reversible process. Time flows in only one direction, forward. While history itself is a sunk cost —past errors cannot be erased or reversed—the lessons that can be learned from history and its sunk costs are highly valuable. History should be mined as thoroughly as possible for these lessons. So should the history of projects, and the money spent on them. But in making decisions, the magnitude of sunk, historical costs has no relevance and deserves to be ignored. However, learning to do this is far easier said than done.

The wisdom of ignoring sunk costs arouses controversy. Many management experts disagree with the economist's conventional wisdom. Management professor Theodore Levitt has commented that "costs have the same natural tendency to rise as rocks have to fall. They also have a natural tendency to be denied and to resist being accounted for: 'I didn't incur and can't control them. They were here before I was. Anyhow they're overhead.'"

The logic of decision making that emphasizes variable costs and marginal costs, and that treats overhead—costs incurred for administration and general management—as a fixed cost that is inevitable and inescapable in the short run, must not be abused to justify excessive wasteful overheads. Decentralized organizations in particular are susceptible to "fixed cost shirking," where no unit, division, or product group accepts responsibility for them. "All incentives are to deny them and to deny their allocability in a fair way," Levitt notes, ".. the usual result is that a big pool of unabsorbed costs sloshes loosely around the corporation, left irresponsibly to be covered somehow, and , in the end, corporately, where nobody is accountable. Where nobody is accountable, nobody is responsible. Nobody with real responsibilities benefits from trying to contain or eliminate the costs that slosh around in this pool. Anybody who tries only gets hassles." It is therefore vital that the same efforts that go into decisions about closing plants, or continuing to operate them, and to choosing the best level of production—decisions that by nature should ignore fixed or sunk costs—should be invested in efforts to slash needless overhead and fixed costs. One way to do that is to make sure every single dollar of those costs has a "parent"—someone who is responsible for bearing them, noting them in profit-and-loss statements, and ultimately paring them to the minimum possible level.[10]

Paying sunk costs far *more* than their due is a common error. As Levitt notes, paying fixed costs far less than their due is also common. So is decision making based on average (or "unit") costs, when in fact the relevant concept of cost is quite different — *marginal* cost.

THE MARGINAL ROUTE, OR "LIFE AT THE EDGE"

One particular concept of cost is extremely important for executive decision making, but is underplayed and rarely provided or computed by cost accountants. It is known as "incremental cost," or "marginal cost," and is the answer to the key question:

How much will it cost me to produce *one additional unit* of my product, or to supply one more unit of my service?

This is called "marginal" cost not because it is unimportant, at the margin, but because it is incremental, at the end or the margin of the cost structure. For some firms, marginal and average costs are pretty much the same. This occurs when average costs are approximately constant, and hence when it costs about the same to make one more unit as it costs (on average) to make the preceding hundred or thousand units.

However, marginal and average costs often differ. For instance, many businesses—especially ones that require heavy infrastructure and high capital investment, such as airlines or telecommunications—have a cost structure with high average costs. This is true especially when fixed capital costs are taken into account, and when the cost of producing one more unit of output (for instance, one more telephone call, or flying one more passenger) is very low. For a Boeing 727 that is already scheduled to fly between New York and Boston, for instance, and that has empty seats, the cost of flying *one additional* passenger (the marginal cost) between New York and Boston is close to zero. However, the average cost of flying that passenger—computed by taking all the costs of the flight, including fuel, pilots' salaries, flight attendants, capital costs of the plane, and so on, and dividing by 100 or 200 passengers—may be high.

In this situation, it may pay for the airline to fly that passenger, even if the fare he or she pays is very low. The rule of thumb is: as long as the price of the product (in this case, the fare) exceeds the marginal cost, then the company is making a profit *on that particular passenger, or unit of output*. Low marginal costs mean that even low fares can be profitable, provided they turn empty seats (that generate no revenue) into occupied ones, that generate at least *some* revenue. "Profitable," in this sense, means not that the fare covers all costs—probably, it does not—but that it is at least as high as the additional cost that flying the passenger creates.

Businesses with low marginal costs can be made profitable by increasing the degree of use of their capital. There are many ways to do this. Telephone and electricity companies sometimes offer discounts for off-peak use (such as evening and weekends) when marginal costs are low and usage is low. Airlines offer people cheap stand-by flights (on the basis of seat availability at flight time), and special weekend fares when business travellers stay home and planes are less used.

Executives can use the cost data provided by economists and accountants to compute their marginal costs. When such data are not readily available, decision makers can and should call for them. Failing that, they can take average cost data and compute the appropriate marginal cost with relative ease.

Take, for instance, our struggling CPU factory. We return to the conversation between the Exec and Econ.

EXEC: You know, Econ, I am a little uncomfortable about the "five pairs are a full house" thing. I'd like more detailed cost data. I want to know in greater detail what it would cost me, approximately, to make *one more CPU*, at various levels of production.

Why do I want to know this? The reason is—if I can get $30 for each CPU, a low price, I want to be certain that I am not making and selling CPUs that cost me more than I am getting. That would be unprofitable. At the same time, if I can make a CPU for less than $30, then I am making money on it. With competition fierce, I want to make as much money as I can. And I can't do that if the only data I have are these average-cost numbers for broad ranges of output. Let's get some finer detail filled in on this cost function. I want cost data that has thousand-power magnification, not a wide-angle lens across very broad groups of costs.

ECON: You're quite right. Here are the data you want:

TABLE 4.4

Number of units Produced ('000)	60	70	80	90	100
Total Cost ($'000)	1,848	2,142	2,480	2,934	3,500
Marginal Cost ($)	$12.40	$29.40	$31.60	$45.40	$51.00

EXEC: Explain how you calculated marginal cost.

ECON: Here is an example for marginal cost, between 60,000 and 70,000 CPUs.

First, I filled in the total cost numbers. Producing 70,000 CPUs, rather than 60,000, increased total costs from $1.848 million to $2.142 million. That means that the incremental cost—the addition to total cost—was $294,000.

Now, we could make 10,000 additional CPUs with that added cost. *So the marginal cost, for one CPU, was $29.40,* or $294,000 divided by ten. This is about what it costs us to make one more CPU, and note that it is less than the market price, $30.

EXEC: True! So we probably should go on and produce a little more than 70,000 units, say 72,000 or 73,000, and still have our marginal or incremental cost just under the market price.

ECON: This is good economic logic. You might say this is the business example of "living at the edge." The "edge" here is not the precipice of danger, innovation, risk, or technology, but the fine edge of profit—the difference between what one additional CPU costs the firm, and what it brings in, in revenue, or its price in the market.

Marginal-cost pricing is a rule that is especially helpful in periods of recession or thin markets, because it helps executives squeeze the most they can out of underutilized, expensive capital equipment, and earn revenue that defrays heavy overhead expenses. When you have factories already built, planes already purchased, trucks already in your fleet, they are sunk costs. The question then becomes how best to use them during hard times. Marginal-cost decision making is the way.

Eventually, of course, you have to cover all your costs, including fixed costs. You cannot use marginal-cost pricing forever to minimize losses, because the owners of your capital are going to give up and take their capital where it can earn a profit, instead of make losses. But in the short run, if your capital is "sunk"—stuck in its present use, and cannot be easily or quickly extracted—you have to do the best you can. For our CPU plant, we can nearly break even by using good economic logic, in the short run. But we realize that over the long haul, either prices need to rise, or our costs have to fall, to make it worthwhile to keep the plant open.

Even though the logic of maximizing profit is clear, by making sure that you produce and sell, up to the point where the last unit earns in revenue (price) what it costs (marginal cost)—accountants and accounting texts place very little emphasis on incremental costs. A typical accounting text: Robert N. Anthony and James S. Reece, *Accounting: Text and Cases,* does not mention marginal cost anywhere in its 1,030 pages.

To sum up: There is a vital need for executives to know where their costs are, especially for firms operating in competitive markets, for some of whom the hour is only moments before 12. They need to understand the difference between costs incurred to produce, sell, and transport (variable costs) and those that are not related to the volume of production (fixed costs). They should grasp clearly why some costs (sunk costs—costs incurred in the past), though very large, do not and should not influence decisions about current and present production and marketing strategy, but instead focus clearly on money to be spent now and in the future in relation to present and future revenues. Executives should be familiar with their average costs, or costs per unit, and understand how those average costs change with the speed and intensity of production. They should be able to dissect those unit costs, into average variable costs and average fixed costs. And in addition, they should be able to translate cost data into information on marginal costs—what it cost to make that very last CPU, microchip, or automobile steering wheel.

Knowing what your costs are, and *where* your costs are in relation to those of competitors, is a foundation of business strategy. Such knowledge, supported by the tool of cost functions, can help executives achieve a full house of profit in the risky poker game played in global markets.

Chapter Five

PEOPLE, KNOWLEDGE, AND/OR MACHINES

"The conventional definition of management is getting work done through people. Real management is developing people through work."

— A. H. Abedi

Of all executive decisions, the most crucial involve the creative combination and allocation of labor, capital, and knowledge to create value for customers.

How productive are our workers and our capital, compared to those of our competitors? Should new workers be hired, or old ones fired? Should workers be replaced by machines? Are existing machines (particularly, computers) being well used? Are workers being overpaid, or underpaid? How can productivity be increased? How can organizations be shaped to learn better and faster? These questions and other, similar ones involving the use and allocation of resources always had a prominent place on managers' dockets. But in the 1990s, their importance has grown.

Growing numbers of large and small firms, both profitable and unprofitable ones, are undertaking "restructuring" or "downsizing"—euphemisms for the radical shedding of excess amounts of debt and excess numbers of workers acquired during the heydays of the 1980s. And confronted with shrinking sales, burdensome debt, and growing competition, many executives are calling for help. When they do, bad times for business mean good times for business consultants. In Europe, consultants' fees will approach $10 billion in 1994—25 percent greater than in 1990—of which 40 percent is in Germany alone. Much of their consulting services is not in traditional long-term strategies, but in short-term "crisis management."[1] In the United States, consultants are doing well, too.

Even with the wisest, most experienced consultants at their side, executives ultimately bear responsibility for hard decisions. The cost-value logic of economics can be a powerful aid for executives already grappling with restructuring or who fear they might need to one day.

Many crisis decisions about labor and capital boil down to an assessment of how much a reduction in the number of labor hours, or machine hours, will save the company, versus how much it will cost in reduced output and product quality. This type of choice is one that cost-value logic is well suited to organize.

MARGINAL PRODUCT—THE SIMPLE ARITHMETIC OF PRICES, PRODUCTIVITY, AND COSTS

Cost-value logic, applied to labor and capital, rests on the constant comparison of what labor and capital do for the firm, in comparison to what the firm does for them. As always, the cost-value logic applies not to the entire body of labor and capital the firm employs, but to changes in labor and capital—people and machines who are to be added to, or subtracted from, the payroll.

The concept of "the marginal product of labor and capital" is the tool this chapter highlights. It is closely related to the notion of "marginal cost" explained in chapter 4, and is yet another instance of how economic thinking stresses decision making on "increments"—small marginal changes to existing amounts of resources—in place of "totals" or "averages"—relating to the entire existing inventory of resources and output. The logic of marginal product can be helpful in tactical "restructuring." But it is also highly applicable to long-term strategy aimed at giving companies enduring advantage over their competitors.

Marginal product is the specific application of cost-value logic, in the context of primary resources like labor and capital. Applied to labor and capital, cost-value logic asks:

- What does one more hour of labor or capital *cost*?
- What does one more hour of labor or one more machine hour *contribute* to the firm's output of goods or services?

This is "marginal product." Its use is in quantifying the value of an added amount of labor or machinery, in a way that permits comparison with their cost. The notion of marginal cost is not limited solely to labor and capital—it is applicable to other resources, even information, though their marginal product is often much harder to pin down.

The cost of labor and capital should, like all costs, be evaluated as opportunity costs, including hidden ones. Labor may have zero cost if workers who are not gainfully employed at present are used in a productive fashion. Using such labor means the company's payroll does not increase, yet its sales and output do. Capital may have a substantial cost, though a hidden one, even when the firm's own money is used, if such funds could be profitably invested elsewhere.

Estimates of the marginal product of labor and capital are often not readily available. They are not provided by standard accounting data in regular income statements. They are best obtained with the aid of economists and production engineers, by carefully tracking the relationship between the number of labor hours and machine hours used and the number of units of output. Marginal product is the inverse of marginal cost, explained in chapter 4. Marginal cost shows *the added cost incurred in producing an additional unit of output*. Marginal product shows *the added output accruing to an additional labor hour or machine hour*. If the cost of those labor and machine hours is known, then marginal product is simply marginal cost inverted:

TABLE 5.1

Marginal Cost	*Marginal Product*
Addition to Cost divided by Addition to Output	Addition to Output divided by Addition to (Labor or Capital) Input

If the cost of a labor hour or machine hour is known, then it is simple to go from the amount of labor or capital added to the additional cost by multiplying the quantity of labor or capital by labor's price or capital's price.

Economists often speak about the "dual" relation between cost functions and production functions, meaning that if you know one, you can derive (or at least infer a great deal about) the other. Indeed, knowledge of the production function—the detailed relation between labor and capital resources and total output of goods or services—is often the best way to construct cost functions.

Pumping Oil

A concrete example of a production function is the following, which shows the relationship between two inputs: the diameter of a crude-oil pipeline, in inches, and the horsepower of its pumping stations (in thousands of horsepower); and one output, the total amount of crude oil, in thousands of barrels, pumped through the 1,500-kilometer pipeline during 24 hours:[2]

TABLE 5.2

Inputs		Output
Diameter (in.)	Horsepower ('00 hp.)	Throughput ('000 bbl./day)
8	10	25
10	20	47
15	30	109
20	40	200
25	50	320
30	60	469

Knowledge of the production function is highly revealing. It shows, for instance, that large-diameter pipelines are more economical than small-diameter ones. To see this, increase diameter while holding horsepower constant:

TABLE 5.3

Diameter (in.)	Horsepower ('00 hp.)	Throughput ('000 bbl./day)	Marginal Product of Diameter*
8	10	25	–
10	10	36	11
15	10	73	37
20	10	120	47
25	10	176	56
30	10	242	66
35	10	316	74

*Change in throughput, for a 5-inch increase in diameter.

Doubling the diameter of the pipeline from, say, 10 inches to 20 inches, boosts throughput by nearly three and one-half times. This stems from the fact that the volume of a pipe varies with the square of the pipe's diameter. Clearly, larger-diameter pipelines are more economical than small-diameter ones—a so-called "economy of scale."

The same function also reveals that if the pipeline has too small a diameter, and we wish to pump more oil by boosting the power of the pumping stations at a later date, that will prove quite expensive:

TABLE 5.4

Diameter (in.)	Horsepower ('00 hp.)	Throughput ('000 bbl/day)	Marginal Product of Horse Power
25	10	176	—
25	20	228	52
25	30	265	37
25	40	294	29
25	50	320	26
25	60	342	22
25	70	362	20

Raising the horsepower to seven times its initial level, to 70,000 HP. from only 10,000, boosts throughput only by about double. This is because oil, when pumped through a limited-diameter pipe, becomes stickier and friction increases as the horsepower rises. These are all calculations that come from actual production data.

The above three tables can be used to compare the marginal product of diameter and of horsepower. The added throughput accruing to each additional 5 inches of diameter grows from 37,000 bbl., when diameter rises from 10 to 15 inches, to 66,000 bbl., when diameter rises from 25 to 30 inches.

In contrast, the added throughput accruing to each additional 10,000 horsepower of pumping power drops from 52,000 bbl., when HP. rises from 10 to 20 thousand, to only 20,000 bbl., when HP. rises from 60 to 70 thousand. This is an instance of the so-called "law of diminishing returns"—not a law at all, since as seen above the input "diameter" completely violates it—which will be discussed below.

In the same way that marginal cost and marginal product are related, so are average cost and average product. Average product is the ratio between total output of goods and services for a firm, or a division, and the number of labor hours needed to produce them. Like average cost, it is a kind of running history of marginal product, taken over the history of production from the first unit down to the last. Rising average product usually implies lower average costs, and lower prices.

The earliest example of the benefits of higher productivity was detailed by Adam Smith, in his example of the pin factory. The most dramatic example was Henry Ford's Model T automobile.

A Million Pins a Day, A Car Every 10 Seconds:

Business success depends on two things: designing a first-rate product, and then producing it at high quality and reasonable cost. Henry Ford built a tough, light compact prototype he called the Model T in 1908, helped by a new invention known as vanadium steel that was three time tougher than ordinary steel. His next task was to produce Model T's faster and cheaper.

Changes in average product are often used to track productivity. We have noted Henry Ford's remarkable progress in reducing the number of minutes needed to assemble a car—from 12.5 hours down to 90 minutes—and hence in raising the average and marginal product of labor. As a result the labor time per car was sharply lowered, and by the same token, the number of cars per hour was dramatically increased—reaching, at its peak, one car rolling off the revolutionary assembly line every 10 seconds.

In the language of marginal product, Henry Ford introduced a sweeping series of innovations in production technology, that made the marginal product of labor (and capital) higher and higher. Each time he cut the assembly time in half, he doubled the marginal product of a labor hour. These dramatic improvements in costs and productivity made it possible for him to lower prices drastically for his Model T, raise wages (in fact, double them), cut the workday for his workers from 10 hours to 8, and at the same time pocket enormous profits.

"The way to make automobiles," he said in 1903, is to make one automobile like another automobile; *just as one pin is like another pin...*"[3]

John Kenneth Galbraith, one of the most influential contemporary economists, once remarked that to his knowledge, he had never paid a significant visit to a factory. Two centuries ago, Adam Smith did not make that claim. The first chapter of his famous *Wealth of Nations* (1776) opens with a detailed description of a pin factory, in which "each person might be considered as making four thousand eight hundred pins a day." If Smith did not actually visit such an establishment—he likely did—he certainly acquired first-rate information on it.

The pin factory was economics' earliest example of what Adam Smith called the "division of labor"—boosting productivity by splitting large tasks into many smaller ones, and assigning each task to one worker. As workers got better and better at that task, the time it took them to perform it shrank, and hence the cost of making the article declined too. In this sense, Henry Ford did not invent the notion of automation, though he was by far the earliest and most successful implementer of it.

Smith explained why workers were so productive. The 18 separate tasks needed to make a pin were assigned to 18 different workers. This saved time moving from one workbench to another, and made each worker more facile and faster at each individual task. While the work may have become much more dull and less varied, it certainly was faster and more productive. Smith thought this division of labor made pin workers' productivity 240 times higher than if each worker did all 18 tasks—possibly an exaggeration.[4]

Today, one worker in a British pin factory can make 167 times more pins—more than 800,000 pins per day—than a worker could make in 1776.[5] This rise in productivity is significant for two related reasons. It makes pins—and nearly everything else—much cheaper, in terms of labor hours per pin, and it makes a labor hour more valuable, giving labor the income it needs to buy pins and other things, in vastly greater quantities than in 1776.

Why are pin workers more productive? One reason for "the massive long-run increase in labor productivity is attributable to technical progress—the substitution of machines for hand operations," economist Clifford Pratten explains. The speed of pin-making machines rose from 45 pins a minute in 1830 to 500 per minute now—and some workers control as many as 24 machines. One consequence of dividing up the 18 tasks was to enable engineers to design machines to do each one. Henry Ford's car factory was a great leap forward, but nothing more than a sophisticated successor to Adam Smith's pin factory.

At the start of Ford's efforts to make cars faster and cheaper, they were assembled in one place from a pile of parts, and it took 728 hours. In Ford's initial innovation, the chassis (body frame) of a Model T was pulled for 250 feet along the factory floor by a winch. Workers trailed along it, picked up parts carefully spaced along the 250-foot stretch and fitted them to the body. This was the first assembly line. This cut the time to assemble one car in half, from 12.5 hours to five and one-half. A longer line, and more specialized workers, halved assembly time again. Next, an automatic conveyer belt—the first—based on the overhead trolley that moved beef in Chicago meatpacking plants, was built, and assembly time fell by half once more, to 93 minutes—$1/500$ the time it took for stationary assembly. Adam Smith's claim that division of labor increased pin productivity 240 times may have been exaggerated—but Henry Ford's version of division of labor boosted productivity by 500 times, and thousands of Model T cars existed to prove it.

The gains were very large, for workers, consumers, and for the Ford Motor Company. Workers' higher productivity led to higher wages. Higher productivity led to lower costs, and hence to cheaper cars. The 1910 Model T was priced at $780; in four years, its sticker price fell by more than half, to $360, and Ford's annual sales topped $100 million. Ford's plant became more and more productive—where once it took 12.5 hours to make a car, Ford got that time down to one minute and ultimately, every 10 seconds. A total of 15,456,868 Model T's were produced, and the world was never the same.[6]

Henry Ford's recipe for success was to combine, creatively, labor and capital, in a way that made both exceedingly productive. While Ford was to quickly lose its own competitive advantage to other car companies—first General Motors, then Chrysler—the United States led the world in this industry until the 1970s. It lost its lead, when it forgot the main lesson taught by Henry Ford—the crucial value of productive workers in creating low-cost, high-value products that generate high profits—a lesson which, if anything, is starker and clearer today.

From these examples, it might seem that improving the marginal product of labor is a simple process that depends in technological breakthroughs or "great leaps forward." That conclusion is wrong. Improving productivity, whether through technology (better pin machines) or other innovations (dividing up tasks so workers can specialize) depends on the skills, ability, and education of labor, in a continual day-to-day struggle to do humdrum things just a little better.

HUMAN RESOURCES HOLD THE KEY

Goods and services are produced with labor, capital, materials, technology, and "knowledge," or know-how. Of those five components, which creates the largest, most enduring advantage for companies?

It is becoming increasingly clear that the main—perhaps the only—source of such advantage lies in people—their skills, motivation, and the knowledge and capital that they need. It is in this area that executives will earn their pay, in the coming decade. And for this reason, the ability to measure how well, or how poorly, people are performing, will grow in importance.

The reason *people*—and their skill in using knowledge—is now at the forefront of competitive advantage is straightforward. Productive people are the least footloose, and ironically the scarcest, of all the basic resources. Once you acquire them, they are more likely to stay put.[7]

Over the long haul, the substitution of new man-made materials for ones nature once supplied—plastic and ceramics, for example, in place of steel—has sharply lowered the scarcity value of traditional materials. And in the short term, huge supplies of nickel, steel, iron, and aluminum thrown onto world markets from the ex-USSR, especially Russia, have made the cost of materials a shrinking part of overall marginal costs. In the past decade, for instance, U.S. steel consumption has fallen by over one-fourth.

Capital, too, has become relatively plentiful, despite the decline of national savings in the industrial nations. The advent of the global capital market now means that a company, or a nation, with a good product or idea can borrow the money to develop and produce it, and can acquire the machinery to do so. In the nineteenth century, and later in the twentieth, large pools of saving in America, Britain, and Germany gave those countries the ability to create modern factories and infrastructure. Today, countries like Thailand and Malaysia can dip into those savings, as debt or as equity, to build their own industrial base.

Nor are technology and knowledge infallible creators of advantage. Like capital, both technology and know-how are highly mobile, racing from one country (the "discoverer") to another with great speed, defying feverish attempts to corral them or monopolize them. Japanese firms produced not only 30 million video recorders a year, at their peak, even though VCR technology originated in the United States, but also millions of compact-disk recorders, although the Dutch company Philips first developed its technology. Singapore produced no computer disk drives in 1980;

by 1982 it was the world's leading producer of them, even though the product was developed in the United States.

Labor is the most crucial of the four production factors, because in today's global marketplace it is the least mobile. A skilled, highly-motivated labor force is for most companies and even most countries the main enduring source of competitive advantage, exports, and growth. Literate, motivated workers enable Thailand, Indonesia, Singapore, Hong Kong, Taiwan, and Malaysia to capture growing amounts of "offshore" production from North American, Japanese, and European firms. Motorola, for instance, has concentrated much of its cellular-phone production in Malaysia. Technology, financial capital, physical capital (machines), and materials move there in order to reach the skilled, relatively cheap Malaysian labor. Howard Head had his oversize Prince tennis racket, with a light tubular aluminum frame, produced by Kunnan Lo, a Taiwanese company. "We didn't go to Taiwan because we could get rackets cheaper there," Head explained later. "We went to Taiwan because the work ethic was so strong. I still remember watching them in that plant—they were dedicated to their work the way earlier American craftsmen were."[8]

Labor has an additional advantage: under the right conditions, labor gets better with time, with age, and with experience, unlike existing technology and machines, which almost always get worse. Under the right conditions, people learn, often very quickly. Machines don't.

If human resources—skilled hard-working productive people—are the key to corporate advantage, then you would think that the executives in charge of this important functional area are well paid and well heeded. But this is not the case. A survey of salaries of nine key functional areas heads—finance, research, sales, production, marketing, information systems, engineering, materials, and personnel—for 10 European countries reveals that in most countries, personnel ranks as lowest-paid or close to it. Moreover, many personnel heads are not members of the executive board that makes key decisions, even those involving restructuring or large-scale layoffs, which human resource heads will be expected to implement.[9] According to MIT labor relations expert Thomas Kochan, while human resources are a key element of competitive strategy, for the most part human-resource executives have little say in formulating overall business strategy:

> In the U.S., personnel and labor-relations managers have historically been left out of business-strategy discussions. Most human-resource executives are in a low power position relative to their peers in management. They earn on average only 60 percent of what financial executives get. The human-resource profession seemed to accept the notion that their job was to adapt to the competitive strategies chosen by the firm and to match labor practices to those strategies. That simply doesn't work anymore. That is the fundamental lesson. In Europe and Japan, this is not the case.[10]

In Japan, Kochan notes, personnel V-Ps earn as much as financial V-Ps. There, how well a firm's *human* capital is managed is thought to be as important or more so to the firm's well-being as how well its financial capital is invested. Indeed, it surely is.

The old-style adversarial model of labor-management relations, where "management ran the shop and labor grieved," no longer works, Kochan says. In that system, collective bargaining was tied to narrow semi-skilled jobs and operated independent of education, training, and human-resource development. Today, flexible work assignments, performance-linked compensation, employment security, and involvement of workers in management make the old "them against us" model as obsolete as kerosene lamps. Yet many firms are slow to dump it.

Managers know that to succeed, competitive strategy needs a bottom-up approach. Everyone in the company, down to the shipping clerks, has to understand what the strategy is and what each worker must do to make it work. Xerox, for instance, has done this successfully for a decade in revamping the company and its products. Yet this new-style industrial relations built on mutual commitment and trust is being implemented more slowly in America than in, say, Germany or France. Kochan estimates that only 20–45 percent of medium- and large-sized U.S. firms integrate human-resource factors in business strategy sessions.[11]

Two countries exemplify the key role of human resources in creating successful global businesses—Hong Kong and Mauritius. Each is a country that enjoyed a rapid increase in its standard of living by means of a human-resource focused strategy applied with energy and consistency, not unlike the way a chief executive might steer a large company. Each has important lessons for executive decision making.

MARGINAL PRODUCTIVITY IN MAURITIUS AND HONG KONG

To better understand the concept of marginal product, let us consider what is perhaps the most famous economics theory in history—Malthus's Essay on the Principle of Population.

"Nature has scattered the seeds of life abroad with the most profuse and liberal hand," Malthus reasoned, in 1798. But "she has been comparatively sparing in the room, and the nourishment necessary to rear them." As growing amounts of labor work on a constant amount of farm land, the addition to total food production, caused by an added number of workers, gets smaller and smaller—the so-called law of diminishing returns. Ultimately, "the race of man cannot," Malthus said gloomily—bequeathing to economics its inescapable nickname, the "Dismal Science"—"by any efforts of reason, escape from it."

Malthus was right that for given amounts of land and capital, added amounts of labor lead to ever-smaller increases in production. Even today, many countries struggle desperately to keep living standards from falling; when their population doubles itself every two decades, food production too must double at the same pace, and that is a tough task.

But while land cannot be reproduced in large amounts, other things that make labor more productive and that work to increase labor's marginal product—machines and knowledge—can. If Malthus' Essay on Population was a smash hit at the end of the eighteenth century, the twentieth century has provided several practical refutations of it—at least, for the time being. Since Malthus wrote his famous Essay, far from declining, the marginal and average product of labor have risen dramatically. In the United Kingdom and the United States, labor's average productivity has risen by perhaps 20 times since Malthus and with it, standards of living have soared. But a small, densely populated island in the

Indian Ocean—Mauritius—and a fragile enclave off the coast of China—Hong Kong—provide an even more dramatic counterexample to Malthus, and a lesson or two for managers.

Mauritius: Following World War II, little Mauritius, with a population of over a million, had five big strikes against it—its small size, lack of natural resources, overdependence on a single crop (sugar), ethnic frictions (its population is a mosaic of Europeans, Creoles, Chinese, and Hindus, and Moslems of Indian origin), and remoteness from major markets. In a "beauty contest" for nations most likely to attain rapid growth, I would have picked Mauritius to finish dead last.

In fact, Mauritius has been among the winners. Since 1984, Mauritius has doubled its per capita income, which is now over $2,200—one of the few once-poor countries to leap the $2,000 threshold. In 1983, one worker in every five was unemployed; in 1988, fewer than one in 25 was jobless. Inflation has generally been low. The World Bank and International Monetary Fund use it as a model for other nations.

What was Mauritius' recipe? Start with an educated labor force. Even in 1960, elementary education was universal. Between 1960 and 1985, high-school enrollment doubled, from one student out of every four high-school-age youths, to one in two. Mauritians are highly literate, their educational system is excellent, and the University of Mauritius trains islanders well for roles in business and government. Add stable government. Mauritius is a parliamentary democracy with a fine human rights record. Then, toss in some free-market economics. The Mauritius government favors free markets and has acted to create them. In 1984, tariffs were slashed, import quotas removed, and an Export Processing Zone (EPZ) created, where goods are made for export without bureaucratic constraints on imports of goods or capital. (Geographically, the whole island is an EPZ). Asian exporters, mainly from Hong Kong as well as Taiwan and Singapore, chose Mauritius as a site for off-shore production. Capital flooded in to the EPZ. Some 600 manufacturing firms began operating there. They soon made Mauritius the world's third-largest exporter of woollen goods— literally, "rags to riches." A dozen African countries are now emulating Mauritius's EPZ.

Mauritius still faces tough challenges. In economics, as in baseball, promotion to the major leagues brings stiffer competition. High demand for labor has brought wage increases and made its work force less attractive for foreign capital, causing concern that factories may shift to other, lower-wage nations. In response, Mauritius seeks a new role as an "outsourcer" for U.S. and European firms, and is trying to diversify into jewellery, plastics, and perhaps even petrochemicals, and away from textiles. Remarkably, other countries are already bidding for Mauritius's relatively new factories.

Hong Kong: This tiny city remains desperately crowded (in some districts, over 400,000 persons per square mile), and short of housing and other infrastructure. Yet it is highly prosperous. Hong Kong soared from poverty—with per capita GNP of about $800 in 1970—to a prosperous $15,000 per head in 1992, the level of the less wealthy Western European nations.

In 1961, three-quarters of Hong Kong's working population had elementary or high-school education. Only a fifth of the working populace had no education at all. This was a direct result of the massive migration of educated people from mainland China, who came from urban areas and had substantial schooling. This well-educated intelligent labor force became the foundation of Hong Kong's success in manufacturing, built on high productivity and moderate wages.

The new, crucial role played by skilled labor does not bode well for the United States, which has been struggling with an elementary and secondary educational system that leaves many students functionally illiterate or innumerate, or has them drop out of it entirely before graduating. The loudest complaints about America's educational system have come not from parents or politicians. They have come from employers, forced to hire high school graduates who can't read or do simple math. Rebuilding the school system will take years. In the meantime, why don't U.S. companies act now to invest in training programs that foster general skills? Some do, but many don't. American firms spend $30 billion a year on training and personnel development—under 2 percent of wages and far less in per capita terms than America's competitors. The vast majority of these training dollars are spent by big companies on management development.

TRACKING PRODUCTIVITY: CARS AND BIKES

Tracking the marginal and average product of workers, in comparison with workers at rival plants, is a vital task of executives. The crucial importance of such benchmarking cannot be overemphasized. The car industry is a graphic example. America's Big Three lost substantial market share to Japanese competitors in the 1970s and 1980s. (There are signs they are winning it back in the 1990s, however). Early warning signals that this was about to happen existed in the early 1960s. By 1965, Toyota already had a 50 percent higher level of vehicle productivity (cars per worker, adjusted for such differences as vertical integration, capacity utilization, and labor hour differences) than the Big Three, and by 1975, its advantage grew to 160 percent. On an unadjusted basis—computed by dividing the number of vehicles by the number of production workers—as early as 1957, a Toyota worker made 13 vehicles a year, while a GM worker made 6 and a Ford worker 10. Close attention to those figures—if Big Three executives had been carefully tracking them—might have sounded alarm bells long before they actually went off, perhaps in sufficient time to prevent much of the lost market share.

Detailed productivity data provide a fuller picture of Japan's productivity advantage, at its peak around 1982. Changing dies (the machines that shape metal parts like fenders) took 5 minutes in Japan as against 4–6 hours in the United States; assembling a small car took 30 hours in Japan, versus over 50 in the United States.

The result of their higher productivity was to give Japanese car manufacturers a major advantage in global markets, one that not even higher ocean freight, custom duties, marketing, and distribution could begin to offset. Since then, according to Cusumano, in Japanese car facilities, "physical productivity, which reflects the 'throughput' speed for completing products and the amount of labor required, has been roughly twice the levels of most U.S. plants."[12]

(Belatedly, there are signs American and European firms have caught up with Japanese productivity in car production. While some producers still take 30 labor hours to assemble an automobile, the best producers are down to 10 hours for small cars, Nissan's Micra and some models of Opel, and perhaps even less than that for some plants in Japan.)[13]

Another example is the motorcycle industry. Much of what was written about cars can be repeated, replacing "car" with "motorcycle." The British motorcycle makers Norton-Villiers-Triumph once enjoyed success, sales, profits, and high market share. They found that position rapidly eroding in the late 1960s and early 1970s, in the face of fierce competition from the Japanese producers Kawasaki, Yamaha, and Honda.

After the British government funnelled large sums of money into the industry, with no seeming benefit, the Minister of Industry Eric Varley hired a consulting firm, Boston Consulting Group, to analyze the problem. Their report, one of the landmark classics of its kind, was written principally by Bruce Henderson.[14] The study was commissioned in April 1972 and completed within four months, by July.

Henderson found that each Honda worker turned out the equivalent of 200 bikes a year. The British worker rate varied from 10 to 16. In terms of value added, each British worker added $9,000 to the materials they used; a Honda worker added nearly $40,000. As a result, the Japanese pay scale was substantially higher than that in Britain ($13 an hour compared with $11)— yet Japanese unit costs were lower, because their advantage in productivity was greater than their higher wage costs.

To understand the link between prices, costs, wages, and marginal product, recall the tool of comparative advantage discussed in Chapter 3. Suppose we assume that what the average worker produces (average product) and what the last worker produces (marginal product) are roughly equal. Using the "marginal product" tool, we can see that Japan's ratio of marginal product to wage costs compared to that in the UK was:

TABLE 5.5

	Japan	UK
Marginal Product/yr	$40,000	$9,000
Labor Cost/yr*	$25,000	$21,000
Ratio of Marginal Product to Wage	1.6	0.43

*Based on 40-hour work week and 48 work weeks per year.

Clearly, even though Japanese workers were paid nearly 20 percent more per hour, their productivity was some four times greater than British workers. This gave Japan a huge comparative advantage in motorbikes. Its workers created value added of 1.6 times their wage. British workers created value added of less than half what they were paid. No wonder that the British firm began with half of the American market for its medium- and large-size bikes as late as 1969—and ended with only 9 percent for medium models and 19 percent for large ones after only four years, by 1973.

Productivity—whether marginal product or average product—is always a ratio, between a measure of total performance (output, or sales) and a measure of inputs (labor hours, or machine hours). This ratio can be increased either by raising the performance (the numerator) while keeping the inputs steady, or alternately, by keeping the performance constant while slashing the inputs (the denominator). Alternately, existing amounts of labor and capital can be employed, but at lower levels of compensation. Increasingly, it has become fashionable to adopt the latter approach, calling it "restructuring," dumping large numbers of workers and capital while maintaining prevailing levels of production. Close to half of all unemployed American workers today believe that they will never get their jobs back. Two decades ago, that figure was around 20 percent. Job loss came mainly as a result of short-term downturns, and laid-off workers knew that when demand picked up they would be rehired. For many unemployed workers today, that hope no longer exists.

THE EMPLOYMENT CRISIS

The question is, why were excessive amounts of labor and capital acquired in the first place? And how effective is restructuring as a tool for greater efficiency and productivity? How should it best be done?

Since much of "restructuring" is focused on getting rid of excessive numbers of workers, we focus on labor. The tools of comparative advantage and marginal product show that cost-cutting by slashing wages and payrolls can be very expensive. As former

Chrysler CEO and board chairman Lee Iacocca once said: "some managers seek economy above all—and are willing to pay any price to achieve it."

A wise executive will employ labor up to the point where the last amounts of it are worth what they cost. (Any more would be unprofitable; any less would unnecessarily give up small or large incremental profits, on labor hours that were worth more than they cost).

Comparative advantage and marginal product illuminate the controversial issue of competition with countries whose wages are very low. It is sometimes argued that such low-wage countries—for example, Mexico, where manufacturing wages are about $2.50 an hour, compared with $11 in the United States—comprise unmatchable competition for jobs, hence goods made there should be kept out by high tariffs.

According to cost-value logic, cheap wages do not necessarily imply cheap prices of goods. In the case of Honda versus Norton Villiers Triumph cited above, Japanese wages were substantially higher than those in Britain, yet costs and prices were lower, because of Japan's edge in productivity.

Prices and costs are determined by a two-bladed scissors—what labor and capital do for the firm, compared to what the firm pays them. In some cases—perhaps in most cases—high-productivity, high-wage strategies are more cost-effective than low-wage, low-productivity ones.

Again, Henry Ford provides an early and powerful example. By 1913, production of the Model T had become highly mechanized, with specialized workers performing one of numerous small assembly tasks. The result was boring, alienating work in comparison with how workers who took great pride in their skills once built cars by hand. Labor unrest grew, but pressure to speed up production and reduce costs was severe and relentless. So many workers quit, that to keep 100 men working on his line during the year of 1913 Ford at one point had to hire a thousand—a ten-to-one turnover ratio. No sooner did workers acquire a skill than they upped and quit, wasting the initial investment in them. Ford's assembly-line revolution was about to break apart on the rocks of crumbling labor relations.

Henry Ford's solution was to double daily wages, from $2.50 to $5.00. While that big wage hike was seen by some as a gesture of generosity on the part of grateful management to its productive workers, it was in fact an act of desperation, aimed at hiring the best workers and then keeping them from quitting. Besides, it was an exercise in simple cost-value logic applied to capital and labor. It made little sense, Ford thought, to match highly productive, and expensive, machines, with unproductive, cheap labor. Expensive capital needs productive, and expensive, labor. He was right. Ten thousand workers stormed Ford's plant the day after his electrifying $5-a-day announcement. Turnover plummeted, productivity rose, and Ford's assembly-line revolution continued. It was one of the earliest, and most vivid, instances of saving huge sums in costs by actually raising wages.

Many executives react to stiffening competition by trying to cut wages, rather than increase them. This was the approach of many U.S. firms in the early 1980s, including General Electric's electric-motor division. GE competed with nonunion Emerson Electric, who paid $7.20 an hour compared with GE's $11. Both companies had plants in Singapore and in Mexico, where wages were 80 cents to $1.50 an hour. Faced with falling sales and 2 percent profit margins, the division head acted decisively. Hourly workers were assessed a pay cut of $1 an hour, to under $10, and were told to forego scheduled pay increases of another $1.30. In return, the jobs of 5,400 workers were guaranteed, and $200 million were invested in new equipment and product development. Pay cuts did save $25 million a year. But it was a Pyrrhic victory, because worker morale dropped and productivity dived. The electric-motor division now has a new strategy, one based on retaining existing wage levels but offsetting its wage disadvantage (compared to Emerson Electric) by raising productivity and efficiency through such steps as teamwork, job rotation, inventory systems, and quality control. According to a senior GE executive, "we now see that the productivity available is really extraordinary."[15]

Are people valuable assets—or variable overhead costs? When the hard times end, as they must and will, companies will shake out into two groups—those that have struggled to preserve and enhance their human resources and those that practiced "slash and burn." The cost-value logic of economics states clearly which group will endure and prevail.

Ironically, the country that made the high-wage, high-productivity formula work best—Japan—is now being forced to retrench and in some cases abandon it, squeezed by the realities of cost-value logic. A major cause is the rising cost of capital in Japan. In the late 1980s, the real cost of capital (adjusted for inflation) was only 4.5 percent, compared with 5.9 percent for American companies. But U.S. interest rates dropped rapidly after that, while Tokyo's stock market collapsed—and efforts to prop it up led to higher interest rates. As a result, U.S. and Japanese firms nearly switched roles. Japanese firms now pay 5 percent for their capital, and American firms, 4.4 percent.

One consequence has been that Japan's heavy investment in industrial assembly robots in the 1980s, to replace assembly line workers (a bargain then, saving one worker at a cost of 5—10 million yen) has become a costly luxury [at 20 million yen per saved worker—too costly]. Labor-saving equipment has now become more expensive than the wages it saves, at Japan's new, higher cost of capital. Nissan Motor's new plant on Kyushu, with 500 robots, is idle and useless.

Once unthinkable, Japanese firms are now laying off thousands of workers. Sony Electric cut 3,000 from its work force by 1995. TDK, the world's largest manufacturer of magnetic tape, told 50 mid-level managers to stay home, in return for 90 percent of their salaries until they turn 60.[16] Other larger cuts are likely to come.

Pay for Performance

A common-sense approach to boosting productivity is to link the bottom of the cost-value scissors with the top, tying what workers get from their company in pay with what they contribute to it in output. This was the approach of Warren Buffett, legendary founder of Berkshire Hathaway, who invested heavily in Salomon Brothers and then took over to run it when his investment seemed in danger. Salomon Brothers, Wall Street's leading trading house, relies on the skills and knowledge of its workers, and its major cost of doing business is wages and salaries: a total $1.6 billion. Yet because of antiquated cost accounting, no one really knew how individuals or divisions were performing. This was especially true of Salomon Brothers' $4 billion in capital. Buffett redesigned Salomon Brothers' cost accounting, in order to learn which business units had the highest costs, where the company's operating capital was being employed, and where profits were coming from. Overhead expenses were assigned to business units. Then compensation was linked directly to each operation's earnings. Moreover, cost savings were treated as if they contributed as much to profits as increases in revenues—which, dollar for dollar, they do. The result: $1.4 billion in pre-tax profits in 1992, a third higher than one year earlier. One proven approach to improving performance is to have workers redefine themselves as shareholders (with an abiding interest in the company's profitability) instead of just wage earners. Much of Salomon Brothers' compensation to senior management was in the form of shares.[17]

Overall, despite the Salmon Brothers example, the evidence linking higher productivity directly with profit sharing is quite weak. So is the evidence that ESOPs—employee stock ownership plans, that give workers a shareholder's stake in their firm—raise productivity. There is, however, evidence that firms with an *organized program for employee participation in company decision making* have higher productivity gains than companies without such programs. Such plans also enhance the productivity bonus accruing from profit sharing. The principle seems simple—workers who act as if they were in part owners and managers work better than those who act is if they were only hired labor.[18]

Productivity is ultimately the responsibility of management, like everything that happens inside the firm. But is it *responsive* to management? There is evidence that it is. A study by Thomas Hout, V-P of Boston Consulting Group, argues that successful companies "know how to get people working together to come up with the right answers before anyone else." He finds that fast and innovative companies "have a better staffing balance, suggesting more interaction among the functions during the development process, with the design engineers getting more input, context and support from other functions. Such interaction increases the odds that the product will work, sell, and make a profit."[19]

The key role of teamwork is about to undergo a severe test at Boeing, maker of Boeing 767 civilian aircraft. Boeing has promised United Parcel Service a new all-cargo version of its 767 plane in 33 months (including both design and construction), instead of the usual 42 months. It will achieve this by putting a team of 400 employees at one location and organizing them into "cross-functional" teams, with design, production, planning, and tooling workers in each team. Slashing product cycle time by one-fourth is a major achievement—it means that Boeing gets to market with its product nearly a year before its competitors. In an age when many products are similar with respect to price and quality, faster delivery can be a decisive advantage.

Another key element of productivity gains is the notion of "continuous improvement"—the positive application of the Chinese "death by a thousand cuts" torture, as "higher output and efficiency by a thousand small improvements." In general, one of the greatest failings American firms is the concentration on improving products, rather than processes—in other words, emphasis on making better things, instead of making things better. New processes are all too often like baseball expansion teams: warmly welcomed by all at first, then bogged down in confusion and disorder deep in the league basement. Many companies expect to buy new processes "off the shelf"—machines complete with manuals, service engineers, and software—and ready to run at top efficiency. But often this expectation is not borne out in practice. Weeks and months of close cooperation among workers, managers, and engineers are necessary. And once the system is in place, continual tinkering is needed to make it work better.[20]

KNOWLEDGE AND PRODUCTIVITY

The crucial importance of labor and knowledge in the modern economy was brought home by one of the most striking graphs I ever saw, which came out in a research report by SRI International, with the underplayed caption, "The Post-Industrial Society: Shift in Economic Activity Already Made." The graph shows two major revolutions in the way people earn their living. The first came when the fraction of the U.S. labor force working in agriculture fell below that in industry, for the first time, in around 1905—about the time Henry Ford's Model T was a gleam in his eye. The second happened as early as 1955, when the number of people employed by information-related employers—education, media, publishing, software, databases, consulting—overtook those working in industry, for the first time. (See Figure 5.1.)

America's chief business today is not business but information. This has been true for decades, though we have been slow to recognize it. The implications for executive decision making are sweeping, because information is a decidedly different product than cars or TVs, and the labor that produces information is quite different from labor that makes VCRs or personal computers.

In my early days as a rookie journalist, one of my managing editors told me about an argument he had with a lawyer friend. "You journalists," said the lawyer, "are like people standing on the bank of a river, dipping pails into it at random and spilling it into our troughs. You add nothing, you do nothing productive to the water."

"True," said the managing editor. "We dip pails into the stream. Then we clean the water, purify it, distill it, send it in to the right pipes and the right homes at low cost and nearly instantly. Our 'water' is lifegiving. Without it society would shrivel."

If water in the stream is information, then knowledge is the product distilled, purified, and organized, after clever pails have dipped into the information stream. This is the function of increasing numbers of firms and people. This is how many of us earn our living. And though we have been slow to realize it, it is a fundamentally different task from assembling an automobile.

Knowledge, unlike bread or fuel, expands, the more it is consumed and the more it is shared with others. One of the basic tasks of executives is to ensure that the pool of knowledge existing within a company moves freely and swiftly from those who have it to those who need it.[21] I have argued that the command economies of the ex-USSR and Eastern Europe collapsed not because of planning but because the flow of information was rigidly limited as a means of controlling society.[22] A modern industrial system where nearly everyone is purposely kept in the dark about nearly everything cannot possibly work.

FIGURE 5.1
Percentage of U.S. Labor Force in Agriculture, Industry, Information, and Services

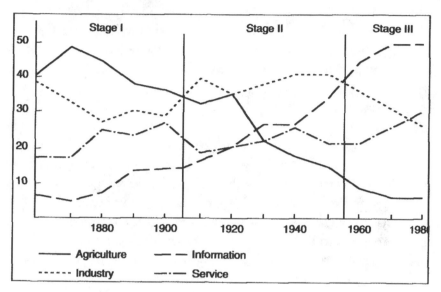

Source: SRI International, "The Post-Industrial Society: Shift in Economic Activity Already Made," cited in Stewart Brand, *The MIT Media Lab* (Viking Penguin, New York, 1987). Reprinted with permission of SRI International, Menlo Park, California.

Many of the executives I taught over the years—even those from information industries—are still hung up on a basic fallacy whose origins lie in Marxist thinking—that only something tangible, a product, has true value, while a service has no value or derivative value based on its contribution to putting out a product. In *Das Kapital,* Book II, chapter 3, Marx wrote, "nothing can have value without being an *object of utility*. If it be useless, the labor contained in it is not useful, cannot be reckoned as labor and cannot therefore create value." Under Marxist economic accounting methods, production of services is not counted in the socialist equivalent of Gross Domestic Product, and for years the USSR published data only on "net material product," meaning goods, excluding services. This was based on a fundamental misunderstanding. Not only are services of value, in the knowledge-based society, information services are of *crucial* value, and often how well they are used spells success or failure for companies. And for the successful production and distribution of information services, a smart, skilled, and educated labor force is vital.

Ultimately, people do not buy products. They purchase services that those products yield. When consumer purchases are seen in the right light, as attempts to buy things that solve problems, it is clear that it is the attributes of products—what products do for you—and not the products themselves, that are crucial. Dartmouth University professor James Bryant Quinn observes insightfully that "products are a happy way of capturing services." A car embodies convenient transportation service, he claims, and it will until we can either physically move you in some other manner or give you the same experience through, say, electronics.[23]

This new view of business affects every aspect of executive decision making. The total quality movement, for instance, tries to find new ways to improve the various services that a product provides, at every stage. Re-engineering breaks down the production processes and tries to improve a sequence of services that ultimately leads to the final, ultimate package of services sold in the marketplace.

The ultimate service is knowledge. In the new workplace, people who know how to create knowledge, and then use it, will be the most important part of the workforce. And knowledge itself will replace land, machines, unskilled labor and raw materials, and even managerial ability, as the crucial factor of production—in fact, it already has. Our awareness of this has been somewhat obscured by the fact that huge investments made by U.S. firms over the past decade in information systems have yielded disappointing results in immediate productivity gains and profitability.

$1 TRILLION IS MISSING IN PRODUCTIVITY DATA

"We see computers everywhere . . . except in the productivity statistics," Nobel laureate in economics Robert Solow once remarked.

Over the past decade, American corporations spent the huge amount of $1 trillion on various types of information technology—computers, networks, and software. The results were very poor. U.S. productivity growth averaged 3 percent a year up to

1973; since then, it grew only 1 percent a year on average, despite the massive investments in computing power.

MIT scholar Geoffrey Brooke thinks the wide adoption of information technology, and the productivity slowdown, are related. His explanation: "the more information there is, the more time you have to spend converting it (into knowledge). We've made it easy to produce, collect and transmit information. We haven't made it easy to consume information. Consuming information is just as slow as it always was."[24] The result is the so-called productivity paradox: computers' enormous potential for improving productivity, and the huge investment in them, coupled with no discernible effect on output or productivity at all.

Help, however, is on the way. New advances in computers and software are indeed making it easy to consume the enormous wave of knowledge produced in recent decades. A large dataset by MIT researcher Erik Byrnjolfsson for some 380 companies shows very high rates of return on investment in computer capital—for 1987–1991, between 54 and 68 percent a year.[25] Two things have occurred in the past five years that have greatly enhanced the value of computers. First, their power has grown by at least a factor of 10, making possible many applications previously unthinkable (for instance, management of computer-based credit-collection systems). Second, many firms have at long last undertaken the sweeping organizational changes that new information technology requires in order to justify its costs. They have gotten rid of layers of managers and workers made unnecessary by information systems.

The problem with the information technology investment was that it was mainly used to serve its masters—managers—rather than the other "slaves"—people who really needed it, those who produce, service, supply, maintain, and design products and services. A study by Princeton University economist Alan Krueger showed that "workers who use computers on their job earn roughly a 10 to 15 percent higher wage rate." This suggests that they are approximately 10 to 15 percent more productive than comparable workers without computers.[26] For years computers created more managers, instead of replacing existing ones as they were intended. As Paul Strassman has shown, companies who used information technology productively employed it principally to market, produce, distribute, and develop goods and services, rather than to manage or organize.[27]

The paradoxical result of information technology was to add layers of managers (to handle and manage it), rather than get rid of managers made superfluous by the ability of top executives to call upon their screens information they once needed underlings to process, refine, and analyze. Hayes, Wheelwright, and Clark observed, "one should bring in a computer, companies learned through painful experience, only after one's information system has been cleaned up and systematized." Most companies, however, first brought in the computer—and then did the cleanup. The result was to delay by long years the keenly anticipated productivity fruits that computers and related information systems bore.[28]

Most sweeping trends in business are a combination of good news and bad news. This is true of the rapid gains in productivity made possible by new information technology. The bad news is that very large numbers of people, some of them highly skilled and educated, are losing their jobs, with no hope of ever getting them back. In 1992, according to one estimate, a half million clerical and technical positions were wiped out in the United States. At the same time, the economy grew. The result of higher output and lower employment is, by definition, higher productivity. This is in part good news. Viewed from a long historical perspective, the short-run pain caused by job loss induced through productivity gains has been more than offset by the long-run increase in living standards such gains enable. The stresses on weak points of the economy are considerable, however. Once only blue-collar workers were subject to layoffs or firing—now, even highly educated workers and mid-to-senior level managers are becoming redundant. For those people, it is small comfort to know that society is better off, when they themselves are substantially worse off and may not in fact find gainful employment for the rest of their lives.

The knowledge economy will radically change the way executives make decisions about labor, capital and knowledge. Here are some implications.

Fact: Knowledge, unlike labor, capital, or materials, expands, the more widely it is shared and the more intensively it is used.

Implication: Executives will have to find innovative ways to foster cooperation, both within their firm and between their firm and others, including bitter rivals, ways that lead to wider sharing of knowledge.

Fact: Knowledge is created, shared, and disseminated faster and better in smaller organizations rather than larger ones.

Implication: Executives will need to find ways to reshape their organizations, turning big clumsy units into smaller faster-reacting ones, in which knowledge can zip to all its participants with enough speed to permit quick reactions to changing conditions in markets and technology.

Fact: The average cost of knowledge is extremely high, but the marginal cost of enlightening one more person or group is very small, once the knowledge exists.

Implication: More knowledge-based products and services will be sold like country-club memberships, to subscribers, rather than piece-by-piece.

T.S. Eliot once wrote, in his poem "The Rock": "Where is the knowledge we have lost in information?" It took $1 trillion, but American firms are now finding the knowledge lost in the ocean of information and information technology they bought. The result will be revolutionary, both for executives and for the workers they manage.

Postscript: The epigraph that led off this chapter is good advice. It was given, however, by Aga Hasan Abedi, who founded a bank known as the Bank for Credit and Commerce International (BCCI), which allegedly fleeced wealthy Arab oil sheikhs and thousands of small depositors alike in forty countries of some $15 billion. There are few areas where preaching and practice diverge more widely than those involving the management of people, knowledge, and machines.

Chapter Six

FROM VOLUME
TO VARIETY

Increasingly, executives are challenged to attain two objectives that are, if not contradictory, at least moderately hostile to one another:

- achieve high-volume production for mass markets; and at the same time,
- provide individually tailored, high-quality customized goods and services, that suit the personal needs of each customer.

They must do this, while continually lowering costs and raising efficiency and productivity, all the while ensuring a broad range of high-quality products that meet customer needs. In short: volume and variety.

The National Bicycle Industrial Co., a Japanese subsidiary of Matsushita, is a good example of how the volume-versus-variety circle can be squared. This company offers, in Japan, over 11 million variations of its 18 models of racing, road, and mountain bikes. After deciding to buy one of the company's bicycles, a typical customer might well think he had mistaken the bike shop for an exclusive tailor. Shopkeepers measure the customer's body dimensions on a special frame. They then note the customer's choice of model, size, color, and design. The specifications are then faxed to the factory.

At the factory, a computer creates custom blueprints for the bicycle. Robots measure, weld, and paint the frame to order. Then skilled workers apply the finishing touches, including the customer's name silkscreened onto the frame.

Thanks in part to the clever blend of well-trained employees, computers, and well-programmed robots, the cost of this tailor-made bicycle is not significantly higher than an off-the-rack standard model. The combination of high value and low price enables the National Bicycle Industrial Co. to attain high-volume sales, which in turn make the high investment in its robot technology worthwhile.

This chapter focuses on the concepts of "scale" (volume) and "scope" (variety). The tool it presents is a concept designed to help executives figure out to what extent there are cost savings in high-volume production (economies of scale), or in broadening the company's range of goods and services (economics of scope), or both.

Accompanying the tool is a message—a new industrial revolution is brewing. Consumers are no longer willing to settle for a standard "any color if black" Model T product, where all fifteen million units look like they were cloned from the same "cell" or design, no matter how inexpensive. They are demanding, and getting, a wide range of sizes, shapes, and colors. Mass production is now giving way to mass customization. Managing this revolution demands radical shifts in the way company heads organize their firms, develop and market their products, choose their technologies, and define their businesses.

THE ORIGINS OF SCALE AND SCOPE

Like all revolutions, this one signalled its coming long ago. Harvard business historian Alfred Chandler, Jr., in his sweeping comparison of capitalism in Britain, Germany, and America, traces its origins to two courageous business decisions made over a century ago, in the United States and Germany.[1]

In America, in 1882, John D. Rockefeller's Standard Oil Company (precursor of Exxon) dominated the production of kerosene.

Kerosene was at that time the key product refined from crude oil and was by far America's largest nonfarm export. The alliance of some 40 companies linked to Standard Oil made 90 percent of all the kerosene produced in the United States and had a stranglehold monopoly on its market. With this rather comfortable, profitable cartel, a new Standard Oil Trust was formed.[2] It created a central corporate office, Chandler relates, which undertook to close down small inefficient refineries and raise capital to build three enormous new ones, in which fully a quarter of world production was concentrated. The main objective was to face a growing challenge to Standard Oil in Europe. Russia's Caspian Sea oil fields began to produce and ship kerosene to Standard Oil's profitable European market. While this threat was still only a potential one—Standard Oil had most of the European market—the company acted fast to meet it, by building giant cost-efficient refineries.

The huge scale of production made possible impressive cost reductions. In 1880, plants with 2,000-barrel-a-day capacity made kerosene for 2.5 cents a gallon. In 1885, plants with three times that capacity could make kerosene for less than half a penny per gallon. The result of these "economies of scale" was to double the profit per gallon of kerosene from half a cent to a full penny. More important, it became possible for Standard Oil to price its kerosene in Europe competitively relative to Russian kerosene, even though the American product had much higher shipping costs.

No competitor could match those costs, or compete with the investment and technology muscle that the resulting cash flow permitted. The success of the decision to shoot for scale, Chandler stresses, lay not in the huge refinery and its technology, but in the management skills required to run it well, coordinating the raw materials, production, shipping, and distribution of a highly complex interdependent system. Trust executives had those skills. Without them, the investment in scale would have failed.[3]

In Germany, at roughly the same juncture in history, three large chemical companies—Bayer, Hoechst, and BASF—were also making enormous investments in huge plants for making dyes. Their objective was somewhat different from that of Standard Oil. Until then, they had made a wide variety of dyes and drugs in a large number of small dedicated production facilities. Why not build huge plants able to produce hundreds of different dyes and drugs, using the same basic chemical stock? they asked. Once the plant was in place, making another, new dye in it would add little to total costs. This was a case of cost-cutting through "economies of scope"—lowering unit costs by making new and different products with the same facility, rather than by making larger volumes of the same product.

Scope economies, like Standard Oil's scale economies, slashed costs dramatically. For instance, the cost of one kilogram of red alizarin, a new synthetic dye, fell from 270 marks in 1869 to 9 marks in 1886. As with high-volume production, high-scope production required high-quality management to handle the vast array of different products, making sure each was made in the right amounts, in the appropriate way, and sent to the correct destination on schedule. Like scale, scope demanded first-rate executives. As with the Standard Oil Trust, managerial skill was a crucial input.

Once attained, the huge cost advantages of scale and scope gave the companies who created them first an almost insurmountable competitive advantage. "In some instances," Chandler notes, "the first company to build a plant of minimum efficient scale and to recruit the essential management team remained the leader in its industry for decades."[4] Exxon is still one of the largest oil companies in the world, and third largest industrial company in America. And Bayer, Hoechst, and BASF dominate world markets for chemicals.

————

How are cost-savings through scope and scale defined and measured?

Economies of scale are *reductions in average and marginal costs that result from the increased size of an operating unit*. Such savings stem from many factors. Among them are the ability to divide up tasks into ever-smaller ones—as Adam Smith explained in his pin-factory example—making laborers ever more speedy and efficient in each one; savings in quantity purchases of components and raw materials; use of equipment too expensive to justify for smaller-scale output; and the spreading of fixed overhead over ever-larger volumes of output.

Economies of scope are *reductions in average and marginal costs that result from using facilities and processes in a single operating unit to produce a larger variety of goods or services.* The basis of scope economies is "joint" production—several different product lines sharing the same manufacturing, distribution, and marketing facility. The German chemical firms' new dye plants, or the National Bicycle Industrial Co.'s tailor-made bikes, are examples.

The scale strategy of Standard Oil and the scope strategy of the German chemical firms are not unrelated. To enjoy scope economies, large-scale plants have to be built. And the huge refineries of Standard Oil that captured economies of scale, also permitted wide scope—by altering the production process, a wide variety of petroleum products could be made, ranging from heavy bunker fuel and diesel oil to gasoline, in the Trust's huge new refineries. The precise quantitative link between "scale" and "scope" economies will be shown in detail below.

THE VOLUME AND/OR VARIETY MATRIX

How do executives know if their firm enjoys economies of scale and scope? And how are the two sources of cost savings related?

One way to answer these questions is a cost matrix, or two-way table, showing total costs (including overhead, distribution, and marketing) as they vary with different amounts of output for two or more products. The example shown here is for two hypothetical products, but could easily be expanded to three or more products or services.

Consider Wal-Mart, America's largest chain of discount retail stores. Wal-Mart founder Sam Walton became a multi-billionaire through his intuitive understanding of huge economies of scale and scope in his business. Wal-Mart currently has $55 billion in annual sales, with 20 percent annual growth. It has a resultant strategic problem—find new markets and products to sustain that remarkable growth rate.

Suppose Wal-Mart sells "clothes and appliances" (lumped together as X) in huge stores with 100,000 sq. ft. or more of floor space. Wal-Mart considers adding groceries—treated as product Y—to some of its stores, in so-called Supercenters.[5]

Is that a good idea? Will it lower costs?

To check this, build a total-cost matrix for X (clothes and appliances) and Y (groceries), varying with different amounts of X and Y. In this matrix, each entry, or element, shows the total cost (both fixed costs, such as the land and building, and variable costs, including salaries of employees) of selling various amounts of X and Y.

This total cost matrix is simply a systematic listing of the total cost of producing varying amounts of Wal-Mart's two basic products, set up in spreadsheet form.

It enables us to answer the questions in the following checklist, in order:

1. *Are there single-product economies of scale?* These are cost savings ocurring *when the amount of one good, say Y (groceries) is held constant, while another is increased.* Hold Y constant at, for instance, zero (that is, no groceries at all are sold in the store). Expand X from 1 to 2 to 3 to 4. Test what happens to total costs.

In the above example, with Y equal zero, quadrupling X, from 1 *unit to 4 (thousand) only doubles total costs. This implies considerable* single-product economies of scale for clothes and appliances—a fact that many of Wal-Mart's smaller competitors have bitterly learned. This holds true equally for all values of Y, whether Y = 1, 2, 3, or 4.

2. *Are there economies of scope?* To check this, compare the total cost of selling given amounts of Y and X in *separate* facilities with the cost of selling them together in the same facility. This involves testing whether:

TOTAL COST (Clothes and Appliances, No Groceries)

+

TOTAL COST (Groceries, No Clothes and Appliances)

is *greater than, equal to,* or *less than:*

TOTAL COST (Clothes and Appliances & Groceries
in the Same Store)

TABLE 6.1

Total Cost of Selling X and Y ($ m.)

Amounts of X ('000 units per day)

		0	1	2	3	4
	0	10	15	20	25	30
Amounts						
	1	15	19	23	27	31
of						
	2	20	23	27	20	32
Y						
('000 units	3	25	27	29	31	33
per day)						
	4	30	31	32	33	34

This comparison must be carried out for comparable quantities—for instance, when 5 units of Y and zero X are sold, and when 5 units of X are sold and zero Y (each in separate stores); compared with selling 5 units of X and 5 units of Y together in the same store.

There are economies of scope if selling X and Y together in the same store is cheaper than selling the same amounts of X and Y separately, in separate ones. There are diseconomies of scope if it is cheaper to sell them separately than together.

In the above table, for X = 0 and Y = 4 (that is, a store which sells 4 units of groceries but no clothing and appliances), total costs are 30. For Y = 0 and X = 4 (that is, a store which sells 4 units of clothing and appliances but no groceries), total costs are also 30. For two separate stores, which together supply 4 units of clothing and appliances and 4 units of groceries, total costs are 30 + 30 = 60. In one combined store, from the matrix, total costs of X = 4 and Y = 4 amount to only 34. This is a considerable saving, compared to 60.

3. *Are there multiproduct economies of scale?* These are cost reductions resulting from expanding the *scale of business* for both X and Y together. It is found by travelling along the main diagonal of the matrix, doubling X and Y together, and then checking to see whether total costs double, more than double, or less than double.

Multiproduct economies of scale are the net outcome of two separate forces: single-product economies of scale, and economies of scope.

If total costs less than double when output doubles, then there are multiproduct economies of scale. If total costs more than double when output of all products doubles, then there are multiproduct *dis*economies of scale.

In the above example, doubling X and Y, from X=Y=2 to X=Y=4 raises total costs from 27 to only 34. In other words, sales have doubled while total costs have risen by less than 25 percent. The reason is that there are separate, individual economies of scale, in both groceries and in clothing and appliances; and there are major synergies in selling them together.

The cost savings are in fact no mystery. Once you are building a retail facility, you might as well build it jumbo-size, and offer consumers nearly everything they might want to purchase, thus guaranteeing that they leave a considerable part of their disposable income in your cash registers. In this way the fixed costs of the facility are spread over a very large total volume of retail sales. It is not only the facility that spreads its fixed costs over a large volume of sales, but also the customer. If you are driving some distance to, say, a Wal-Mart facility, you might as well spread that "fixed time cost" over a wide range of purchases, thus economizing on gasoline, trips, and energy.

The phenomenal success of Wal-Mart in revolutionizing American retailing—and its imitators in various branches of retailing, including Toys-R-Us in toys, Circuit City stores in appliances, and so forth—is a vivid example of how huge economies of scale and scope together create competitive advantage. Today, retailers seek sites close to major highways, where stores of at least 100,000 sq. ft. can be built. Such stores may be as far as 50 miles from the nearest large population center. Despite this customers seem willing to get into their cars and drive to them, if they have good reason to do so. These are the modern equivalent of the Standard Oil Trust's giant kerosene refineries, applied (perhaps belatedly) to retailing.

To grasp the size of such stores, consider that average aisle length is nearly 100 yards and there are often 20 or more aisles. That means walking up and down each aisle involves travelling well over a mile! If there are four layers of shelves on each aisle, on two sides, this means the store has 8 miles of shelf space. Large numbers of such stores, in chains, generate big cost-savings through scale—quantity purchases of goods, for instance. Each huge store generates economies of scope, enabling display of a wide range of goods, so that customers are sure to find the precise model, price, color, and type of product they want and can afford.

Clearly, it is substantially cheaper to sell food, clothing, and appliances, at a discount, in the same store. There are economies of scale in each, taken separately, and synergies creating economies of scope when they are sold together. Knowing this, one could perhaps have predicted Wal-Mart's incursion into the grocery business, and the fierce competitive battle that will likely result. Some experts predict that within four to five years, Wal-Mart will eclipse the current supermarket leader, Kroger Co., with $22 billion in sales in 1992. In an industry where corner grocery stores could once make a decent living, economies of scale and scope will likely bring an increasing chunk of the $383 billion in annual grocery sales into the coffers of large chains like Wal-Mart. Owners of smaller stores—like small drugstores before them—may be trampled by scale and scope, just like the small refineries and chemical companies were trampled at the end of the nineteenth century. Their strategy will be to offer customers what large chains cannot—personal service, home delivery, proximity to their homes, and so forth—and fewer aisles.

The formula for scale-plus-scope in discount retailing has spread to nearly every type of product, from toys through appliances. Circuit City Stores average 32,000 sq. ft. in size, and in 1990 their 149 outlets offered an average of 2,800 different brand-name items, including 150 different color TVs, 50 VCRs,

30 CD players, 45 models of refrigerators, and 26 washer-dryer pairs. Underlying Circuit City's scope operation was some crucial technology—a mechanized distribution center that let Circuit City replenish its inventories overnight, and provide instant product availability.[6]

The airline industry is a good example of the close linkage between scale and scope. Large planes have lower costs per seat-mile than small planes. This is an economy of scale—the larger the number of passengers on a given route, the larger the plane that can be used, hence the lower the costs. In order to facilitate use of big planes instead of small ones, airlines have moved to a hub-and-spoke system, in which small "feeder" routes ("spokes") fly passengers to a central "hub." Passengers are flown to the hub from smaller cities in the area and then loaded onto large planes to fly to other hubs or major cities. The larger the scope of operations— that is, the number of routes that feed in to the central hub—the greater the possible savings in economies of scale.

VICES AND VIRTUES OF VARIETY

A wider range of products on the same production and distribution base does not always save costs. Sometimes it actually *increases* them. It is entirely possible, for instance, that there are single-product economies of *scale* but diseconomies of *scope*. If the single-product diseconomies of scope outweigh the scale effects, then this could lead to rising costs as the scale of output grows.

All the logical possibilities of scale and scope are summarized below:

TABLE 6.2
Multiproduct Economies (E) or Diseconomies (D) of Scale

		Economies of Scope?	
		Yes	*No*
Single-Product	*Yes*	E for sure	E or D
Economies of Scale?	*No*	E or D	D for sure

If both single-product scale economies and scope economies work in the same direction—to lower costs, or raise costs—then the overall multiproduct economies of scale will of course reflect the same trend. But if single-product scale and scope work in opposite directions, then the overall effect, in multiproduct economies of scale, will depend on which effect is stronger. For instance, there could be single-product economies of scale, but they might be offset by "negative synergies"—diseconomies of scope, stemming from one product interfering with another, perhaps through by-products or congestion—meaning that overall, it is cheaper to expand production of two products separately, in different facilities, rather than the same one.

Roads are an example. Roads *for cars only*, with heavy trucks banned, enjoy single-product economies of scale—the larger the traffic volume on the road, the cheaper the cost per car, especially when the indirect costs of congestion (time lost by being stuck in traffic jams) is taken into account. (Congestion costs are generally very large—a case where time [lost] really is money.) Roads for trucks only similarly enjoy (single-product) economies of scale.

But when *both* trucks and cars travel on the same road, there are "diseconomies of scope," because trucks and cars get in each other's way.[7] The author of a study exploring this issue suggests examining "whether to separate auto and truck traffic" as a way of making transportation budgets more economical. A similar problem appears to exist in passenger and freight railroad services. "Keeping tracks smooth enough for passenger trains, but heavy enough to withstand the axle loadings of freight trains, can indeed be costly... [causing] diseconomies of scope," H. Youn Kim has argued.[8]

Bigness is not always a guarantee of low costs. During the merger boom of the 1980s, Michael Blumenthal, CEO of a large computer firm Burroughs, bid nearly $5 billion for a slightly bigger competitor in the mainframe computer market, Sperry. He reasoned that by doubling in size, the combined firm could cut its production, administrative, and service costs, generating profits that would enable them to chase expensive, innovative research neither could pay for on its own. Possibly, he reasoned, they might even be able to challenge mighty IBM.

The merged firm, Unisys, did not fulfill its promise. Its losses mounted, partly due to the cost of servicing the $4 billion in debt acquired in order to create the merger. More important, Burroughs and Sperry had incompatible standards; Unisys could not phase out either company's product line, so it had to keep spending duplicative R&D investments to maintain both.

MASS CUSTOMIZATION: THE NEW PARADIGM

Some observers believe that economies of scope, as exemplified by Wal-Mart, have implications far beyond the area of mass retailing—they comprise no less than a new paradigm, or comprehensive model, of capitalism itself. As B. Joseph Pine II has explained, mass customization is a synthesis of the two long-competing systems of management: the mass production of standard products, and individual tailoring of products and services to the precise desires and needs of each consumer or group of consumers.[9]

Mass production is based on cost-savings through economies of scale—of the kind Henry Ford created, by making 15 million Model T's. Mass customization is based on cost savings by building a large variety of products with the same basic set of components.

Part of the rise of mass customization was made possible by new technologies—like the clever robots used by the Japanese bicycle company that know how to translate information about the buyer's body measurements into a precisely produced bicycle frame, or flexible manufacturing that permits the programming of assembly robots to put together thousands of different automobile models, each with its own specific color and package of options, without delaying the entire line. But a major part rests on intelligent managers and workers. Economies of scope, more than scale, rely on highly skilled production workers, and managers. Take, for instance, the Coopersburg, Pa., company, Lutron Electronics.

Lutron makes lighting controls for homes and offices. It is the market leader—with no serious competitor in sight. Lutron offers over 11,000 different controls, across over a dozen product lines. The vast majority of its products are shipped in lots of under 100 units each. In its electronic lighting system, for example, no system has ever been reproduced twice—each is different.

Lutron enjoys economies of scale, because it uses standard components produced on a single assembly line. This captures the benefits of the first industrial revolution of mass production. But Lutron also enjoys the bounties of the second industrial revolution, of mass customization. It hires skilled engineers and invests large amounts of time and money in training them. The engineers spend long periods of time with Lutron's customers—even to the extent of eating up all the company's profits on that particular sale—to learn the customer's needs. First, they design a basic product line. Then they work with each customer to adapt it to his or her exact needs. From, say, 100 different models for purchase, engineering and production experts trim the line down to 15–20 standardized components, which can later be configured into the 100 different models.

Lutron's chairman, Joel Spira, describes the process: "Chaos increases new business. Order increases profits." Mass customization, more than anything, is the simultaneous existence of chaos and order—variety and volume, lions and lambs forced to lie down together by good management and good technology, applied by well-trained workers.[10]

Motorola's Pager Division is a good example of how a "scope" strategy can keep a business alive. (A pager, or beeper, signals the person carrying it to contact his or her office or employer.) In the 1980s, B. Joseph Pine II reports, Japanese companies invaded the U.S. market and sold their pagers for half the going $200 price of American ones. By 1985 most of the U.S. producers had been forced out of business. Motorola knew that for its pager to survive, it needed a radical solution. Standard cost-reduction efforts would not be enough. Its answer was to assemble a new team to design a new manufacturing process for its Bravo pagers. The goal set for the team was to build a line yielding economies of scale—on volumes of one unit—as well as economies of scope. Today, a Motorola salesperson meets with a customer and designs the pagers that precisely suit that customer's needs. The specifications are sent by computer modem to Motorola's company headquarters in Schaumburg, Illinois. From there, orders go out automatically to IBM mainframe computers at the factory in Boynton Beach, Florida, and from there to a set of Hewlett-Packard computers on the factory floor that control 27 Seiko robots. The total elapsed time, from receipt of the customer's specifications to the first pager starting its jaunt down the assembly line: 15 to 20 minutes. About an hour later the first pager is inspected, labelled, and boxed for shipping. It is far more attractive to the customer than a standard off-the-shelf model. The added value lets the seller ask for a higher price. The sophisticated technology ensures that the cost of creating such value is not prohibitive.

The key to mass customization is good design. Motorola began to revitalize its Bravo pagers by redesigning them for robotic production, with 109 of its parts on electronic circuit boards that enabled a high degree of customization. Those boards made possible 29 million different variations of the pager. To be successful, it is now recognized that design needs to be integrated with manufacturing right from the time the product is just an idea. Redesign can rescue unsuccessful products. For example, after finding its costs soaring through proliferation of models and types of power tools, Skil Corp. reorganized by redesigning its products—using, for instance, the same handle for all its models of power drills. The savings were large, without impairing the variety of models that customers had come to demand.

MASS CUSTOMIZATION AND THE BUSINESS CYCLE

Technology emerges in waves. It is one of the ironies of business that major new developments in technology often emerge during society's blackest eras, depressions. Television, for instance, a major consumer electronics product, was discovered during the Great Depression of the 1930s. Depressions occur, by some accounts, when technologies and related products and services run out of steam. Products mature as they saturate markets and consumers find no reason to buy more of them. Meanwhile, firms overinvest in productive capacity for such mature products, based on overoptimistic forecasts of sales. As profits shrink and markets cease to grow, labor and capital are sloughed off as managers try to cut costs. The result is a long-term decline in economic activity, accompanied by high unemployment, deflation, and idle factories.

In 1920, the Russian economist Nikolai Kondratiev observed that such long-wave cycles seem to happen every 60 years. He noted previous depressions that began in 1814 (at the end of the Napoleonic Wars) and 1873. By his calculation, the next long-wave downturn should begin around 1930. It did, heralded by the Wall Street Collapse in 1929.

It is now about 60 years after the onset of the third long-wave cycle, the Great Depression of the thirties. Are we again at the onset of another secular downturn? The answer is unclear. What is clear, however, is that the global economy's major products—automobiles, computers, consumer electronics—are all mature products. It is this fact, more than any other, that is dominating the shift in paradigm from mass production to mass customization.

In such mature markets, companies face flat sales. As costs rise, profit margins are squeezed ever lower. One response is to create new and different varieties of old, familiar products. But such "niche" markets tend to be small in size and hence limited in profit potential. The adjective of "mass customization" is at least as important as the noun—a key principle of management remains the necessity for mass-market sales, to achieve rapid growth. The solution to this dilemma is to move out into foreign markets. As Professor Theodore Levitt has noted:

> possibilities expand for people to have exactly what they wish, and at mass-produced prices—prices that are low not so much because of improved or flexible manufacturing but rather because of global scale economies. The kinds of small market segments common in Switzerland now appear also in Sri Lanka and Swaziland. Everywhere people learn from the same communal messenger, while prices descend into increasingly attractive reach. Additively, similar small preferences in many places cumulate into global bigness in all places. No product category—consumer or industrial, tangible or intangible—is exempt. All products everywhere undergo the transformation from huge monolithic segments into porous little ones. Though consumption thus gets pluralized and miniaturized, its global aggregate gets magnified. The competitive possibilities for scale and scope become compelling. *Those who act on these possibilities capture economizing advantages, to the envy and regret of those who only sit and wait.*[11]

"That," Levitt concludes, "is the only way to capture the scale economies necessary to get and keep costs down, get access to low-cost suppliers, and generate sufficient cash to finance the development and innovations that competitiveness requires."

A kind of two-stage sequence can be discerned in many products. Initially, economies of scale dominate, as companies race to cut costs through high-volume large-scale production not unlike the kind that drove automobile production. Later, as the product matures, economies of scope dominate, as companies try to lure customers to make purchases by expanding the variety of models, adding a dazzling array of bells and whistles to familiar products. The fact that economies of scope now are achieving growing importance suggests that many of the world's major products are now mature ones, mellowing into middle-age and approaching saturation.

A technologically simple product like earphones, for instance, is an example. According to Akio Morita, today one can buy more than 200 different models made by a dozen producers, in a single store.[12] Videocassette recorders (VCRs) are another example. The initial round of competition was fought on scale, as companies struggled to boost volume, lower costs and prices, and expand their market share. At its height, the market for VCRs reached 30 million units a year. Such levels of mass production permitted great cost savings and generated high profits. Now, as sales decline in mature markets, VCRs will become the arena for competition through scope, as competitors seek to offer attractive new features to customers.

Economies of scope are sometimes related to a similar notion drawn from the theory of finance—reducing costly risk by diversification, or spreading it across a large number of assets or projects. Experts have cautioned against applying this false analogy, inferring wrong conclusions from noncomparable contexts. Holding a portfolio of five or ten stocks can help preserve its overall rate of return, while diminishing the risk entailed—when some of the stocks rise, while others fall, the fluctuations tend to cancel out. But for companies, investing limited R&D resources in, say, a "portfolio" of five or ten technologies can be disastrous, because they may fail to achieve excellence and leadership in any one of them.

Simple proliferation of variety is not what is meant by "mass customization." Variety creates a bewildering array of possibilities, many of which no one wants. Customization goes to great lengths to produce a particular variety—perhaps one of several million possibilities—*provided customers want to buy it and are willing to pay the price*. Toyota may be an example. In its efforts in the late 1980's to make varied, individually customized products, Toyota found its production costs soared. There may still have been economies of scale in long production runs of individual car components—but product development costs soared and so did the costs of holding large inventories. Toyota found that 80 percent of its product varieties accounted for only 20 percent of its sales. As a result, Toyota pulled back from its mass-customization strategy and cut its range of different offerings by a fifth.[13] Other Japanese automobile companies, like Mitsubishi, Nissan, and Mazda, had similar experiences.

The cautionary tale of Toyota empasizes that the two-way cost matrix presented earlier tells only part of the story—albeit an important part. The value and price arms of the cost-value-price triangle also need to be considered. It makes little sense to proliferate varieties of products and services, even at falling production cost, if consumers don't need or want them. Such products ultimately prove extremely costly, because they end up sitting in warehouses, forlorn and unneeded—like many of Toyota's slick new technological features—and eventually are written off as a sunk cost, generating little or no revenue. Business strategies built on mass customization and economies of scope are not the same as churning out, and stockpiling, varieties of products, in the wistful hope someone will want one of them. Above all, scope is driven by, and based on, the pull of demand, implemented by a production system that makes it possible to translate that demand very quickly—in the case of Motorola or the National Bicycle Industrial Co., within minutes or hours—into a usable, suitable product. It is the ear of technology shaping into concrete form what it hears the voice of the market asking for.

MINITEL: SCOPE OVER PHONE LINES

Knowledge has become a major source of economies of scope, through so-called "network economics." To see how networks cut costs as they expand, apply a simple formula for the number of connections between any two people in a network with N people: $(N)(N-1)/2$. A network comprising, say, 5 persons, has 5 times $4 / 2 = 10$ possible paths, or links, among them. Each of the 5 persons is connected with 4 others, making 20 links—to avoid double counting (X linked to Y means Y is linked to X), divide 20 by 2, giving 10. Adding a sixth person increases the number of paths to 6 times $5 / 2 = 15$. That is, by increasing the number of members of the network by 20 percent, the total number of paths (which measures the value, or usefulness, of the network) has risen by 50 percent, from 10 to 15. In general, network paths grow in proportion to the square of the number of "nodes" or members. Sharing knowledge becomes more and more cost-effective, the more people there are who are engaged in sharing it. A major function of management has become the facilitation of knowledge sharing among parts of the organization, including from one country's operation to that in another perhaps distant country.

As chapter 5 argued, knowledge—and the people who know how to use it—have become increasingly crucial factors of production. More than any other such factor, knowledge (especially when it is networked) enjoys large economies of scale and scope. The growing importance of networks as a means of creating valuable services for individuals and businesses, transmitting data, films, TV programs, videotex, and so on, is a further example of the shift from mass production to mass customization. Each home can tailor-make its own viewing choices (scope), thanks to scale economies inherent in networked facilities.

Knowledge-based services are inherently driven by scope. Once you have reached a consumer's home with fiber-optic cable—capable of carrying massive amounts of data, voice, and picture information—you can provide that consumer with a dazzling array of services, including choice of thousands of videotaped movies on demand, home shopping, interactive TV programs, hundreds of cable TV channels from dozens of countries, database information, video games...and other services not yet dreamed up. But which customized services will prove to be the "killer application"—the creator of mass markets? The answer is not yet clear; the voice of the market has not yet spoken. What is clear is that somewhere in the combination of "multimedia" there is a massive market to provide consumers with a variety of services tailored to their needs.

One example of network economies of scope in a knowledge-based industry is France Telecom's videotex system known as Minitel. Videotex is a computer-based system that transmits text and graphics, to a terminal screen hooked up to a phone line. The information is usually sent as "pages," chosen from a set of "menus."

France is the acknowledged world leader in this type of electronic retailing. Virtually every French citizen has had access to Teletel (the name for the French videotex system) for the past six years. In the United States, similar services—for instance the IBM-Sears joint venture known as Prodigy—have had modest success, despite vaunted U.S. expertise in telecommunications. Most of the world's videotex activity now occurs in Europe, which has 6 million active users, of whom some 5 million are in France. In contrast, there are only about a million users in the United States.

Professor Tawfik Jelassi, an expert on information technology at INSEAD, the business school in Fontainebleu, France, explains why. Jelassi's case studies of the Minitel system tell an important and meaningful tale for executives facing the mass-customization revolution.

A 1978 report to the French government, Jelassi relates, warned that "for France, the American domination of telecommunications and computers is a threat to independence." As a result, the French government, through France Telecom, initiated an experiment late that same year to get back onto the global playing field—Minitel videotex terminals, which offered an electronic phone directory service in Rouen, and other services in the Paris area.

France Telecom invested heavily in the Minitel system, installing a half-million computer terminals across the nation. This investment was a major gamble. It involved first setting up a costly infrastructure, then inviting people and businesses to make use of it. There was absolutely no guarantee they would do so.

The idea worked. Today there are nearly 6 million Minitel terminals all over France—one for every ten persons. Some

15,000 different services are offered through it, a powerful and classic example of providing a wide and growing range of products at decreasing cost for each one, by building on a single technologically advanced infrastructure. In addition to the electronic directory, Minitel terminals now offer information services, professional databases, banking services, electronic mail, order processing, cash management, portfolio management, and accounting. And the list is growing daily, limited only by the imagination of small and large businesses and their customers.

France Telecom's dilemma, Jelassi notes, was "how to launch a mass-market product for which market demand did not yet exist." This is a classic chicken-and-egg problem. Demand for the product is created by saturating the country with videotex terminals. But who would invest massively in such terminals without first being assured of the demand for their services? The answer: a government with deep pockets, clear purpose, and a national technology strategy. France Telecom put in place a half-million Minitel units all over France, free of charge. (Second-generation terminals are rented for a monthly fee, generally quite low.) Users paid only according to calls they made, with measured-service call traffic France Telecom's only revenue source.

The first service was a highly convenient electronic phone directory that anchored the new service and, Professor Jelassi observes, "allowed customers to get used to it, while providing a major incentive to start using it." As early as 1983, the system would not only *find* numbers but also dial them.

But France Telecom is not resting on its laurels. The new competitive frontier is known as ISDN (for integrated services digital network), which transmits voice, text, and images, all in one digital package that can be sent along existing telephone lines. Commercial first-generation ISDN now exists throughout France. It enhances videotex because, for example, it lets buyers see sharp images of sellers' products on their screens, perhaps accompanied by a soft-voiced sales pitch. By 1992, Jelassi estimates that $150 billion had been invested in ISDN. And that is just the beginning. Second-generation ISDN will require replacement of copper wires with fiber-optic cables, a huge investment; but it will carry massive amounts of data at great speed, and its screen pictures will be remarkably sharp. With it, vacationers shopping for a resort will experience the sights and sounds of their destination on the screen, tour through it, and then decide whether to buy. The economies of scope that ISDN makes possible are limited only by the creativity and imagination of the managers who are now, in Europe and America, dreaming up ISDN-based services.[14]

THE INTELLIGENT ORGANIZATION

The successful integration of volume and variety—scope and scale— forces executives to think carefully about the structure of their organization. The way firms do their business stems directly from the nature of that business. For high-volume mass-market sales based on low prices, a hierarchical organization, with managers directing supervisors who in turn boss low-skill workers, makes sense. But high-volume sales based on relatively high-value high-priced products, generated by individually tailored products, demand quick transfer of knowledge, fast internal communication, high capability for learning, and high overall intelligence. Hierarchies are not suitable for this type of firm. It needs a "flat" organization, with as many links as possible among its components. What its workers need is not orders given by superiors, but information and knowledge flowing from others in the organization—marketing experts reporting to production and design engineers, sales personnel reporting to those in marketing, and so on.

Transforming a volume business into a volume-and-variety one is no easy task. It means shaping the ability of a small or large organization to learn, to change, and to adapt. The tool discussed in the next chapter—the learning curve—has often been presented as a technical, engineering formula, linking cumulative output to historical average cost. But in fact, the learning curve is a living, breathing economic entity, one that can be enhanced through smart management or ruined by bad decision making. Managing learning curves, like all the tools discussed here, is crucially dependent on the visible hand of the manager, in contrast with economics' single-minded obsession with the "invisible hand" of anonymous market forces.

Chapter Seven

RACING DOWN THE LEARNING CURVE

Experience—the name we give to our mistakes.

Recognizing errors and correcting them is one of the most basic—and most difficult—tasks that organizations undertake. It is indeed important to dissect our errors carefully, and to take steps to eliminate them.

This chapter focuses on a tool that helps managers and workers perform that task: the learning curve. The learning curve is literally a graphic record of cost improvements as producers gain experience and increase the total number of cars, TV sets, VCRs or aircraft that their plants and assembly lines turn out.

Learning curves, and their close cousins, experience curves, show the reduction in average and marginal costs as cumulative production rises. Learning curves show how average (per-unit) *variable* costs change through experience. Experience curves figure in fixed costs as well and portray changes in average all-inclusive costs. Both are shown in relation to lifetime, or cumulated, production. They are a concrete expression of how line workers, supervisors, and top management learn to do things better. Learning curves depend on the organization's skill at, and dedication to, getting better with each new batch of output. They are practical tools that embody an old but important principle: the more you do something, the better you get at it.

Executives have two main jobs—to make new and better things (improved goods and services), and to make things the firm already produces faster, cheaper, and of higher quality. Learning curves are invaluable aids for the latter. In some industries, such as aircraft production, learning curves are like highways—they lead in predictable fashion from one destination to another and can be highly useful for forecasting and strategy. In other sectors, they are far less stable.

Learning curves are a key component of a kind of closed-loop strategy racetrack that exists in many markets. This track works as follows:

- As production volume increases, unit costs fall.
- As unit costs fall, companies can lower their prices without impairing profitability or cash flow.
- As prices fall, consumer demand grows and market share rises.
- As market share rises, resulting profits make it possible to make investments in marketing and technology that further lower costs.
- And as unit costs fall . . . and so on.

A key part of this loop is the first part, the fall in unit costs as cumulative (or lifetime) output rises. This is the learning-curve effect. It explains competitive patterns in such diverse industries as VCRs, motorcycles, aircraft, missiles, and automobiles.

Take personal computers. It is easy to forget that this product is still in its infancy. The first IBM PC came to market as late as August 1981. Like the infancy of all technologically sophisticated products, personal computers began their careers in a dazzling array of different shapes, designs, and approaches, by such players as Osborne, IBM, Texas Instruments, Commodore, and Apple. Gradually, the needs and desires of consumers whittled this array down to a fairly standard dominant design, with a basic set of attributes that buyers came to expect each PC to have.

As PCs mature, the learning-curve racetrack loop kicks in—an inevitable development, though one that seems to have caught some players in the industry by surprise. PCs become a relatively standard commodity, one in which the lowest-cost producer (for acceptable quality) will capture the largest chunk of the market. A survey of the emerging "computer revolution" describes two key principles that will drive this maturing industry:

- the company with the highest unit volume almost always wins, and
- the place to find unit volume is the bottom of the market, where low prices create new customers.[1]

Recognizing this, both Compaq and IBM—firms which once enjoyed success by extracting large price premiums for the quality their brand name implied—have moved to slash prices, increase volume, and reduce costs. After adopting a mass-market low-cost strategy, Compaq managed to slash its costs by 30 percent in only eight months. It was not simple. As Dell Computer Co. founder and CEO Michael Dell succinctly summarizes: "Ideas are a commodity. Execution of them is not."[2]

The videocassette recorder (VCR) industry is another good example of a learning-curve-driven market. Although the basic technology of the VCR was pioneered by an American firm, Ampex, in the 1950s, and remained the industry standard into the 1980s, no American company managed to produce and commercialize a videorecorder for the consumer market. In contrast, JVC (Victor Corp. of Japan, ironically, originally a subsidiary of the Victor Co. of America), the subsidiary of the largest Japanese consumer electronics firm Matsushita, assembled a special team to design a video home system (VHS). The project manager, whose team included experts in marketing, production, and design, was told not to ask what was technologically possible—often, the chief aim of design engineers—but rather "to determine what consumers wanted in a home VCR and then to develop the technology to meet those requirements." The emphasis was placed on "producibility"—the ability to manufacture VCRs with steady, substantial cost reductions driven by the learning curve, rather than creation of technological excellence (which might possibly have been difficult or impossible to mass produce). The result was the VHS technology that ultimately surpassed what some experts regard as a technologically superior one, Sony's Betamax system, and that was eventually licensed by JVC to seven other Japanese firms in 1977. It yielded a design synthesis "well matched to the needs of the mass market"—a necessary condition for the very creation of such a mass market.

By 1978, worldwide demand exceeded one million units. World demand doubled every year between 1978 and 1981. At its peak in 1986, 35 million VCRs were produced, 88 percent of them by Japanese firms. Unit prices dropped rapidly, and the firms with the largest market share were able to raise their shares even further by drastic price cuts. It was a classic market-share race driven by mass-production and learning-curve cost cuts.[3]

How could a technologically superior product—Betamax—lose out to a less sophisticated product—VHS—in the fierce competition for consumers' hearts and dollars? It happens all the time. The ability to manufacture large quantities of a product, at acceptable quality, and achieve low prices through cost reductions driven by learning curves holds the key. This is a brief and accurate summary of what occurred in many industries, including automobiles and motorcycles.

Learning curves are not only a good way to manage and predict a company's own cost structure, they are also helpful in estimating unit costs of competitors. Here is an example of how a college professor, Princeton University's Uwe Reinhardt, managed to deduce with reasonable accuracy the bleak prospects of a technologically superior civilian aircraft—the pioneering Lockheed L-1011 Tristar—without any help from Lockheed itself, when the first production model was rolling off the assembly line in Palmdale, California.[4]

...BUT WILL IT FLY?

In the summer of 1971, Lockheed was in trouble. Once one of America's leading aircraft manufacturers, Lockheed stumbled over a contract to make an air force transport plane, the C-5A. Cost overruns gobbled up its cash and endangered Lockheed's plans to start producing its new wide-body civilian jetliner, the L-1011 Tristar, then nearing the end of 42 months of research, development, evaluation, and testing. The Tristar had 3 engines, one of them perched on its tail mount, and could carry between 260 and 400 passengers. Despite the Tristar's promise, banks would not lend Lockheed money to build its Tristar plant.

Lockheed was not the first aircraft manufacturer to find itself in hot water over a widebody plane. Boeing, too, was nearly bankrupted by the expense of developing its 747 Jumbo, saving itself only by slashing its work force by over 60 percent in 1971.[5]

To raise the money to put its Tristar into production, Lockheed went to the United States Congress and asked it to guarantee a quarter-billion-dollar loan. On a close vote — the Senate approved the request by a single vote, 49–48 — Lockheed got its guarantee. During the Congressional debate, controversy arose over whether the Tristar program was economically sound — that is, whether the market price of the product would be sufficient to cover the costs of making it. (The billion dollars Lockheed had already spent, in developing the plane, were sunk costs, or water under the bridge, and hence were not relevant in this debate; see chapter 2).

Using the learning-curve concept, Reinhardt was able to piece together an accurate estimate of future production costs per plane, even though some of the planes would be produced 10 or 15 years later. He based his analysis on the learning curve, first discovered by a keen-sighted engineer named T. P. Wright, in 1925. Wright, then commander of what later became Wright-Patterson Air Force Base in Dayton, Ohio, noticed that in aircraft production, as more and more planes were produced, the average time needed to - assemble each additional one declined. The rate of decline, he observed, seemed to be about 20 percent of the average costs per plane (averaged over all planes ever assembled), each time the number of planes assembled doubled. This means, Wright observed, that if the average per-plane cost in making 4 planes was, say, $1 million, then that unit cost would fall to $800,000 after 8 planes had been made, and $640,000 after 16 planes were produced. Through learning by doing, workers got better and faster at their jobs and costs fell. Wright later wrote up his observation in a short article, published in 1936.[6] The learning curve's fingerprint came to be associated with the "learning-curve coefficient"—the ratio between average costs after production doubles, compared with their level before the doubling. The above example, for instance, has a "0.8" or 80 percent learning curve.

Published estimates of Tristar production costs in 1971 guessed that per-plane costs might look as follows:

After the 150th Tristar: $15.5 million
After the 300th Tristar: $12 million

This means that doubling Tristar production, from 150 to 300, would reduce unit production costs by 77.4 percent, since $12 million is 77.4 percent of $15 million. Reinhardt found that this "77 percent learning curve" estimate cross-checked well with studies of other aircraft and with T. P. Wright's original 80 percent learning curve estimate.

It was known that the very first production model of the Tristar to roll off the assembly line at its Palmdale, California, plant, would cost around $100 million. (Note that this is not a prototype, of which several were built for testing purposes, but a real production model for sale to customers. Prototypes are generally hand-made and are far more costly.) The first and second planes (the first doubling), would cost on average, taken together, only 77 percent of $100 m., or $77 million. (Note that since $77 million is an average of the cost of the first plane and the cost of the second plane, the *marginal* cost of the second plane was much lower than $77 million—in fact, $54 million.)

To build a complete cost schedule for the Tristar, from the first plane through the one-thousandth, do the following:

- List each doubling of production: 1, 2, 4, 8, 16 planes, and so on.
- Each time a doubling occurs, multiply the previous average cost by 0.77, reflecting the 23 percent fall in unit costs.

The pattern of average per-plane costs that results is as follows (in million of dollars):

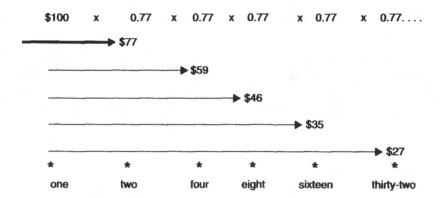

These calculations produce the following table, which is a complete "map" of Tristar production costs, from the first through the 1,024th:

TABLE 7.1

Learning Curve for the Lockheed L-1011 Tristar
Widebody Aircraft

Cumulative No. of Tristars Ever Produced	Average Per-Plane Production Costs ($ million)
1	$100
2	77
4	59
8	46
16	35
32	27
64	21
128	16
256	12
512	10
1024	7

Translated into a graph, this table becomes a learning curve. (See figure 7.1) What it reveals is the enormous advantage that exists in large-volume production. The average cost of a Tristar after 1,024 have been made, is only one-fourteenth that of the first Tristar, $100 million. Line workers, parts suppliers, managers, and toolmakers become on average 14 times more productive after a decade or so of doing more or less the same job, time after time, and working to learn and get better at it. The learning curve should not be interpreted as a kind of automatic dividend that nature pays to large-scale producers, but rather the fruits of hard work and cooperation between managers and workers, striving to improve what they do each time a new model rolls off the line.

Obviously, it takes much less time to go from 1 to 2 planes, than from 512 to 1,024. The second plane is probably produced in the first month or so. At a rate of 4 planes per month—Lockheed's goal for its Palmdale plant, never actually attained—reaching the milestone of the 1,024th plane (Lockheed never did!) from the 512th, will take $512/4$ = nearly 128 months, or nearly 11 years! Thus, the first cost reduction of 23 percent happens right from the start, but the tenth cost reduction of 23 percent takes more than a decade. In other words, the learning curve is a fairly predictable ski slope down which factories travel—but unlike the trails at Aspen or Vail, factories need to work harder and harder to avoid slowing down. This is in part why Alfred Chandler, Jr., sometimes calls the cost savings in large-scale production "economies of speed," because they depend in part on the intensity with which productive capacity is put to use. Cost savings, he observes, are always organizational in nature, and "depend on knowledge, skill, experience and teamwork—on the organized human capabilities essential to exploit the potential of technological processes."[7]

What does the Tristar learning curve tell us? For one thing, it permits an educated guess about whether Lockheed will make or lose money on the whole project. The original asking price for the Tristar was $14.7 million, driven down even before the first model was sold by fierce competition from two other players, Airbus Industries (Europe) and McDonnell-Douglas' DC-10. The price later climbed a bit, averaging around $15.5 million.

FIGURE 7.1

Learning Curve for L-1011 Tristar: Average Production Cost per Plane

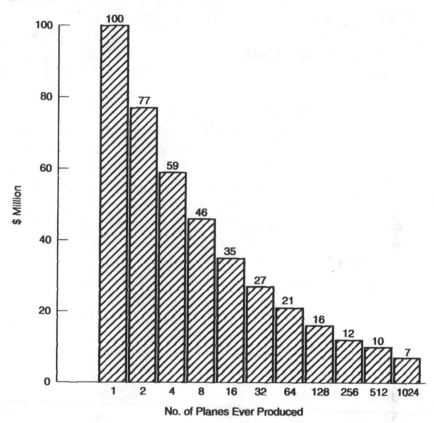

Looking at the table, one sees that the variable cost of making Tristars falls below what they are sold for—their market price—sometime after 128 planes have been made. This, of course, does not take into account the billion-dollar fixed costs already spent. Nor does it take into account the fact that some of those 128 planes are made and sold far in the future, meaning that the present value of the revenue they bring in is worth far less than the $15.5 million price. (Clearly, a bird in the hand today, $15.5 million in 1973, is worth more than one in a distant bush, $15.5 million in 1985.)

The combined use of revenue estimates and cost estimates—often based on the learning curve—is known as break-even analysis. Its objective is to reveal how many units must be produced and sold in order to cover costs. There are different types of break-even points, depending on whether only variable costs, or total costs, including fixed costs such as research, development, evaluation and testing, are covered by sales revenue. Using the learning curve tool, Reinhardt was able to argue that the Tristar was not a viable money-making project, even without a single piece of information volunteered by Lockheed itself. Lockheed would lose money on the Tristar, Reinhardt predicted in 1973.

Was he right? It turns out that he was. Lockheed nearly foundered because of mounting losses on the Tristar and other aircraft projects. It rescued itself mainly by redefining its core business and becoming a major aerospace and defense producer just at a time when the U.S. administration was rapidly expanding defense spending, in the early 1980s. But the real story behind the Tristar is far more fascinating than the economics of learning curves and involves politics, bribery, international scandal, and intrigue— none of which, unfortunately, is directly relevant to this book.

Learning curves have a close cousin—experience curves. To move from a learning curve to an experience curve, add the fixed costs (those unrelated to actual production of, say, motorcycles, planes, or cars) and calculate overall unit costs as cumulative output rises. For instance, it cost Lockheed an estimated $1 billion between 1968 and 1971 to design the Tristar, do the necessary research, evaluate the prototypes, and then test them completely (T&E). (In today's dollars, that billion would amount to at least $3 billion—which explains in part why many bitter rivals find it a good idea to join forces in designing new aircraft, rather than go it alone.) Dividing that billion dollars by the total number of Tristars ever produced provides average fixed costs—fixed costs per plane. Then, adding average variable cost (computed from the learning curve tool) to average fixed cost, yields average total cost (see table 7.2). The experience curve shows how average total costs decline as the number of planes continues to double.

The table provides a complete picture of estimated production costs for the Tristar.

Another valuable bit of information can be extracted from learning curves. Sometimes executives like to know the point in a product's production history when the company begins to make a

TABLE 7.2
Predicted Average Costs of L-1011 Tristar
($ million)

Total No. of Planes	Total RDT&E Fixed Costs	Average Fixed Costs	Average Variable Cost	Average Total Cost	Marginal Cost
1	1000	1000	100	1,100	100
2	1000	500	77	577	49
4	1000	250	59	309	38
8	1000	125	46	171	29
16	1000	63	35	98	23
32	1000	31	27	58	18
64	1000	16	21	37	14
128	1000	8	16	24	11
256	1000	4	12	16	8
512	1000	2	10	12	6
1024	1000	1	7	8	5

marginal profit—that is, how many units need to be made until the last one adds more to sales revenue (its price) than it costs the company to make (marginal cost)? In this example, we might ask, which Tristar is the first to cost less to make than it adds to Lockheed coffers when sold? To compute this, we need to figure out marginal cost, also in relation to the number of planes ever produced. It turns out that if average production costs fall by a constant percentage, for each doubling, then so do marginal costs; marginal cost differs from average cost only by a constant multiplicative factor.[8]

If we know that each Tristar sells for about $15.5 million, the table provides three useful pieces of information.

• It shows that something over 256 planes have to be sold to cover all costs, including fixed ones.

- Over 128 planes have to be produced and sold, to cover only the production costs.
- Somewhere between the 32nd and 64th plane, the cost of making one more plane falls below the price that plane gets when sold.

These are three different types of break-even points and each is useful and revealing to executives trying to track the losses and profits a product will generate.

Realistic comparison of sales forecasts with break-even points can help managers decide whether a project is worth undertaking from the outset.[9]

LEARNING IN CURVES IN ACTION: AIR TO AIR MISSILES

Like aircraft, developing and producing a sophisticated radar-guided air to air missile for the United States and its allies is a long process, taking 15 years or more. The so-called AMRAAM missile—Advanced Medium Range Air-to-Air Missile—was initiated in 1978, at the onset of a large expansion in American defense spending. It matured in the late 1980s, just when major cuts in defense spending began. This shift in direction caused the program's managers to encounter fierce sensitivity to cost on the part of Congress and its overseers. Only the intelligent and shrewd use of cost reductions through learning-curve effects enabled the program's managers to rescue it, bring it to fruition and completion, at costs well within those budgeted initially.[10]

The objective of the AMRAAM project was to develop a new generation of air-to-air missiles that would be lightweight, accurate, reliable, cost-effective, compatible with many types of aircraft, and able to destroy enemy aircraft beyond visual range of the pilot. Apart from batches made for the U.S. Air Force, they were sold to Korea, Turkey, the UK, and Norway.

Production of the missile began in 1986, just when defense spending was reaching its peak and cost sensitivity was growing. The managers of the project introduced competition among those supplying components for the missile to create incentives for cost savings. A huge database was developed to identify targets for cost reductions, based on projected learning curves. The missile itself was broken down into fairly small subsystems, and each subsystem had its own learning curve constructed, with its own learning-curve parameter. These curves were continuously refined as learning progressed and new technologies were harnessed. They enabled the program managers to track costs as they progressed and establish attainable cost targets—unlike the common process in which costs are tallied at the end of the project, and often show enormous overruns at a time when nothing can be done to correct them. (The process of analyzing subsystems of a product, and working to make each more cost-effective, while continually enhancing quality or performance standards, is known as value engineering.)

The first lot, or batch, of AMRAAM missiles (180 in total) had an average unit cost of $1.8 million in 1987. A year later, the next batch had unit costs that were 44 percent lower: $1.0 million each. By the time the ninth batch was produced in 1993, per-missile costs were down to $400,000. The substantial cost savings helped the program avoid intense scrutiny and challenge by Congress. The savings were achieved, according to program directors, by "making learning curves a common language at all levels in the procurement process from the factory floor to the Undersecretary of Defense." Learning curves, it is said, were used in every phase of the program to analyze alternate production plans and acquisition strategies. Not solely the logic, but the *language* of learning curves, too, is important—the language of continual improvement, correcting errors, while adopting thousands of small measures each of which contributes to ever-lower costs without impairing the value, performance, and quality of the product itself (see table 7.3).

BRITISH MOTORCYCLES: LEARNING-CURVE AUTOPSY

One of the earliest groups to use learning curves as the basis for analyzing strategy and competitive forces in markets was the Boston Consulting Group (BCG).[11] Mentioned in chapter 5, the BCG Report used the learning curve as a kind of lens, through

TABLE 7.3
Average Unit Cost of AMRAAM Missile Hardware

Lot #	1	2	3	4	5	6	7	8	9
No. of Units	180	412	900	900	900	891	1463	1023	1062
Unit Cost ($'000)	1800	1000	600	550	540	500	400	400	400

which to dissect the motorbike industry. It was commissioned by the British House of Commons and the Secretary of State for Industry, Eric Varley. They were troubled by the rapid deterioration of Britain's motorcycle industry and its key producer, Norton-Villiers-Triumph, which was rapidly losing market share at home and abroad to Japanese competitors and had undergone several expensive reorganizations, including sale of some plants to workers or to entrepreneurs, with heavy investment of government money in subsidies.

This carefully documented report is a graphic early example of the learning-curve closed loop described at the beginning of the chapter.[12] While it purports to offer strategy alternatives for the British firms, it is in fact more a postmortem or autopsy than a plan or prognostication—it reveals a state of decay in Britain so advanced that it was obvious the industry could not be salvaged. The report is significant, because it described what later happened to American and British firms in the automobile industry, and to some extent, in consumer electronics. Had the learning-curve tool been fully understood, and had the appropriate lessons been learned from the motorcycle case, then auto and electronics firms might have saved themselves lost sales, market share, and market leadership ten years later.

The BCG report found that "the British motorcycle industry has lost share of world markets very dramatically," and sought to discover why. In 1974–75, Honda, the largest competitor, sold 2 million units. British firms sold only 1 percent of that—20,000. The reason was in part "a concern for short-term profitability" by British firms, who during the 1960s withdrew from any market segment that faced Japanese competition. Initially, Japan produced small bikes. Both British and American motorcycle producers scorned the small-bike market. In 1965, William Davidson, son of the founder of Harley-Davidson (the only U.S. motorcycle company still alive in 1980) and then its president, scoffed, "Basically we do not believe in the lightweight market."[13] The British shared his view. They both ignored the fact that penurious young buyers, who buy 125-cc displacement bikes in their twenties, will later buy 1200-cc bikes when they become more affluent, in their thirties and forties. This is precisely what happened. Japanese motorbike companies gradually worked their way up the price scale, growing and maturing with their customers. In America, Honda sold thousands of small bikes with the slogan, "You meet the nicest people on a Honda" (a slogan first suggested by a college student). This was a strategy that would later be applied to perfection in the automobile market.

Between 1969 and 1973, in the profitable large-bike market in the United States, British companies sold a constant 30,000 units annually; Japanese volume soared from 27,000 in 1969 to 218,000 four years later. The British firms sagged because they could not compete on costs with the Japanese. This, the BCG experts found, stemmed from two factors: technology and scale. Honda had a 1,400-worker subsidiary whose sole task was to make machine tools for Honda that incorporated the latest advances in technology. The British suppliers used general-purpose machine tools obtained from outside suppliers, which offered no unique competitive advantage.

As British volume stagnated, so did unit costs—the British firms stalled on the learning-curve turnpike. At the same time, Japanese firms enjoyed rapid volume growth. While doubling production again and again, they managed to drive their unit costs ever lower, racing down the steeply sloped learning-curve turnpike at breakneck speed. The high production volumes made possible capital-intensive production and resulting high productivity—assembly-line operations not unlike Henry Ford's. The Japanese firms designed their motorcycles with a view to low-cost production; the British firms designed them based on "pure engineering considerations" largely independent of how cheaply the designs could be made. Japanese firms worked closely with their parts suppliers.

Some of the Japanese bike firms, like Suzuki and Honda, were car companies as well. This gave them access to parts suppliers who also could enjoy learning-curve savings through volume production. In contrast, the British companies, which were exclusively motorbike producers, had to use suppliers who treated them as poor cousins to their more profitable car-producer clients. All these factors gave Japanese producers huge cost advantages based on high-volume low-cost high-market-share strategies. In 1960, Japan exported only 4 percent of its motorcycle production. But they had attained high-volume low-cost production for their domestic market, and that learning-curve experience at home served them well in later competition in global markets. Japanese firms did their homework in their local market. What they learned there aided them after graduation to the tougher school of global markets in the late 1960s. This is the basis of Harvard Business School Professor Michael Porter's theory of how countries attain global competitive advantage. First, he argues, firms battle fiercely in the domestic market and acquire valuable skills; successful firms, hardened by battle at home, take their newly won competitive abilities into even tougher world markets. The fiercer the fight at home, the more likely they are to endure and prevail abroad.

The BCG report describes in painful detail the precise disease that killed Norton-Villiers-Triumph. Long-term success depended on matching Japanese sales volume. British firms, though, confined their managerial vision to existing low-volume equipment and methods, dropping market segments where they faced competition. Over time, they were pushed out of the 175-, 250-, 350-, 500-, and finally, 650-cc models, in the same way General Patton's tanks rolled back German forces in Europe after D-Day, in 1944—step by step, city by city, town by town, ridge by ridge. Moreover, the presence of the ultimately fatal illness was not completely obvious, because total sales of British motorbikes remained stable, at around 80,000 units a year through the 1960s. But the continuous segment-retreat signalled impending death—it was only a matter of time.

A similar pattern very nearly occurred in the United States. Like the British firms, Harley-Davidson initially failed to perceive and meet the Japanese challenge. By 1980 Harley-Davidson was the only American motorcycle producer who had survived, while scores of other producers had died during the course of the century. But half the motorcycles that came off its assembly lines were defective. Its models leaked oil on the showroom floor, as small cans underneath them showed. Its market share was down to a miniscule 3.3 percent, compared to Honda's 55 percent, Yamaha's 19 percent, Kawasaki's 10 percent, and Suzuki's 12 percent. In 1985, Harley was reportedly hours from bankruptcy.[14]

"Up until 1979, the total market was going up, so I could increase volume and compare myself against last year and decide I did fine," Harley president Richard Teerlink observed. "But how did I do against my competitor? Not so hot. Because he was gaining market share." Harley proved the Japanese were dumping bikes—selling them below cost in the United States in the mid-1970s—but no action was taken.

Meanwhile, "Harley came unglued," said Vaughn Beals, Harley's board chairman. "When you're busy trying to make products as fast as you can, you forget designs are outdated. There wasn't the research there should have been. Quality and labor relations went to pot. They [Japanese competition] came to town with first-class products and ours were not up to snuff."

Eleven Harley executives borrowed millions in 1981 to buy the company from its owner, AMF Inc. They began to make major changes. The first thing the new team did was to visit Japanese motorcycle facilities. Often, imitating successful competitors is a fast and cheap form of learning. What they found was not some mystical robot technology but rather, "the intelligent efficient organization of the company's employees and production systems." Harley set out to do the same. But it needed time. And meanwhile its share of the heavyweight cycle market had fallen to 12.5 percent, while Honda grabbed more than half of what was once Harley's principal market territory. Japanese manufacturers started to stockpile motorcycles in their dealerships. A price war loomed, and it looked like Harley was doomed to loose it. The learning curve was on the side of the opposition.

Vaughn Beals went to Washington and begged for help. The administration and U.S. Congress were receptive. The International Trade Commission ruled in 1983 that Harley was imperiled by the flood of foreign imports—and how it was! The White House imposed a five-year tariff on large-displacement motorcycles, starting at a stiff 45 percent. The Japanese reacted fast by downsizing, shifting to lighter models not subject to the tariff. Meanwhile, Harley rolled up its collective sleeves.

Harley executives, including Willie Davidson (grandson of the company's founder) went out to biker rallies on new "Hogs" (the nickname of large Harley-Davidson bikes) and conducted effective curbside market research. Harley adopted computer-aided design. They blended their heritage and tradition with state-of-the-art high-tech production. Quality circles were instituted. So was statistical process control (SPC). Statistical quality charts were hung up on the factory floor for all to see. Models were mixed on the assembly line, preventing boredom and keeping workers sharp. Harley says it succeeded in raising its productivity by half, cut its inventory by two-thirds, and gained a threefold increase in quality. A new Sportster model with low price reclaimed market share, increased its volume, guaranteed resale value, and managed to hold the line on its price.

By 1986, Harley again led in the super-heavyweight class. Harley diversified, went public, and paid off much of its debt. In May 1987, a full year ahead of the five-year limit, Harley's executives voluntarily relinquished the 45 percent tariff wall, signalling Harley's readiness to compete openly in free markets. By 1988, Harley had caught up with Honda and rebuilt its market share from an eighth of the market to 40 percent.

Beals notes that "while we were the beneficiaries of a protectionist program, we feel very strongly that it is not in the country's best interest to have a protectionist environment. Those guys in Washington who want to make headlines and buy votes by showing how supportive they are of labor, they are the worst enemies labor's got. That petrifies me."

Harley-Davidson is still not out of the woods, and continues to face fierce competition from foreign rivals. But it returned from the brink of collapse and bankruptcy by putting the learning curve to work in its favor rather than against it.

Teerlink claims that "the true future of America lies in the employees, not in the financial wheeler-dealers who are buying and selling corporations as if they are chattel. Too many financial people got to the top and they didn't view their businesses as living, breathing things. They viewed them instead as financial portfolios, and so they managed them not very humanely. And as a consequence, they were looking for short-term profitability, not long-term viability.*The guy on the factory floor knew what was wrong. The problem is, nobody would listen to him."*

THE ENEMIES OF LEARNING CURVES: BUILDING A TRUTHFUL ORGANIZATION

Harvard Business School psychologist Chris Argyris has proof that "the guy on the factory floor knew what was wrong." He describes a meeting of a dozen first-line supervisors at an industrial plant—not Harley-Davidson—at which they built "a list of factors that had led to poor quality products and unnecessary costs." They identified more than 30 areas of inefficiency and ranked them for possible action. They then selected six on which they promised to take action—and did. Three months later, those six areas had all been improved and "management estimated the likely savings to be about $210,000." Top management provided champagne and dinner to celebrate the achievement. At the dinner, Argyris asked the supervisors how long they had known that these defects and related superfluous costs existed.

"For one to three years," they responded. "It was common knowledge."

Why had the supervisors not acted to remedy the inefficiencies they knew existed? What, Argyris asked, led you not to take action until these seminars?

The answer, Argyris and others have argued in a series of books and articles, is *"defensive behavior"*—actions individuals take to forestall embarrassment or threat, when they are faced with failure or errors. Defensive behavior is the arch enemy of learning curves. It can at times totally defeat them. In the instance described above, "the cost-reduction program was judged a success. However, the related question [how can its underlying *causes* be corrected, i.e. how can the sources of X-inefficiency be removed, not just the proximate consequences] was not asked by those who manage it."[15]

The question is—why?

Learning, Argyris argues, is the "detection and correction of error." An error is "any mismatch between our intentions and what actually happens." Errors in organizations lead to organizational defensive routines—"any policy, practice, or action that prevents the people involved from being embarrassed or threatened, and at the same time, prevents them from learning how to reduce the causes of the embarrassment or threat." Faced with strategies that go awry and businesses that are crumbling, human nature becomes vigorously defensive. People blame others, evade responsibility, avoid making hard decisions, and resist change. Organizational learning is stymied by such routines, which, it has been found, are pervasive across cultures and across all types of organizations, including corporations, schools, government bureaucracies, and military units. "Human beings show remarkable ingenuity for self-protection," Argyris argues "They can create individual and organizational defenses that are powerful and in which that power is largely in the service of poor to mediocre performance as well as of antilearning." [16]

Argyris has studied over 6,000 managers and administrators in a large number of countries. He found that defensive behavior is found among organizations in every nation, no matter what their culture or background, or size of the group—indeed wherever people come together in groups and work to achieve their goals.

Researchers focus on how to "unfreeze" organizations, how to help them learn *how* to learn and how to change. The core issues—what makes organizations ineffective, how can they become better at attaining their goals, and how, in particular, can one build an organization that is good at detecting and correcting its own errors, especially embarrassing and painful ones—are precisely those addressed, independently, by the X-efficiency literature.

Quality control is an example. When it reveals excessive defects, efforts are made to examine the production process and line workers to discover and remove the cause. This is simple learning and may operate to reduce static X-inefficiency. But a better approach would ask: Should we entirely revamp our whole production process and shoot for zero defects? Should we retrain all our workers, perhaps having them run quality-control procedures rather than use special quality inspectors? This more complex type of learning asks whether "procedures" should be entirely eliminated and replaced by something better.

Companies need special "thermostats," Argyris has argued, the kind of thermostats that "could ask, 'why am I set at 68 degrees?' and then explore whether or not some other temperature might more efficiently achieve the goal of heating the room." Such thermostats are difficult to build. The reason is that complex learning often demands as a first step the admission of failure or error. But the smarter the executives, and the better-trained and educated an organization's professionals are, the less willing they are to face failure or admit mistakes and make the needed changes, and the steeper the fortifications they build against true learning. Smart people are generally unaccustomed to failure. Recognizing and admitting it, and accepting responsibility for it in front of fellow workers, is one of the hardest things in the world for accomplished people to do. When it is suggested their performance may have been less than perfect, they react with feelings of guilt and anger and resistance to change. Quality-control circles are a good example of defensive behavior and persistence of errors. One study found that 70 percent of such circles disbanded within two years of their formation, despite convincing evidence that they contribute to an organization's efficiency.[17]

The crux of the "defensive behavior" problem, as Argyris defines it, is this—*precisely the same learning system that helps companies run day-to-day operations smoothly can "freeze" them when new directions are urgently required.*

Borrowing from electrical engineering, Argyris coined the terms *"single-loop"* and *"double-loop"* learning to illustrate the fundamental difference between two necessary but often rival modes of learning. *Single-loop learning* is analogous to a thermostat. When the room temperature rises, the thermostat turns off the heat. When the temperature falls, it turns it back on. The loop is: temperature-thermostat-temperature. This is a type of feedback system all businesses need for smooth daily operation. Quality control is an example. Discovery of excessive defective units triggers checks on the production line to isolate the source. It can help achieve such goals as reducing the number of sub-par units.

Successful companies need good single-loop systems for day-to-day operations. Yet paradoxically, the better companies are at single-loop learning, the less likely they may be to adopt the double-loop variety for long-run planning. This is learning that evaluates not only existing processes but steps *outside* them to ask: Is this the right way to do things? Should we do basic things differently? Should we change our goals, and our strategies for attaining them? In addition to the temperature-thermostat loop, it adds a *second*, or double loop that questions the very need for, and functioning of, the single-loop thermostat itself.

Argyris describes an experiment he ran many years ago with a large bank. The bank implemented a set of rules for staffing its branches. A carefully constructed [single-loop] formula determined how many savings tellers, commercial tellers, and so forth, were needed in each one. According to the rules, as business expanded, more and more people were hired. The formula, a single-loop kind of "thermostat," seemed to work well. But Argyris and his colleagues suggested a double-loop experiment. "Let us work with the employees at half your branches," they said, "and let *them* design how many workers to bring in. If they hire fewer people than what your rules imply, then they should get some of the economic (as well as psychological) rewards." (That is, part of the cost reduction should go to them as bonuses.) This is "double-loop" learning, because they replace the single-loop staffing formulae with a system that checks and evaluates the rules themselves. The bank agreed.

"We found that the double-loop branches genuinely resisted hiring new people until they were sure they were needed," Argyris said. "If commercial business increased and the savings teller was not doing much, fine, she simply walked over and helped out. By the end of the year, these branches were doing as much or more business as the other branches, but had one-quarter fewer employees." General Foods had similar successes in a pet food plant, he told me, decreasing layers of management and reducing staffing by 30 percent, with no decline in output, compared to a similar plant.

What practical steps can managers take to make their organizations flexible, able to learn, and good at persistently re-evaluating their goals and how they achieve them?

Here are some of Argyris's recommendations:

- *Start at the top.* If mid-level managers practice open "double-loop" inquiry and their CEO does not, explosions may result. Changes in the way organizations learn must start with the CEO and top management group itself.
- Encourage people's capacity *to confront their own ideas* and re-examine basic assumptions. Help them "create a window in to their own mind."
- *While advocating your own positions,* principles, and values, combine them with inquiry and a lot of self-reflection, to *invite both yourself and others to challenge them.* Ask, can what I just said be "disconfirmed" (refuted) by data? If it can, why not do it? If so, how? What would we need to know?
- Be *aware* of how and when you yourself react defensively to criticism, and work hard to forestall any possibility of it. This takes a lot of practice. People rarely face the fact that they can produce double-loop solutions to organizational problems once they decide they wish to do so.
- *Encourage others* (and yourself) to say what they know, yet are afraid to. Foster the notion, in your own behavior and that of others, that questioning others' reasoning is not a sign of mistrust or an indication of disloyalty, but a valuable opportunity for learning.

Truthfulness, it turns out, may be one of management's most underrated tools—not because managers think lying is smart, but because they wrongly doubt their ability to handle the embarassment and threat that hard truth brings in its wake. Truth and trust are powerful allies of the learning curve. It should always be recalled that the learning curve is in no way an automatic, lockstep machine that reduces costs simply because more and more units of output are produced. Learning is a process that needs to be managed, encouraged, facilitated, and speeded. It does not happen by itself. More than a few organizations learn slowly or not all, and ultimately stumble through their inability to react to changes in their environment.

PERILS OF THE LEARNING CURVE

Even when organizations are rebuilt on foundations of truth, rather than defensiveness, and even when learning curves are steep and smooth, the promises learning curves bring for cost reduction, expanded market share, and resulting higher profits, are not without accompanying perils. The major danger is this—if for some reason you are forced off the learning curve turnpike (perhaps by the need to match newer competing models with a new one of your own), and start again at the very top of the slope, you will lose piles of money, especially if you do this significantly later than your competitors. Meanwhile, the old learning curve you happen to be on runs out of steam, because it takes ever-growing periods of time to attain new doublings, and resulting new cost reductions. Time is thus on the side of the innovating attacker, who assaults established firms locked into aging products and aging learning curves. That is why there are major advantages to innovation.

Henry Ford's mass-produced Model T enjoyed startling learning-curve cost savings. The number of Model T's doubled 14 times, to over 15 million in cumulative production. The learning curve for Model T's was an 85 percent one—meaning each doubling lowered average costs by 15 percent. This means that after the 14th doubling, the unit cost of a Model T was only 10 percent (0.85 multiplied by itself 14 times, or 0.10) of the cost of the first model; moreover, the marginal cost (the cost of the fifteenth million model) was probably only 6 or 7 percent of the cost of the first one. Thus, even while the price of the Model T was falling (in constant 1958 dollars, adjusted for inflation) from around $4,000 to about $900, the Ford Motor Co. was piling up huge profits, because its unit costs were dropping far faster than the price, while the price reductions got its market share up to a dominant 55 percent position in 1921. Ford Motor Co. dominated the automobile industry.

But a competitor, Alfred P. Sloan's General Motors, began offering heavier cars with more comfortable, closed bodies. Ford's Model T had an open-car design and a light chassis. Hence, as Sloan wrote, "'in less than two years [by 1923], the closed body made the already obsolescing design of the Model T noncompetitive as an engineering design.'... The old master had failed to master change.... His precious volume, which was the foundation of his position, was fast disappearing. He could not continue losing sales and maintain his profits. And so, for engineering and market reasons, the Model T fell."[18] Ford fell to a dynamic innovating attacker, and its impressive learning curve could not save it.

In May 1927 Henry Ford shut down the huge River Rouge plant to retool. It took over a year, and hundreds of millions of dollars. From that point, the learning and experience curves change direction, beginning an upward march that led Ford to lower market share and the edge of bankruptcy. Ford did come out with a new product—the Model A. But as William Abernathy and Kenneth Wayne note, Ford abandoned the learning curve for a new strategy based on continual performance-maximizing (rather than cost-reduction), with ever-higher product prices. List prices rose from 1930 through 1965 by two-and-one-half times (adjusted for inflation). Ford's long devotion to the experience-curve strategy, the authors note, made the transition to another strategy difficult and very costly. New strategies require new patterns of thinking and decision making, and organizations trained in old habits find it hard to shake them. This is where executive leadership is crucial, and the Ford Motor Co. lacked it.

Not every successful, profitable company has to follow a high-market-share strategy built on learning curves. There is an alternative—a niche strategy where companies focus on a particular product line, market segment, or geographic area, trying to achieve distinctive competence in their specialty. Such firms can usually command a premium price for their products, based on perceived uniqueness and high quality. In some ways, the Japanese car producers' single-minded pursuit of the luxury-car market is an example. Such cars claim a high price premium for perceived extra-high quality, and are a niche market. They generate profits not through especially high-volume production, but through very high quality in production and design, which creates premium prices from customers who are not price-sensitive in their demand.

"The worst position to occupy," Michael Hergert observes, "is at intermediate levels of market share. These firms are 'stuck in the middle' in the sense that they are neither large enough to produce at low costs nor specialized enough to be viewed as unique to be able to charge premium price."[19] Generally, as new industries mature, a shakeout occurs, in which large firms with big cost advantages and high market share (based on learning curve cost-savings) co-exist with smaller "niche" firms who make differentiated products immune to learning-curve competition because the production volume is quite small. The mid-size firms tend to merge into the larger ones, split into smaller units, or simply disappear. A decade ago, Anheuser-Busch (Budweiser) and Philip Morris (Miller), had large market shares, while Coors, for instance, did well in its smaller niche. Schlitz, trapped in between, performed more poorly. Coors ultimately shifted from its niche position to becoming a national-market player aiming at high market share.

Aside from the perils of innovation, and the "uncurved" economics of niches, there is a third cautionary lesson to be learned about learning curves: Sometimes, stepping on the gas, to speed up progress down the learning curve, actually slows you down. To illustrate, we turn again to our hapless Tristar.

In 1979, Lockheed announced loss write-offs reflecting problems in its Tristar production line in California. Lockheed had, in 1977–78, achieved a production rate of only 24 planes a year, or two a month—half of its originally planned level. This meant that learning-curve savings came far slower than expected, as the company was moving down its learning curve at a slower rate than anticipated.

It was then decided to speed up production. To boost its output rate fourfold, Lockheed hired 5,500 new employees. Many of them were unskilled, according to Lockheed chairman Roy Andersen. The booming California economy created a shortage of skilled workers and machinists and necessitated hiring those without experience. The six-week training programs proved insufficient. The result was hikes in Tristar production costs, long lead times for some materials, and late deliveries in other materials from suppliers. "The company [Lockheed]," *Aviation Week* observed, "is struggling with learning curve problems." Rather than move down the learning curve, the company was plucked by circumstances from a lower position on the curve and dumped back near the start, much higher up, as new employees had to undergo the learning process nearly from the start.[20]

"While Lockheed officials believe Tristar sales will continue past the 300 mark, they say it is unlikely that the program will ever break even," *Aviation Week* concluded in 1979. This proved correct. When the last Tristar was produced in 1985, losses on the program totalled hundreds of millions of dollars. Basic learning curve and demand analysis back in 1973 had forecasted this result. Unlike Ford, which had to retool to make a new product, thus shifting to a new and higher learning curve, Lockheed stumbled on the need to try to move down an existing curve faster—and found itself pushed back up on the curve, much like a game-board player who ends up in "Jail" and on release has to start again at Square One.

THE POLITICAL ECONOMY OF LEARNING CURVES

I conclude this chapter by showing that the economics of learning curves and the politics of budget appropriations mix very badly. The reason is simple: learning-curve strategies build on cost-savings through high-volume production while budget appropriations often rest on cutting back on unit volume in times of budget cutting. We need look no further than the defense industry for yet another example.

The latest chapter in this endless saga, whose plot never seems to change, is the YF-22 next-generation fighter aircraft, built by Lockheed and Boeing, and representing the largest single acquisition program of the Pentagon.[21] The U.S. Air Force currently has 648 jets on order, at a total cost of $96 billion. About 40 percent of that sum is development costs—money already spent. The remaining $56 billion are production costs. That works out to $56 billion/648 or $87 million per plane.

The Pentagon, facing budget cuts, is considering reducing the total number of planes produced to 442. That will push Lockheed back up its learning curve and increase per-plane costs to an estimated $130 million. The total production costs of 442 planes— 442 times $130 million per plane—works out to the same number as 648 planes times $87 million per plane, or about $56 billion. Often, when the total number of planes is reduced, the length of time over which they are produced is also lengthened, reducing the budgeted expenditures per fiscal year. But this too proves costly—it simply slows the learning process and causes unit costs to be higher than they would be if production were speedier.

There may be further rounds of cutbacks in the program, trying to save money by reducing the total number produced. But such savings, if they exist at all, are minimal. And this has happened before. The hapless B-2 bomber program was ordinarily scheduled to produce 132 aircraft. Continuous cutbacks in budget appropriations ultimately led to production of only 20 aircraft. The per-aircraft cost soared, making the plane prohibitively expensive and wasteful. The F-22 may meet the same fate. There are signs total production may be fewer than 300.

Other countries have performed a similar dance. Canada's Avro Arrow fighter aircraft, in the 1960s, was cancelled, as Canada realized that it could not achieve sufficient scale of production to make the per-plane cost reasonable, nor could it rescue the program by producing smaller numbers. Israel cancelled its Lavie fighter aircraft program, after several attempts to rescue it by scheduling ever-smaller numbers for production and failing to realize significant savings.

The politics of learning curves are especially fierce. As Congress cuts back the number of planes to be produced, the per-plane cost rises as contracting firms slip backward on the learning curve. Political opposition to the aircraft then mounts, as Members of Congress rebel against its increasing costliness. Further cuts in production may result, and ultimately the entire program is endangered. Moreover, cutbacks in one program often endanger others. Companies load fixed costs from one cancelled program onto the burdened back of other programs, making them increasingly more costly—this has happened to some degree with the F-22 aircraft, as subcontracters try to shift overhead costs from cancelled programs onto this one.

Learning curves are a great boon to consumers, because they make possible dramatic reductions in price. But one must always keep in mind the perils of learning-curve economics, that always accompany their promise and potential. Every manager would love to replicate the learning curve of, say, silicon transistors, for instance, which fell in price from around $40–$50 in 1954, when they were discovered, to 40–50 cents in 1968, after two billion had been produced! Or, of polyvinylchloride, whose price per pound (adjusted for inflation) dropped from 60 cents in 1945 to a little over 10 cents, after the industry had accumulated experience in making 20 billion pounds of it. But such dramatic cost reductions can't happen unless conditions are right. Of primary importance are the consumers and their psychology.

Indeed, after seven chapters of detailed discussions of costs, it is high time to recall the nearly-forgotten consumer, and turn to the analysis of supply and demand. The next chapter focuses on a tool that helps executives understand the key forces that shape whether or not consumers buy their product, and the degree to which buyers are sensitive to changes in the product's price.

Chapter 8

MARKETS AND DEMAND

How to Listen to Your Customer

Good executives create customers. Great ones create markets.

But how do they do it?

Market creation and market demand are topics that economics should have much to say about. Economics' main focus for over two centuries has been the analysis of markets. Like boxers, microeconomics textbooks lead with their best punch—they generally plunge right in to supply and demand in the earliest chapters. So, when Econ speak to Exec about demand, there should be an embarrassment of riches.

Instead, there is mainly embarrassment—trillions of words and graphs and symbols, that together reveal large gaps of ignorance when it comes to edifying managers. The reason is simple. Supply—what sellers choose to put up for sale, at various prices—is driven in large part by cost—what it costs the sellers to make their product. For this reason, the first seven chapters of this book have been devoted to various aspects of cost estimation. Generally, executives surveyed after taking some sort of microeconomics course report that the economic tools focusing on costs were of greatest and most frequent use to them.[1]

Supply is in part subjective, driven by psychology—workers' motivation for instance—but it is in the main objective, concerning such things as resources (labor, capital, materials) and technology (the way those resources are combined).

In contrast, demand—what consumers purchase, at various prices—is principally psychological. It rests on the value that customers perceive in goods or services, and is driven by a very large variety of assorted factors, including price, income, habit, fashion, greed, exclusiveness, scarcity, reliability, comfort, and the desire to impress others. Often, the subjective nature of value-creation means that what truly creates value for customers remains something of a mystery.

Economists approach demand by assuming what they call a "utility function," which is a mapping, or relationship, between the amounts of a product or service consumers buy and the amount of satisfaction they presumably derive from them. But this mapping—unlike, for instance, cost functions—is an opaque black box. "Utility" is not directly observable, and attempts to infer its nature from behavior are somewhat circular, along the lines of "people buy what they want, and want what they buy." When managers ask, what do economists know about demand that is immediately useful for decision making, the cloth is often thin and threadbare indeed. It often comes down to little more than "lower prices bring higher quantities demanded"—which is sometimes not true (as when, for instance, people judge an article's quality by its price).

The paucity of economic tools for demand analysis is betrayed by many of the demand diagrams in textbooks. These diagrams usually feature the quantity demanded, on one axis, and the price of the product on the other. Yet for a great many goods and services, price is no longer the single most dominating factor. For industrial goods, for instance, price now takes second place in buyers' surveys to quality.

The tool this chapter presents is the demand function—the relation between the amount and type of products consumers buy, and the characteristics of those products and their economic and social environment. Its purpose is to help executives better understand the key factors that drive demand for their products, and those of their competitors, in order to make better decisions with regard to prices, advertising, production, R&D, marketing, and distribution.

There are 13 distinct forces that shape market demand. By sheer coincidence, they arrange themselves neatly in alphabetical order. They are shown in table 8.1.

TABLE 8.1
Thirteen Forces that Shape What People Buy

A aptness
  B bandwagons and bubbles
    C cost, or price
      D demographics
        E elasticity, or sensitivity to price
          F fashion and fads
            G greed
              H habit
                I income
                  J jazz
                    K knowledge
                      L loyalty
                        M minds and money

You cannot say it often enough, or loud enough, executives tell themselves repeatedly: "Never lose touch with your customers." Analyzing these 13 forces can help executives stay in touch with their markets and amplify the noisy, static-ridden signals consumers send them, to better understand why people "vote" for their products with their hard-earned disposable income. Often, the greatest difficulty is to hear not what customers are telling you, but what they are *not* saying. The price for subacute hearing is steep.

For instance, First Boston Corp. was one of America's most successful investment banking firm in the 1980s. It "became a powerhouse in mergers, mortgage trading and Eurobonds," all of them growing, profitable markets at that time. But market demand shifted—apparently without clearly telling First Boston executives. The new growth markets for investment banks in the 1990s became currency trading, money management, and foreign stocks and bonds. First Boston failed to re-allocate its resources to these new markets. This shows, the *Wall Street Journal* observed, "how difficult it is for any Wall Street firm to manage the allocation of resources from one area to another as markets wax and wane."[2] The same difficulty exists for non-Wall Street firms.

APTNESS

Huge new markets are created when enterprising individuals become aware of customers' needs—*and find an apt way to satisfy them*—even before the customers themselves are aware of them. Sears, Roebuck is a good example.

Richard Warren Sears, age 23, was running a railroad station agency in remote North Redwood, Minnesota, when by chance he was offered a consignment of watches the local retailer had refused. He sold the watches to other station agents at a reasonable price and enjoyed booming sales. His success led him to found the Sears Watch Co. in 1886 (the year Coca-Cola was founded in Atlanta). His business strategy was one of low prices to generate high volume and was an immediate success.

In 1893, Sears asked himself the key question, "What business am I in?" and found, to his surprise, the answer was not "the watch business" but "the mail order business." His company issued a small 64-page booklet of items that could be ordered by mail, including guns, sewing machines, clothing, jewelry, and silverware. That small booklet ultimately grew into the 1,500-page volume that reached all parts of rural and urban America.

The Sears catalog was a means to supply appropriate goods at reasonable prices that met the needs of its buyers—mainly farmers in rural communities, who had only limited access to retail stores. Sears's emphasis on volume sales predated Henry Ford's strategy of volume production, and was no less revolutionary. Like Henry Ford, Sears believed "the strongest argument for the average customer was a sensationally low price." Sears's costs were cheaper than local retailers, because he bought in huge volumes. He once ordered a thousand dozen pairs of pants from a startled supplier. Perhaps you ought to take a trial order of a hundred dozen to see if they sell? the supplier suggested. I've already sold all thousand dozen, Sears replied.

The Sears catalog listened to the muffled voice of its buyers with keen hearing. In 1906, the railroads decided to divide America into time zones, in order to run an efficient train schedule "by the clock." Until then, farmers rose with the sun, worked until dusk, and then quit. But when trains had to be met at a precise hour, they needed watches. They got most of them from the Sears catalog, which began an aggressive campaign to sell watches to the newly time-conscious rural residents.

Two products symbolize Sears's legendary skill at providing apt products: sewing machines, and cream separators. In 1897, Sears was selling, through his catalog, sewing machines at about $17, a third to a sixth of the price of nationally advertised brands. He continued slashing his prices, pressuring the manufacturer to lower his price to Sears again and again, until by the turn of the century, the price of a sewing machine was down to $7.65. A similar process occurred, with even more spectacular results for profits, with cream separators—devices that saved farmers hours of labor by mechanically skimming the cream off milk, and generated about one in every six dollars of profit. (That story will be told later in this chapter.) Sewing machines and cream separators: devices that saved time and labor, for the home and the farm—apt products, at apt prices, that solved problems for farmers and their wives that were not even recognized as problems.[3]

Problems, industrialist Henry J. Kaiser once said, are opportunities in work clothes. Like the neighborhood bully roaming his territory and seeking trouble, some managers build products by looking for trouble—problems that they and their firm can solve. George Hatsopolous is a good example. Trained as an engineer and author of a leading textbook on thermodynamics, Hatsopolous shifted from academe to business, becoming an entrepreneur and founding a highly successful company called Thermo Electron. Hatsopolous's company has "core competencies"— skills in various technologies, including for instance treatment of environmental wastes and heat transfer. By serving on public committees—he was president of the Boston Federal Reserve Bank for a time—Hatsopolous becomes intimately involved with his community and learns first-hand about its problems. He then tries to match his company's problem-solving capability with the problems that need solving. To raise capital, he founds new companies—with their own stock offerings—built not around *products* but around specific problem-solving *technologies*. These companies work under the overall umbrella of the parent firm but enjoy much independence. The key to Hatsopolous's success is his knack of making an apt match between technology and the problems it is able to solve.

Hatsopolous and other successful product innovators embody the old adage that necessity is the mother of invention. They seek out necessity and use their knowledge to resolve it. More often than not, however, the process works the other way around—invention is the mother of necessity, meaning that inventions create markets to satisfy needs that did not previously exist. The invention of television, by Americans Zworykin and Farnsworth, in 1923 and 1927, was not related to the inventors' wish to create a multibillion dollar market, but to their curiosity in trying to see how pictures might be transmitted electronically. Penicillin was discovered by a chance observation of Alexander Fleming, who noticed small defensive islands around spots of mould in a Petri dish. The need for it was tremendous—as witnessed by the lives it saved during World War II—but that was not why it was discovered. Rather, it was the keen eye and curiosity of a researcher.

Necessity is always there, human appetites being what they are, notes economic historian Joel Mokyr, but the ability to satisfy them is not always present. The demand for technology is derived from the demand for the goods and services that technology helps make. A common error of technologists seeking to make and sell a product is to become enamoured with their technology and overlook the specific need it meets—if any. The aptness of the match between technology (solutions) and needs (problems) is a major determinant of product success.[4]

BANDWAGONS AND BUBBLES

Bandwagons are large, ornate wagons in which circus bands ride. Once, when the circus came to town, it was announced by bandwagons followed by large crowds of adults and children, who tagged along behind, drawn by the excitement and the crowds. Bandwagons have largely disappeared, but they still exist strongly in markets; they have come to mean demand arising not from intrinsic needs but simply because other people are buying. Like the crowds who come to meet the circus, the larger the crowd, the more nonparticipants are attracted to join in.[5]

Bandwagon effects can sometimes be manufactured out of very little, simply by making a lot of noise. Joe Nakash, chairman of Jordache Enterprises, one of the creators of the designer-jeans fad, is an adherent. "We scream louder," he observed, in 1982. "If you scream louder, you do better." His company was founded in 1978 and in four years reached sales of $370 million. Jordache sold 1.2 million pairs of jeans a month partly by guessing at a burgeoning bandwagon—American teenagers were ready to shift from scruffy torn jeans to expensive "smart" tight-fitting ones—and partly by creating it, with clever advertising and snob-appeal prices $20 above standard models.[6] The history of marketing is replete with bandwagons, from hula hoops, pet rocks, smurfs, through gerbils and Jurassic Park dinosaurs, and even, in the 1920s, chameleons attached to women's blouses with small gold chains. Cellular phones are a recent instance of a powerful bandwagon—world demand for them has grown faster than the rosiest forecasts.

Bandwagons are especially powerful in markets for assets, such as stocks, bonds, currency, and property. The more powerful the bandwagon, the greater the potential for "bubbles." A financial bubble is a rapid increase in the price of assets that occurs without fundamental, underlying reasons (such as a new-product announcement, or oil discovery). The South Sea Bubble, 1711–20, is a graphic case in point. To help pay off England's £9 million in debt, the British government created the South Sea Co. in 1711 with a monopoly on England's trade with Spanish ports in South America, then let bondholders trade in their bonds for stock in this company. (Britain and Spain were at war or at loggerheads for most of the following decade, a circumstance unlikely to foster huge profits from booming trade between them.) From time to time new stock was issued. As a trading firm, the company was a flop. But in January 1720, the company got into a bidding war with the Bank of England to buy up England's national debt. It won, thanks to bribery and chicanery. From that moment, all hell broke loose. Its stock rose from £128 a share, on Jan. 1, 1720, to £1,000 a share at the end of June. The bubble then burst and the stock fell back to £160 by the end of the year. Among those who lost money was perhaps one of civilization's smartest persons, Sir Isaac Newton, who lost £20,000 in speculations on South Sea stock. He said later, "I can calculate the motions of the heavenly bodies, but not the madness of people." A conservative banker, who resisted the bandwagon and then jumped on it by buying stock at £500 per share, said, "when the rest of the world are mad, we must imitate them in some measure"—perhaps the epitaph of all such bandwagon bubbles, advice that human beings seem determined to follow with dogged persistence.[7]

Bandwagon effects are not all bad. They ultimately bring order to some chaotic markets by making it clear which product characteristics people find especially desirable. (See, for instance, the discussion later in this chapter of the Model T.) When a standard product emerges from this chaos, it often can be mass-produced, bringing large and rapid reductions in price and making the product available widely to a mass market. Market bandwagons, like circus ones, stress that shopping is a social act, one in which the influence of others is pervasive and powerful. The immense social energy embodied in bandwagons is like Niagara Falls—very hard to harness, but it is of great benefit to those who succeed. Ultimately, cognitive psychologist Stanley Schachter observed, *price is a social fact*. Prices, Princeton economist William Baumol once observed, *are relationships among people*, expressed as relationships among things (like money, goods, and assets.) Of all the significant facts one can list about prices, their social and psychological nature, reflecting how people interact, is probably the most important of all.

COSTS AND PRICES

This brings us to prices. In 1976, economist Charles Schultze observed, 10 million cars, 1.5 million houses, 2 billion bushels of wheat, and 10 billion soft-drink bottles were produced in the United States. This was roughly coincident with consumer demands. It happened in response "to the intricate meshing of the signals and incentives provided by the price system.... Prices...

signaled consumer wishes to producers and the costs of fulfilling those wishes to consumers, and gave both the incentive to make appropriate choices."

"I am increasingly convinced," Schultze observed, "no one but economists (and not all of them) really understands what is in this black box. Somehow the cars get into the showrooms and the loaves of bread onto the grocery shelves, but the whole thing is like an oft-repeated high-wire act: we don't really understand how it's possible but it's been done so often we are no longer surprised."[8]

Prices are to the market economy what red cells are to the human body—they both direct vital life-giving resources to the right place at the right time, with little interference or direction. As Milton Friedman has observed, we take for granted that little pat of butter that magically appears on our tray in an airliner at 30,000 feet above the Atlantic. One of the small miracles of the price system is how it manages to get highly perishable products across long distances, to just the right place, at the right time, at the right price, where someone wants to buy them. Take, for instance, Dutch Masters daffodils, grown in the Netherlands, and sold in Alaska, at Carrs Supermarkets. How does this small miracle that transports delicate flowers from Netherlands to willing customers half a globe away while they are still fresh, at affordable prices, occur?

The process begins at Aalsmeer, the world's largest flower auction, where 14 million cut flowers and 1.5 million potted plants are sold every day, in the world's largest commercial building, a 6 million-sq. ft. structure large enough to enclose nine football fields. At 6:30 A.M., buyers take their places in one of five auction halls, each seating 300–600 buyers, with rows of tiered seats. A complex computer system tracks the 50–150,000 transactions each morning. During the previous day and night, nurseries deliver their products, prepacked in boxes or containers. Each is tagged with a slip showing the number of flowers and the grower's name. Each buyer gets a numbered plate that, inserted into a slot in their seat, electronically records their position and unlocks a push-button console on their desks. At dawn, trolleys roll chrysanthemums, irises, and anthuriums out to center stage. Information about the flowers flashes across electronic screens. At this Dutch auction, a clock's single hand points to 100 guilders, at the 12 o'clock position, and begins to move counterclockwise, down to one cent. The first buyer to push the button on the control console stops the clock; he or she then tells the auctioneer how much of the product is being purchased. The transaction is recorded by computer. The clock is reset, and the next lot of flowers is sold in the same way, until all of it is sold.

Computers prepare invoices and the buyers' purchases are stacked on a trailer with his or her number on it. It takes only 15 minutes for the flowers to reach the buyer from the time he or she "stopped the clock." Flowers bought at the morning auction reach New York at 11 P.M. that same night. At 4 A.M. the next day they are on sale at New York's 28th Street market. To reach Alaska, it takes a bit longer—but not much. The top seller at the Aalsmeer market is not tulips—Holland's best-known export—but in fact roses. A billion roses in 150 varieties are sold ever year, compared with "only" 313 million tulips.[9] While the process uses complex state-of-the-art technology, ultimately it is a reflection of "relationships among people"—Dutch flower-growers meeting the needs of Alaskans half-a-world away, who want and need the color and beauty of roses and daffodils during a dark and cold winter at a reasonable price.

There is some evidence that prices are not what they are cracked up to be—either for consumers or for producers. A study by Princeton University economist Alan Blinder, based on interviews with executives, found that businesses change their prices far less frequently than economic theory suggests they should, even when demand or costs change and greater profits could be made. More than half the companies questioned—in a wide variety of different businesses—typically changed their prices no more than once a year, if at all. Three-quarters change their prices no more than twice a year. There are several possible explanations, though as yet no single convincing one: businesses prefer to cut back on service or extras, rather than raise prices, during strong demand; businesses fear the reaction of competitors, who may not follow suit; and businesses strive to preserve long-term commitments to customers to keep prices steady.[10]

Prices can be highly misleading. To measure them properly, they need to be assessed the same way Einstein asked us to look at the universe—relative to other prices. Gasoline prices are a good example. In 1950, the price of a gallon of gas at the pump was 27 cents; 20 cents of that was for the gas itself, 7 cents was for taxes. In 1970, the price of gasoline was still about 27 cents a gallon— exactly the same. But the value of the dollar had declined in that same period—other consumer goods had on average doubled in price, and in 1970 the dollar could buy only about half what it used to buy in 1950. As a result, the real (inflation-adjusted) price of gasoline had in fact fallen, between 1950 and 1970, by about 50 percent. It was the belief in the likely persistence of this cheap price of gasoline that kept Detroit producing big cars—big cars, after all, meant big profits, it was said.[11]

Sometimes, there are hidden elements to costs and prices. When prices are for some reason too cheap, supply may fail to meet the demand. What results then is queues—long lines of people waiting to buy the product in demand, as happened frequently in the Soviet Union and Eastern Europe. The low money price of the product is illusory—the full price, including the value of the person's time waiting in line, may be quite high. (USSR citizens developed ingenious ways of dealing with this problem, including sending members of the family, such as grandparents, whose time was less costly, to stand in queues for daily groceries.) A study of the gasoline shortage in the United States in 1974, for instance, shows that in cities, the true price of a gallon of gasoline was higher by one-third than its money cost—17.7 cents, at the time— because of the value of time spent waiting in gas lines—and in rural areas, where gas was scarcer, waiting time was equivalent to 30 cents a gallon, or nearly half the money price, in March 1974.[12]

Cost and price focus on an attribute of the product or service. But often, it is more important to know the attributes of those who buy them—the "demographics" of the market.

DEMOGRAPHICS

Demography is the study of population and its characteristics. It is one of the most useful tools in listening to the voice of the market, because it provides exceptionally useful information about buyers without the need for directly eliciting it from them.

Here is an admittedly extreme, but vivid, illustration, of how population size and changes in it can have great impact on the kinds of goods and services people want and need. It shows how one of Britain's major markets—woolen goods—was created by disease-carrying fleas and the impact they had on Britain's population.

In the fourteenth century, bubonic plague—or Black Death—swept through Europe and parts of Asia, killing as many as three of every four persons. The Plague was spread to humans by fleas, who in turn were spread by rats infected with the plague. Bubonic plague halved Britain's population in the 1340s. This also halved the demand for food. At the same time, the survivors had become better off—inheriting the capital wealth of those who perished—and sought to trade their poor clothing for better woolen garments. As a result, much of Britain's land was converted from farm land to pasture for raising sheep. This was perhaps the first, and most powerful, instance of how demographic forces shape markets and often create them.[13]

"Demographics," as advertising and marketing experts refer to them, are data about the number of people in markets and their characteristics—age, gender, family status, occupation, income, wealth, education, etc. People's demand for goods and services varies widely with their age, income, and education. Managers need to have a clear idea who buys their product and whether it is suitable for them. Take Honda for example. Honda's Accord became the best-selling automobile in the United States during 1989–91. Honda was designed as a family car. In 1986, the average age of Accord buyers was 40. By 1990, it had climbed to nearly 45 years, while their average income jumped from $47,000 to $55,000. Honda was rightly concerned that it might be "making family cars for people who no longer needed them" because they no longer had children living at home.[14] The Accord was redesigned, aiming again at 40-year-old buyers; its two-door sports coupe was designed for 35-year-olds.

One of the Great Divides in demographics is age 60. About 17 percent of all Americans are 60 or more—over 40 million out of a total population of around 250 million. They differ in a number of important ways from younger persons. They are far less likely than younger adults to have attended college (fewer than a third, compared to half of those under 60), or even high school. Their *household* incomes are relatively low; but because people over 60 live in small households, they enjoy discretionary income that is a third higher than average.[15]

One of the most powerful demographic influences on markets in the 1980s was the rise of the so-called Yuppies—young, upwardly mobile, professional adults, with relatively high discretionary income and an abiding desire to spend it. Many products enjoyed great success because they appealed to this affluent group. Now, in the 1990s, close on the heels of these Yuppies —the often maligned baby-boomers, aged about 30 to 45—comes a new generation. Dubbed "Yiffies" (Young Individualistic Freedom-Minded Few) in a 1990 *Fortune* article by Alan Deutschman, they were born roughly between the assassination of John F. Kennedy, which signalled a sharp drop in America's birth rate, and Watergate. They are already the prime market for housing and in a few years will become the peak-earning thirty-somethings at whom marketers and ad agencies aim their smart-bomb pitches. And they differ greatly from their predecessors.

For one thing, there are a lot fewer of them—they are almost an endangered species. That fact alone will have a major impact on market demand. After World War II Americans had babies in earnest. Annual births rose by almost a half, from under 3 million in 1945 to over 4.3 million (the peak) in 1957. During the two baby-boom decades, 1945–64, 75 million Americans were born. The number of persons in their twenties more than doubled, from 24 million in 1960 (one person in every 8) to 45 million in 1980 (one person in every five).

Births then started to decline, bottoming out in 1973 at about 3 million (a level lower than at any time since World War II), then rising again. The baby-boomers created a "bulge" that travels along the age pyramid like a cat under a carpet.

This bulge is now becoming middle-aged. As it does, America ages too. In 1900, the median age of Americans— the age that divides the population into equal halves—was 23. It is now 33, and in two decades will exceed 35, as 10 percent of the population shifts from 44-and-under age groups to 45-and-older.

The paucity of baby-busters creates a *crater*. Like the bulge, it too travels relentlessly along the life cycle like the bomb run of a B-52, with consequences as large or larger in magnitude, but precisely opposite in direction. These effects are highly predictable. Since mortality rates are known, once babies are born the size of their "cohort" (people born in the same year) at every age through 100 can be accurately predicted long ahead of time. Despite this, as the baby bulge matured and entered grade school, high school, college, and the labor force, its arrival was greeted by screams of surprise at every stage. No doubt the baby bust will provide similar, equally preventable, Pearl Harbors.

The biggest impact of the baby bust will doubtless be on construction and housing. Economists N. Gregory Mankiw and David N. Weil note that "housing demand rises sharply between ages 20 and 30, and remains approximately flat after age 30." In a 1989 article in *Regional Science and Urban Economics*, they argue that because they are so few, Yiffies are producing a sharp drop in housing demand.

Some people believe the recent collapse in the real estate market is related to the recession, as it surely is in part. According to the National Association of Realtors, the median price of a home fell harder and faster in 1990 than during the 1981–82 recession. In only 14 of 96 cities surveyed did home prices rise by more than the 6.1 percent inflation rate. And in 38 cities, prices actually declined.

But Mankiw and Weil claim the real estate depression will far outlast the current downturn, because of Yiffie demographics. "Housing demand will grow more slowly over the next 20 years than in any time since World War II," they observe, a view shared by many experienced realtors. "Real housing prices [current-dollar prices corrected for inflation] will fall substantially," they conclude, "... and may well reach levels lower than those experienced at any time in the past 40 years." Slow demand for housing will reverberate in such related markets as furniture, building materials, and do-it-yourself tools, and will hit commercial developers, mortgage banks, and real estate agents.

There will, however, be a silver lining. In 1980, home ownership rates began to fall as Yuppies fueled an explosion in home prices that put houses beyond the reach of many young couples. One twenty-something, with a crisp new Ph.D., told me his rent for a one-room flat in Washington, D.C., exceeds his parents' monthly mortgage for a sprawling suburban home bought in

1973, when houses and interest rates were both cheap. (They also benefitted from the eight years of inflation, from 1973 to 1981, which depreciated the dollar and hence lowered the real value of their mortgage debt.) The fall in prices will make houses more affordable for the baby-busters and thus will stimulate demand.

It is not just the Yiffies' small numbers that affect housing and other markets, but also their tendency to stay single. In 1970, about one male in five aged 25–29 had never been married; the proportion in 1987 was one in two. For women, the never-married proportions were one in three in 1987, up from one in ten in 1970.

One young woman told me that in her peer group, if she were to announce her engagement, her friends' reaction would be strong and negative. Getting married is "dumb," they tell her. One reason is that Yiffies observe the high divorce rates of their parents; polls show some 85 percent of twenty-somethings think that they are even *more* likely to divorce than their parents. At the same time, the *value* Yiffies attach to a lasting, stable marriage is high and growing. Since statistics trail values, divorce rates will likely decline in future. There are already early signs of this.

Yiffies are keenly concerned about the ethical implications of what they do and what they buy. And they reject the "greed is good" epitaph of the 1980s. Unlike much of the earlier generation, they do not want "to have it all," because as one twenty-something told me, if you have it all (or think you do)—you don't have it all; you have run out of challenges. *Who* you are, for them, is more important than *what* you are or what you have. Acquiring experiences is more important than accumulating assets.

This pragmatic, value-oriented personality is already finding expression in the marketplace, where marketers increasingly tailor products to fit the changing life-styles of their customers. I spoke about this with Norman Belmonte, president of Milco Industries, a women's apparel manufacturer. "The buying public is moving away from built-in obsolescence—the three-years-and-out type of design," he said. "People now look for more European-type products. They want things that have lasting value. Value orientation is more important than style—even in intimate apparel." Belmonte's company is riding this trend by marketing Sleep Walkers, a practical kind of jogging-suit pyjama that women (particularly those who work) can make dinner in, hop over to the supermarket—and then, if they wish, sleep in.

Yiffies are smart, tough buyers. Some of them took consumerism classes in grade school. They are worried about U.S. competitiveness and hence are receptive to "Buy American" appeals.

Look for Yiffies to buy far more "green" (environmentally safe) products. Many large corporations, like GE, Whirlpool, and 3M, are launching DFD (design for disassembly) projects—products that come apart so that plastic and metal components can be recycled more easily. There is even a Yiffie version of that classic, classy Yuppie product, the BMW. A limited edition called the Z1, available so far only in Europe, can be disassembled from its metal chassis in just 20 minutes for ease in recycling. Its cost is a pricey $55,000.

Yiffies believe they will live less well than their predecessors. This is the first time in memory one generation has passed on a *lower* standard of living to its descendants. What is most remarkable, notes MIT Economist Paul Krugman in his book *The Age of Diminished Expectations,* is not young Americans' *expectation* of lower incomes but their resigned *acceptance* of them—so far.[16] And out of those lower real incomes, Yiffies will need to support the profligate Yuppies' retirement benefits and medical care.[17]

Technology is making it possible to learn far more than ever before about a company's customers—whether they are mainly Yuppies, or Yiffies. So-called point-of-sale computers register the sale of a product, its price, and if desired, data on the person buying it. Apart from making possible better inventory management, through real-time tracking of purchases and demand, the system makes it easier to spot trends, in time to re-order, expand production and purchasing, and take advantage of even minor bandwagons. Executives will soon have at their fingertips precise up-to-the-minute data about what their customers are buying and who those customers are.

Demographically, the United States differs significantly from other countries. It is almost the only industrial country whose population is expected to grow substantially over the next century. A new Bureau of the Census report projects that there will be 383 million Americans (compared with 258 million today) by the year 2050, and that number will continue to grow. In contrast, the populations of Japan, France, and Britain will grow by only 1 to 3 percent, through the year 2025, and the populations of Germany and Italy are expected to decline by 6–7 percent in the same period. There are two main reasons for American population growth: children and immigration. The average number of children per married woman fell below its replacement level—2.1—in the 1970s, but has now regained that level (compared with 1.5–1.6 in Japan and Europe). Meanwhile, immigration has now reached the rates it attained early in this century, at about 1 million a year. These sweeping changes in the number of people, and their age structure, will have important impacts on markets and demand.[18]

ELASTICITY, OR SENSITIVITY TO PRICE

Economists measure the sensitivity of demand to changes in price by "price-elasticity of demand," defined as *the percentage change in the quantity demanded resulting from a 1 percent change in the product's own price.* This is an important tool for executives. It indicates whether, for instance, there is room for further price increases without wiping out large amounts of sales volume, taking advantage of perceived product quality and brand loyalty, or whether such price rises will drive buyers to cheaper, competing products.

More than once, managers find themselves surprised by the degree to which customers respond to price changes. Compaq computers are an example. After years of high profits by charging premium prices for high quality, Compaq found its competitors had narrowed the quality gap and began losing its market share rapidly. In 1991, Compaq did not react quickly enough to rounds of price cuts and had its first quarterly loss ever.

In 1992, Compaq responded by moving into low-price computers with its ProLinea line. In the summer of that year, a month after the new line was introduced, Compaq was not able to meet the demand, having been unprepared for the crush of orders that followed a heavily promoted product introduction. A Compaq executive explained: "We were overwhelmed. The demand is higher than the ability to deliver." The company added shifts to its plants in Houston, Texas, Glasgow, Scotland, and Singapore. The shortage occurred despite Compaq's ability to attain a "machine a minute" rate in its plants—eight times its previous rate.[19]

There are complex statistical methods for measuring price sensitivity of demand. Here are two simple "rules of thumb" methods that give executives a reasonable ballpark guess at the price sensitivity of demand for their product.

• METHOD ONE:

Ask a client two questions:

(a) What do you currently pay for my product? Call this price P1.

(b) At what price would you stop buying my product altogether? Call this price P2.

Price sensitivity is calculated as:

$$P1 / (P2 - P1)$$

The intuitive meaning of this measure is clear. The higher the value of P2, the more they are willing to pay rather than do without—hence, the less price sensitive customers are, and hence the lower the value of the "price sensitivity" parameter.*

The reader can try this method on himself or herself. How sensitive are you to changes in the price of the daily newspaper you buy? Suppose that price is, say, 50 cents. At what price would you stop buying it? $1.00? $1.25? If there is only one daily paper in

---

* Here is the proof: Price-elasticity of demand is $(\Delta Q/Q)/(\Delta P/P)$, or $(\Delta Q/\Delta P)/(Q/P)$. For a straight-line demand curve, the numerator is the inverse of the slope of the line, equal to $Q/(P2-P1)$. The denominator is the ratio of quantity to price, or $Q/P1$. The ratio of these two expressions is $P1/(P2-P1)$, because Q cancels out.

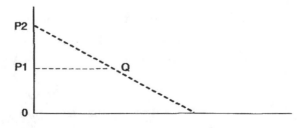

town, chances are your demand is price insensitive. If there are several, and they seem more or less equal in your eyes, a small price increase may lead you to buy the competing paper.

• METHOD TWO:

Picture a proposed 10 percent drop in the price of your product. As seller, you will both gain and lose. You will *gain* from increased sales, as demand reacts to the cheaper price. You will *lose* from lower prices on all units you sell. Price cuts are a tradeoff between gaining higher volume and suffering lower prices on each unit sold. Price-sensitivity of demand tells the executive how the firm comes out on that tradeoff.

Ask yourself two questions, again:

(a) by how much will sales revenue increase owing to higher volume of sales? Let this sum be A.

(b) By how much will sales revenue decrease, owing to the lower price on each unit sold? let this sum be B.

Then, price-sensitivity of demand is the ratio of A/B. Higher price sensitivity means that A will be very large relative to B; low price sensitivity means that in cutting prices, B is larger relative to A, because while few new sales are created by lower prices, all previous sales earn a lower price and hence cause losses in sales revenue.*

The benchmarking point for price sensitivity is when it equals one. If A = B, or if P1 equals (P2-P1), then total sales revenue— the product of the amount sold multiplied by its price—remains

---

* Shown in a diagram: lowering price from P1 to P2 creates two rectangles, "volume gain" (A) and "price loss" (B). Price-sensitivity of demand is the ratio between the two: A/B.

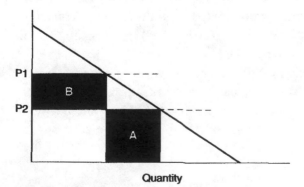

Quantity

the same when prices are raised or lowered (by a small percentage). If price sensitivity is smaller than one, then we say that demand is price insensitive. If it is bigger than one, demand is termed price sensitive.

Price sensitivity is greater the more alternatives and substitutes exist. So, for instance, the price sensitivity of demand for ice cream, in general, is much less than the price sensitivity of demand for Baskin-Robbins or Breyers (the leading two brands). If Baskin-Robbins gets more expensive, you can shift to Breyers. But if all brands get more expensive, the range of substitutes for ice cream is limited, hence overall demand is less likely to fall.

One way to find out what business you are in is to examine the so-called "cross" price-elasticity of demand—the sensitivity of demand for your product, not with respect to its *own* price but with respect to the price of related, competing products. Very high, positive cross-elasticities of demand mean that if your competitor raises his price, and you don't, many of his customers will flock to buy yours. These cross-elasticities are sometimes used to define a "market"—products related by high cross-elasticities of demand are probably good substitutes, hence may be in the same market even though they are quite different in nature. (For example: different forms of entertainment, such as movies and videos.)

A somewhat unusual example of cross-price elasticity analysis is University of Hawaii economist Gerard Russo's study of the demand for physician visits. He finds that such visits are "complementary" with smoking—the more smoking, the more visits. He is also able to measure the cross-price elasticity of demand for physician visits, with respect to the price of cigarettes, and finds it is equal to −0.5. This means that raising the price of cigarettes by 10 percent would lower the number of physician visits by (10 times −0.5 =) 5 percent—a policy Russo thinks is worth considering (perhaps through higher cigarette taxes) as an "important health care policy instrument."[20]

The basis of elasticity, or price-sensitivity, estimates is the concept of the demand curve, a basic tool-in-trade of economists. Figure 8-1 shows the number of Model T Fords sold, between 1908 and 1916, on the X-axis, and the price of the touring car

FIGURE 8.1

Demand for Model T Touring Cars, 1908–16

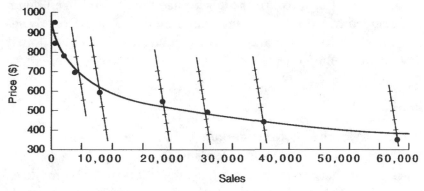

Year	Model T Touring Car Price ($)	Unit Sales
1908	850	5,986
1909	950	12,292
1910	780	19,293
1911	690	40,402
1912	600	78,611
1913	550	182,809
1914	490	260,720
1915	440	355,276
1916	360	577,036

Source: Richard S. Tedlow. *New and Improved: The Story of Mass Marketing in America.* Basic Books: New York, 1990, p. 125.

model on the Y-axis. What it appears to show is a very high degree of price sensitivity of demand, as relatively small reductions in price lead to very large increases in volume.

After all, a fall of only 18 percent in price, between 1915 and 1916, brought about a rise in sales of 62 percent—a price-elasticity of demand equal to 62/18 = 3.44. But a classic paper by economist E. J. Working in 1927 shows the fallacy in this.[21] The curve shown in the figure is not a "true" demand curve, as economist would define it, because it reveals sales over a decade, during which a great many factors other than price underwent major change. *Demand curves show changes in sales, in relation to changes in price, with all other demand factors held constant.* The points shown in the figure are really individual points on a *series* of demand curves that have shifted outward over time—probably, owing to bandwagon effects, as more and more people heard about Model T's, spoke to those who had bought and liked them, and decided that they too should climb on the Model T bandwagon. These shifting demand curves are illustrated by the dotted downward-sloping lines.

FASHION

Related to bandwagon effects are fashion and fads—the social nature of consumption, which leads people to buy things because other people have them or are buying them. In consumer markets, fashion and fads lead to cyclical patterns, in which certain products grow rapidly in sales, then fade away as the market becomes saturated, and yield to new products. (See figure 8.2, for the case of consumer electronics, in which radios yielded to black-and-white TVs, which gave way to color TV, which yielded to Hi-fi stereos, which in turn were conquered by VCRs). In a sense, products have a life cycle just like human beings—birth, growth, maturity, and ultimately death. So-called life cycle analysis of products provides executives with tools to analyze and forecast demand patterns. A typical demand curve for such a product will have a kind of "S" shape—rapid initial growth followed by a decline in growth and ultimately flat sales. This is why innovators—those who design, produce and sell products on the rising part of their S-curve—have an inherent advantage over more conservative firms, who sell mature products on the flat part of their S-curve. Managers have two functions, Peter Drucker observed—marketing (selling existing products) and innovating (creating new ones), and increasing importance attaches to the innovation function.

GREED

Human society, Milton Friedman has implied, is driven by greed. We cannot prevent or eliminate this, he added, but we can simply try to control it.[22]

There are many cases where greed fuels excessive demand that drives price through the ceiling and generates enormous amounts

FIGURE 8.2

Consumer Electronics: The Rise and Fall of Products
(Individual products as Percent of Worldwide Sales in
Consumer Electronics)

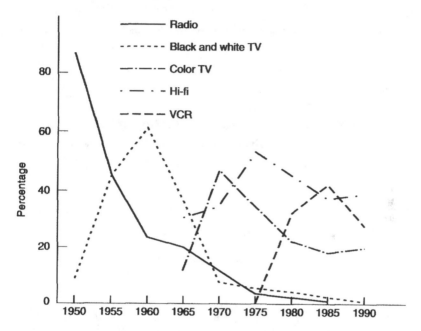

Source: The Ministry of International Trade and Industry; reproduced in "Survey of Consumer Electronics," *Economist,* April 13, 1991, p. 3. © 1991 The Economist Newspaper Group, Inc. Reprinted with permission. Further reproduction prohibited.

The huge consumer electronics industry comes up with a blockbuster product once a decade. Its sales rise to dominate the industry, then fade away quickly as a new product takes over. At present, it is not clear what that new product will be, to succeed the VCR. High definition TV is a possible candidate, or so-called multi-media home-entertainment centers.

of paper wealth—the "bubbles" discussed earlier. The crash of common stocks on the New York Stock Exchange on October 29, 1929, wiped out $14 billion in value; the crash 58 years later, on October 19, 1987, destroyed over $500 billion in wealth. Much of that wealth was "paper" fortunes, created by soaring stock prices—but that fact made its loss no less real to investors. In 1979 the price of an ounce of gold was less than $200. A year later, its price had surged beyond $800 an ounce, hitting a peak of

$850 an ounce on January 21, 1980. By March 17, gold had plummeted to $480. Again, enormous wealth was quickly created, and just as quickly, wiped out. Similarly, silver—which sold for $2 an ounce in the 1970s, topped $50 in mid-January 1980 (driven by its close ally, gold), then collapsed to $14.80 in March of that year. The latest bubble episode is the collapse of land prices in Japan—sliding down from their peak, when the few acres of Emperor Hirohito's palace in downtown Tokyo were theoretically worth all of California.

Financial crises are a frequent occurrence in history; there were 22 serious ones between 1763 and 1929. They are always driven by an earlier period of bubbles, motivated by greed, and have a common element, described by J. M. Barker:

> Whenever you have a group of people thinking the same thing at the same time, you have one of the hardest emotional causes in the world to control.[23]

Executives faced with "groups of people thinking the same thing at the same time" may not be able to control the consequences but they can limit the damage to themselves by trying to think otherwise. Some investors have made large profits by applying the rule of "doing the opposite to what groups of people are thinking at the same time"—the so-called contrarian approach. It is unlikely that the majority is always wrong, any more than that the majority is always right. But right or wrong, excessive majorities can be highly destabilizing in some markets; the trick seems to be to join and then abandon them, well before the bubble bursts.

HABIT

History plays a powerful role in determining consumer behavior, in large part because people are creatures of habit and tend to continue to do what they have done in the past, including the purchase of familiar products. That is one reason why launching new products is so costly—it takes enormous resources and effort to overcome the consumer inertia that keeps people picking the same reassuringly familiar products off the supermarket shelf week after week. An example of habit is the fact that while many people might refuse to sell for, say, a half million dollars, the house they have lived in for 20 years, they would never dream of spending anywhere near that amount for an otherwise equivalent home.[24] Childhood experiences—the things parents, relatives, and friends choose for them to eat, read, hear and observe—have a major impact on their consumer preferences as adults.

Habit tends to make price sensitivity higher, the longer the period of time that passes. For instance, a study of the demand for cigarettes in the United States found that a permanent 10 percent decrease in the price of a pack of cigarettes would cause only a 4 percent rise in smoking a year later—but an 8 percent increase a few years later.[25]

"The past casts a long shadow on the present," Nobel laureate Gary Becker concludes, "through its influence on the formation of present preferences and the present." Becker observes that some companies charge lower prices than pure profit considerations might dictate, possibly to "commit" consumers to their product and generate habit that makes future consumption and sales higher than they might be with high current prices.

The extremest form of habit is addiction. Addiction to drugs, such as cocaine, results in very low price-sensitivity of demand. This creates a severe social dilemma. Drug enforcement is largely aimed at confiscating drugs during and after the time they enter the country. Limiting the amounts that are on the streets simply creates severe shortages and drastically raises the price of such illegal drugs. Higher prices, in turn, do not curtail drug use, but lead to increased crime in order to acquire the resources to buy the high-priced drugs. This has led some experts to suggest legalizing such drugs to break the vicious cost-crime circle.

INCOME

In 1930, Senator Smoot helped push the Smoot-Hawley Tariff through Congress, which imposed tariffs as high as 45 percent on imported goods. The tariff was a reaction to the unemployment that the onset of the Depression was causing. Opposing the tariff was Congresswoman Teresa Norton of New Jersey. Representative Norton argued that the tariff would mean "women whose clothes are already too costly for their purses would have to pay 10% to 75% more for everything that goes to make a woman comfortable," including silk dresses, toilet soap, shoes, and perfumes. Mrs. Norton did some early market research to support her contention. She surveyed "working girls earning $25 per week in a metropolitan area," and found that they spent, per week:

Room $7
Food & Carfare $13
Clothes, etc. $5

That $5 a week, or $260 a year, was divided up among shoes ($30, or 3 pair), a coat $35, 3 hats ($15), several silk dresses ($75), lingerie ($30), 12 pairs of stockings ($20), laundry and cleaning ($15), toilet articles ($25), and extra and emergency ($15).[26]

What is interesting about Rep. Norton's data is the relative paucity of disposable, or discretionary, income that $25-a-week working girls had in those days; three-fourths of their income went on strict necessities, such as room, food, and bus and subway fares. Even in 1929 dollars, $260 a year was not an enormous sum.

By those standards Americans now enjoy much more discretionary income—spending power beyond immediate necessities. Rep. Norton's numbers highlight an important point: Income is a key determinant of demand and is a driver of mass markets. Indeed, sluggish growth in income has been the dark cloud hovering over recent rapid gains in productivity in the United States. As more and more workers are laid off, the output of remaining workers increases. Such gains in efficiency and productivity are offset in part by those who lack jobs.

Demand is always conditional upon purchasing power to support it; without income, demand is imaginary, wishful thinking. This is why such allegedly huge markets as China—with 1.2 billion people—are less attractive than they might seem, because they consist of individuals whose per capita income is only a few hundred dollars—one one-hundredth the spending power of affluent Americans, who now make up a fifth of all U.S. households. China's entire spending power—its Gross Domestic Product—is only about 5 percent that of Europe: $400 billion, in contrast with Europe's $8,000 billion GDP. However, valuing

China's currency at realistic, rather than official, levels doubles GDP.

Some of the most hotly contested market segments in America are those that aim at the "rich"—people with money. Three-eighths of all after-tax income earned in America accrues to only one affluent household in five. Those households have $8 out of every $10 in discretionary (spendable) income, or about $19,000 a year per household, after they have bought such necessities as food, energy, clothing, housing, and transportation. This adds up to $250 billion a year. Many of these affluent families (in fact, nearly two-thirds of them) have money because they are supported by at least two incomes.[27]

Whatever the nature of the market segment you are assaulting, it is important to know both its income, and its *income-sensitivity of demand* for your product—a concept similar to price-sensitivity of demand, reflecting how changes in income affect demand for a particular product. In a growing economy, with rising personal income, products whose demand is highly income sensitive will enjoy faster-growing sales than products whose demand is insensitive to affluence. The objective is to aim at markets with growing incomes, and to sell them products whose demand grows in step with higher incomes.

A rule of thumb exists for measuring income elasticity of demand—inevitably, based on two questions:

(a) What part of your total budget do you spend on Product X?
(b) If you earned a bonus of an additional $1,000, what part of that sum would you spend on Product X?[28]

The ratio of the answers to (b) and (a) is the income elasticity of demand—in other words, the ratio of the marginal expenditure on X, and the average expenditure. Demand for food, for instance, tends to be income insensitive, because people spend additional discretionary income on other things. But demand for "restaurant meals" or "prepared food" is quite income sensitive, because people tend to spend significant parts of added income on having other people prepare their meals, especially if that added income comes from labor that takes away time from meal preparation. The growth of restaurants and fast-food chains is a reflection of the increased proportion of households with two income-earners and the relatively high income-elasticity of demand for out-of-home eating.

JAZZ

Jazz : a) a type of American music, characterized by melodious themes, subtly syncopated dance rhythms, and varied orchestral coloring. b) a quality suggestive of jazz music, esp. in literary style.

New products are far more likely to flop than fizz. Ones that succeed have "jazz," which for products is as hard to define as it is for music—"nonadditive" appeal that comprises far more than just the sum total of attributes or characteristics of that product. Sometimes that jazz is nothing more than Nabisco's idea to put new varieties of peanuts into brightly colored plastic bags, rather than traditional cans and jars (once opened, bags need to be finished, or go stale). Sometimes, it is a whole new concept in technology—like "wireless world" products, including credit-card scanners, modems, faxes, telephones, and computers, all able to communicate with one another seamlessly via satellites, battery-powered, with no wires.[29] Sometimes, "jazz" is no more than an extremely low price. And sometimes, it is simply a way to use an old facility in a startling new fashion—like Williams Co., an owner and builder of gas and oil pipelines, which tugged fiber-optic cables through the pipelines to become the fourth-largest purveyor of long-distance telephone service in the United States, just after AT&T, MCI, and Sprint.[30]

When Richard Sears began selling cream separators at $62.50 (compared with the $100 price of standard models), he was "ablaze with excitement" over the product's prospects. It was "apt"— saving farmers hours of hard work. Those who could afford it were glad to spend the $100, but not many could. Sears's $62.50 model did not sell well. In 1903, Sears added "jazz." He brought out three sizes, at $27, $35, and $39.50. The prices were a sensation. Sales skyrocketed. Between 1902 and 1908 Sears sold nearly $7 million worth of cream separators, and the product became "a bulwark of the company," earning a significant fraction of its total profits. For farmers who used them, cream separators were as "jazzy" as the "wireless world" products about to burst on the consumer electronics scene. They created value, by saving time and work. Sears did not discover them. But he pioneered marketing them. Increasingly, markets will go to those who are good at making things better—producing, distributing, and marketing existing products, as Sears did—rather than to those who are great at making better things—that is, designing new products.

New ideas are relatively scarce in marketing. A recent fad is so-called "value pricing." In automobile sales, value pricing means providing buyers with cars that already have a full package of options, at attractive prices, eliminating haggling with dealers and reducing the need for costly rebates. Value pricing was the basis of Sears, Roebuck, one of the earliest mass merchandisers, and like honesty and Plato, is constantly being rediscovered. In the end, "value for money" is the ultimate "jazz."

KNOWLEDGE

"You can't say it often enough: don't lose touch with the customer."[31] This is the single most-often repeated piece of advice in management literature. It is also the truest, and the hardest to implement.

A great many new products fail to make money for their innovators, despite extensive market testing and investments in market research. Perhaps one new product in 13 succeeds. "The new product battleground is a scene of awful carnage," one market consultant commented. Some market testing yields favorable results, because it mistakes novelty value (and the resulting interest consumers show) with long-lasting market "staying power."[32]

Outback Steakhouse, a chain of 117 restaurants, was founded in 1987. It is America's eighth-fasting-growing new business, over the past five years. It is based on an Australian theme, with shark jaws and boomerangs on the wall. But its food is straight American. Its founder, Chris Sullivan, never even visited Australia before opening his chain. "I might have tried to bring back authentic Australian food, which Americans don't generally like," he explains. "Our company sells American food and Australian fun."[33] Sullivan did no market research—but he knew his market.

Growing numbers of companies that operate in many countries

are learning how valuable knowledge about customers and markets acquired in one country can be when applied to other countries. Unilever's Kuschelweich (cuddles, in German) is a classic example. For years, Unilever struggled to compete with Proctor & Gamble in the fabric-softener market, a market that P&G had created and came to dominate in the United States with its Downy brand and in Europe with Lenor. Nothing worked for Unilever. Its product, known as Comfort, brought major discomfort to Unilever executives and stockholders.

Then one day Unilever's subsidiary in Germany came up with Kuschelweich—a cuddly teddy bear that appeared on the product's package and in its advertising. As a brand symbol, it was perfect. It conveyed trust, softness, love, security, and fond memories. And best of all, it was universal—everyone had some sort of teddy bear as a child. Unilever—a true transnational company (with operations integrated across all countries), as opposed to multinational (with separate unconnected operations in many lands)— quickly transferred the brand and related strategy to other countries—Cajoline in France, Mimosin in Spain, Huggy in Australia, Coccolino in Italy, and Snuggle in the United States. It met with success everywhere. The American teddy-bear product, introduced in the mid-1980s, quickly tripled Unilever's market share in fabric softeners—without a significant change in the product itself.[34]

LOYALTY

The success of Kuschelweis as a brand name shows how important brand names can be. But at the same time, one of the leading business stories of recent years has been the rapid decline of national name brands, and the premium prices they charge. Brands such as Marlboro cigarettes, Kraft cheese, Gerber babyfoods, Frito snacks, and others, that once commanded premiums as high as 45 percent above similar products' prices, have been slashing prices in the face of competition from private-label brands. A survey taken last year found that only three of eight buyers judged some brands in premium categories worth paying more for—compared to 45 percent in 1988. The reason for this change is not obvious. One theory is that the decline of the three-network monopoly on TV advertising—which once meant nearly all consumers could be blanketed by ads on just three channels—as a result of cable TV, has meant that no longer can all consumers be reached, even by the costliest ad campaign. Another is that Yiffies, who are more value conscious, are displacing Yuppies, who in turn are growing older and wiser, and are less brand-disposed.[35]

As Robert Kuttner explains, companies selling identical products that differed only in price would find themselves in cutthroat competition and with minimal profit margins—a Darwinian "survival of the fittest" situation that few executives wish for.[36] In such contexts, efficient firms slash prices to drive out less efficient ones—then swallow the market and boost their prices again. It is perhaps for this reason that there have been far more prosecutions for lowering prices, under American antitrust laws, than for raising them. So-called predatory pricing aims at making competitors extinct. (Federal courts recently ruled that Continental Airlines' suit against American Airlines, claiming that its fare cuts during one competitive summer were predatory, were unfounded; this likely will dampen further such suits in future.)

Companies much prefer to battle one another on the basis of service, quality, convenience, durability, and other product attributes that differentiate one product from another and give companies an edge. Such differentiation lowers price sensitivity and increases repeat purchases. The more unique consumers perceive a product, the greater the price premium they are willing to pay.

Contracts are a new approach to achieving brand loyalty. Ford is trying out a new idea to lock in customers for over a decade. Under this plan, buyers sign a 12-year lease agreement that provides them with a new car every two years, in return for a fixed monthly payment. At the end of the 12 years, customers get to keep the last car.[37]

The erosion of brand loyalty coalesced at a single point in time: so-called Marlboro Friday, April 2, 1993, the day Philip Morris slashed the price of its flagship Marlboro cigarettes, thereby admitting it was losing out to cheaper, nonbrand cigarettes. Wall Street reacted by dumping Philip Morris stock, which lost $13.4 billion in value in a single day. The decline of brands was inevitable, partly because they had become too much of a good thing. In a single year, 1988, companies with strong "mega-brands" were bought up in leveraged buyouts for prices many times the book value of their assets. RJR Nabisco sold for $25 billion, Kraft for $12.9 billion, and Rowntree, $4.5 billion—prices between two and five times their asset values. But mega-brand companies themselves had eroded their own brands, partly by bombarding consumers with special offers and direct promotions that slashed brand prices—creating price awareness and sensitivity, the arch enemy of national brands—and partly by themselves manufacturing products for sale as competing store brands. Moreover, the blizzard of brands was overdone. Americans now have 200 brands of breakfast cereals, the Dutch have 220 types of cigarettes, and even Argentinans enjoy 100 brands of perfume.[38] Perhaps the most unusual brand is one that denies it is one—The Tea That Dares to Be Known by Good Taste Alone, known in supermarket ads as The Tea That Dares.

Name-brand products still account for 80 percent of supermarket sales. Loyalty to brands is not dead. Buyers will continue to search for products they come to know and trust by name, provided the premium they pay is not excessive. Brand loyalty rests securely in the center of the cost-price-value triangle and its announced death is certainly premature. As the CEO of Grand Metropolitan PLC—a mega-brand retailer, with products like J&B Scotch, Smirnoff vodka, and Haagen-Dazs ice cream—George J. Bull claims, "if you can convince consumers that your product tastes better than your competitor's, that it is made with superior ingredients, then you can command a premium price for it."[39]

MINDS AND MONEY

Markets are places where minds and money meet. To understand markets, you need to understand both the *money*—the resources that the major players in the market command—and the *minds* that drive those resources.

The world's largest single market is the foreign exchange market. This market provides a good illustration to sum up this chapter, because all 13 forces mentioned here are at work in this volatile, often-frenzied entity.

Daily, about $1,000 billion change hands, in round-the-clock trading—principally, in dollars, yen, and deutsche marks. This is well over half the total global financial capital transactions under-taken in a given day. It is a market that powerfully affects the lives of everyone, because exchange rates crucially affect jobs, trade, and inflation. Yet a relatively small handful of insiders participates in and dominates it, and few managers or economists are intimate-ly acquainted with it. And it is a market completely electronic in nature, built on two foundations—state-of-the-art network tech-nology and absolute trust.

The principal players are banks—commercial, merchant, and investment—oil companies, multinationals, Central Banks, the Sultan of Brunei and other wealthy individuals. Major players have large foreign exchange trading rooms—typically, with 30 or more professional traders, all hunched in front of computer screens. There are an estimated 20,000 active foreign exchange traders in the United States alone. All the dealers are linked by computer network with one another, and with brokers, who help "make" the market. (The network technology used by brokers is astonishingly primitive. At a New York firm I visited, Noonan, two dozen traders sit in a large room, each with a dozen telephone receivers cradled on chunks of foam rubber in front of them. Each receiver is an open line to foreign exchange dealers. The broker receives buy or sell bids by phone, and literally screams them to his open-line clientele! An experienced foreign exchange trader can grasp the pace and liquidity of the market just by being sensi-tive to the intensity and volume of the screams coming from the broker's room.)

This is a market with no rules except one—if you make a deal, even if you lose your shirt or your job on it, you must pay up. All deals are verbal, made by telephone, with no more legal obligation than the trust binding all the players. Verbal contracts aren't worth the paper they are written on, Samuel Goldwyn once said—but in foreign exchange, if you welsh, don't expect to stay a player. (Phone conversations are taperecorded, in the rare event that a "misunderstanding" arises.) It is a market completely without fric-tion. Broker commissions are miniscule, bid-ask spreads are very small, and a massive amount of trading is carried out simply to get the "feel" of the market—to sense whether players are long or short, tense or loose, whether the market is able to absorb a large amount of dollars without falling or whether even $100 million can drop the exchange rate. And there are no rules. There is no ban on insider trading—what is "insider information" in foreign exchange? "Parking" funds to hide a position is commonplace—such practices in the stock market would lead to jail. Traders more than once have floated false rumours (e.g., President Clinton has been shot!) to help bail out of a wrong position. As far as I know, no one ever went to jail for violating foreign exchange trading rules, because there are none (barring outright fraud).

The market never closes. When New York trading ceases, action moves to Los Angeles and San Francisco, then to Tokyo, Singapore, Australia, the Far East, the Mideast, then on to Frankfurt, Paris, and London, then back to New York, in an unending constant continuum. Active traders who are running a "position" (i.e., hold large amounts of a currency) can literally not afford to sleep. A quick drop in their currency can bankrupt them while they sleep. An acquaintance of mine who trades actively goes jogging with a portable handheld Quotron screen, and checks it every few moments; a quick call from a pay phone can avert disaster—provided he has a quarter in his shorts.

Most trades are conducted in U.S. dollars, for either yen or DM; there are some cross-trades, and traders track cross-rates carefully for arbitrage opportunities. Some currencies are more volatile than others. The Australian and New Zealand dollars ("Aussie" and "Kiwi," as they are known) are especially unstable, as funds flow in and out of those countries in search of high interest rates. Most activity is in spot trades, though there is a rapidly growing market in foreign exchange options, including long options for a year or two.

Successful trading in the market can generate huge profits. Banker's Trust made over $500 million in 1988 from its foreign exchange trading operation, enabling it to write off huge chunks of its uncollectible Latin American debt without foundering.

Only markets where prices fluctuate widely are ones with active trading and speculation. Is the dollar really "worth" 1.8 DM? Perhaps not in purchasing power—but if the market perceives it is, then it is; many nonexperts have made the mistake of basing exchange rate forecasts on what a currency's "true" underlying worth is. They failed to understand that markets are both *money* and *minds*. For nearly a decade, the U.S. dollar appreciated, despite that country's relatively weak economy, because people felt America was a good safe (and profitable) haven to keep money. Economists' predictions that the dollar's fall was imminent repeatedly failed—until it sank precipitously, in 1987.

Success in any market requires possessing knowledge or skill that others lack. Successful traders develop a network of friends and acquaintances, who provide tips, opinions, and even convenient "parking places" for money. The underlying trade of such information is as important to a trader as the overt trade of dollars and the price data common to all. It is this human network that drives the market, and it is one that has to my knowledge not been studied in depth. Often, traders may act on information provided by a distant acquaintance, in, say, Singapore or Melbourne, whom they may never have met face-to-face in their life. And there is a massive amount of duplicity, deceit, deception, lying, and trickery—as well as interludes of selfless friendship and sacrifice.

Corporations with foreign exchange exposures run the risk of losing large sums, and many have in the past. Suppose you earned a billion Italian lire in sales in July 1992. At that time, Italy was part of the so-called Exchange Rate Mechanism (ERM), which linked European community currencies to one another at fixed prices. The French franc, British pound, German mark, Italian lire, and so on, were allowed to fluctuate against one another only within narrow 2.25 percent bands above and below central rates.

You might have felt safe in leaving your lire in Italy. After all, under the ERM Italy promised to keep its currency at close to the prevailing rate, 1,130 lire for one U.S. dollar. At that exchange rate, a billion lire were worth $885,000. Moreover, interest rates in Italy were much higher than in the United States. So, why rush to buy dollars and bring home the Italian earnings?

In mid-September 1992, following massive speculative selling of pounds and lire, both the United Kingdom and Italy dropped out of the ERM as their currencies broke through the "floor"— the lowest permissible exchange rate—and went into near freefall. Some speculators made handsome profits. George Soros, head of the Quantum Fund, is reported to have made $1 billion in profits by betting correctly that Britain would not be able to forestall a large devaluation of sterling. But individuals and businesses with "unhedged" (that is, uninsured against changes in exchange rates) lire and pounds lost heavily.

In July 1993, one U.S. dollar cost 1,583 lire. Your billion Italian lire were worth only $632,000—30 percent fewer dollars than a year earlier. Had you failed to cover yourself against this risk, the loss would have been painful. For smaller businesses, it could even have been life-threatening. Hedging, too, is not without pain—like auto insurance, the cost rises as the roads get riskier.

Ultimately, all consumer demand boils down to minds and money—people's willingness to spend their money on goods and services (minds) and the amount of money they have to spend. Listening to the voice of the customer means knowing a product's attributes well—its aptness, jazz, cost—and knowing equally well the attributes of those who we hope will buy it—their demographics, income, greed, habit, knowledge, loyalty, wants, and needs. Demand is at its core psychological, because our needs are limited, yet our wants are infinitely great. For instance, a family of four could buy food that supplies all its nutritional needs for about $38 a week, yet the average family spends more than three times that sum—its wants are far greater.[40]

The interaction of minds and money is mysterious and often unpredictable. Sometimes, it is not even clear what precisely the minds and money are aiming to buy or sell. In capital markets, for instance, dollars, yen, marks, francs, renminbi (China's currency), stocks, bonds, and options, are bought and sold; a trillion dollars in foreign exchange alone is traded every day. However, it is not pieces of paper, but rather *risk*—the willingness to bear risk, or the ability to avoid risk-bearing—that is traded. A true understanding of capital markets begins by recognizing that, basically, they are markets where risk is bought and sold. The next chapter discusses risk and provides a tool to facilitate decision making under conditions of uncertainty.

Chapter Nine

CALCULATED RISKS

Take calculated risks.

—General George Smith Patton

On June 4, 1944, the eve of D-Day and the risky, massive Allied invasion of Europe, George Patton wrote to his son—at the time an army cadet who would one day become an army general himself.

"Take calculated risks," Patton urged. "That is quite different from being rash."[1] He then led his Third Army (mainly tank forces) onto the beachhead at Normandy, broke through German defenses at Periers and then swept across France in a wide encircling movement. He did this on dangerously low supplies of ammunition and fuel. His Third Army halted only at a heavily defended German line near Metz.

By August, Patton was a major general. The following March, his forces crossed the Rhine.

For some, Patton's daring assault was a rash gamble with soldiers' lives. For him, it was a "calculated risk"—a clear cost-value "tradeoff" choice, giving up the security of safe, short supply lines for the advantage of speed, boldness, and initiative, to keep the enemy off balance, disorganized, and in retreat. Playing for safety, Patton argued, is the riskiest strategy of all in war—and perhaps, he might have added, in business.

Two decades later, IBM faced its own D-day and "played Patton." In 1964, IBM introduced its System/360 family of mainframe computers. The system was a kind of economy of scope, embracing six different models, and had a modular feature that enabled customers to partly design their own configuration. The new computer system was a huge calculated risk. In 1993 dollars, IBM invested $20 billion in it.

After initial delays in bringing the 360s to market, the product became a huge success. IBM doubled its sales dollars (adjusted for inflation) between 1963 and 1966. But, as a senior IBM executive involved with the project noted, this calculated risk may have contained the seeds of IBM's near-destruction. The huge project generated initial chaos and complexity. So an organization was built. This meant hiring new people. IBM's payroll rose far faster than its sales—growing 130 percent in three years. By 1986, at its peak, IBM employed 407,000 people. IBM grew into a risk-averse bureaucracy with an allergy to innovation.[2] For instance, modern computer technology is in large part based on so-called RISC— reduced instruction computing—chips that run powerful workstations. This technology was invented by an IBM scientist in 1974. IBM repeatedly told him to drop the idea, because it was considered valueless.

Executives are paid to take calculated risks. Because most business choices are made under conditions of imperfect information, incomplete or missing data, uncertainty about the future, uncertainty about competitors' actions and business conditions, and sketchy knowledge of technology and markets, nearly all executive decisions are some sort of calculated risk. Moreover, since life offers few opportunities for precise repetition, under identical circumstances, decisions made under uncertainty are one-shot choices, never repeated, with the decision maker never ever knowing for certain whether things might have turned out better if a different choice had been made.

Calculated risks have become the order of the day, because over the past two decades, the world has become a far more uncertain place. Both circumstances and people have become more volatile. Exchange rates, interest rates, commodity prices, and stocks and bonds fluctuate widely. On October 19, 1987, the Dow-Jones

Industrial Average dropped 22.6 percent, or 508 points—compared with only 12.8 percent on October 29, 1929. The Gulf War, collapse of the USSR, civil war in Yugoslavia, the U.S. recession that began in June 1990 while most experts were forecasting continued growth, the global recession, the "flood of the century" in the U.S. Midwest—all these events make the business environment a highly chancy place.

The bond market is a good indicator of uncertainty and volatility. Once, in the 1950s, the bond market was the Wall St. equivalent of a lullaby or a sleeping pill. Today, top-quality corporate bonds leap and dive much like stocks. Not by accident did Tom Wolfe make the protagonist of his novel, *Bonfire of the Vanities,* a bond trader (rather than stockbroker). Observers think the reason is the "magnifying glass" with which investors watch bond-market developments, the instability of interest rates, and the technology that enables bond traders to react instantly to corporate news of any kind.[3]

Dealing with such uncertainties is one of the executive's most important duties. For decision makers uncertainty holds both promise and peril. Peril, because bad choices have very costly consequences. Promise, because those who excel at decision making in a risky environment will have a significant advantage over those who deal with risk by ignoring it, or who underestimate it or in other ways fail to deal with it.

Risk humbles some and enriches others, while scrambling the fortunes of large, powerful companies. Of the 25 largest industrial corporations in the United States in 1900, only two remained on the list by the mid-1960s—General Electric (fifth-largest American industrial firm in 1993) and U.S. Steel (now USX, squeaking in at twenty-fourth).

This chapter offers a tool to help decision makers make better choices under conditions of uncertainty. This tool—expected value—is focused on *evaluating, quantifying and portraying graphically the magnitude and nature of risk, in order to better decide whether it is worth running.* Underlying it is a large body of scholarly research that reveals many of the pitfalls that await unwary managers, as they step through the minefields of chaotic markets and rivalry.

"CRAZY MARKETS, CRAZY GOVERNMENTS"

Uncertainty that executives face has two underlying, often related, basic causes: circumstances and behavior, or in other words: events and people. As two observers put it, less politely, "crazy markets and crazy governments," although realistically non-governmental people should also share some blame.[4]

One type of risk is that created by Nature and circumstance. Patton faced uncertainties about weather, speed and durability of tanks, and other physical conditions. IBM confronted risks with new computer technologies right at the frontiers of science.

A second type of risk is that created by people—the choices that both allies and rivals make, that seriously impact on our own well-being but which for the most part are not subject to our control or knowledge. Patton did not know how the German forces would react to his rapid advance. IBM did not know how its customers would react to the new System/360 nor how its competitors would respond.

Patton and IBM both took calculated risks. A calculated risk is by nature one that weighs the chances against the benefits. In standard cost-value logic under certainty, discussed in earlier chapters, only two questions are employed by the decision maker:

What is it worth? What do I give up to get it?

But under uncertainty, cost-value logic adds a third question: What is it worth? *What are the chances I will get it?* And what do I have to give up in order to get the chance to attain it? We can reduce these three questions back to the original cost-versus-value pair, but the answer to "what is it worth?" becomes more complicated—it becomes a kind of weighted average of several possible outcomes, with the weights represented by likelihood or probability.

So, for example, we might forgo a risk-free bond paying 5 percent to buy shares in a biotechnology firm paying a 25 percent return (one-in-three odds), or zero return (one-in-six) or a 10 percent loss (one-in-two). The overall value of the shares depends crucially on getting the odds right.

ODDS: WORDS...OR NUMBERS?

Making good judgments in the face of uncertainty requires us to quantify the risk as much as possible. In no other area is language more deceiving, befuddling, and imprecise, than in the terms used to describe probability. The vagueness of language in describing risk makes it vital to use a more precise tool—numbers. P. G. Moore once chose ten expressions that express risk or uncertainty. He asked 250 managers to rank the words, in order of the degree of risk or uncertainty they express. The ten phrases were: quite certain, expected, likely, probable, not unreasonable that, possible, hoped, not certain, doubtful, unlikely. Only four of the 250 managers produced identical rankings. The last six of the ten—from "probable" through "unlikely"—had ranks that ranged from "second most certain" to "tenth most certain." Moore repeated the test a month later. He found that even the same manager was not consistent in his or her rankings, which tended to change significantly.[5]

In other words, language is a very imprecise tool when used exclusively to deal with risk. "The usual tests and language habits of our culture," wrote probability expert Leonard Savage, "tend to promote confusion between the ideas of *certainty* and *belief*. They *encourage not only the vice of acting and speaking as though we* are certain when we are not only fairly sure, but also that of acting and speaking as though the opinions we have are worthless when they are not very strong."[6]

Attaching probabilities, or percentages, to forecasts can defeat the vagueness of language. Weather forecasters, for instance, long ago adopted the technique of attaching a likelihood, or probability, to their forecast of rain. People no longer were willing to accept a "likelihood of precipitation," because it was unclear what likelihood meant: 10 percent? 50 percent? 90 percent? The vagueness of the language of risk meant that the forecast of "likely rain" increased, rather than diminished, the uncertainty of the person hearing the forecast.

Other prognosticators would do well to imitate the meteorologist, by being sure to attach probabilities to their predicted scenarios. While such estimates are difficult, a forecast is of little value unless those who make it also inform us what the probability is that it will occur. If you are unable to add such a likelihood, it is probably best not to forecast at all.

The cost-value logic of decision making under uncertainty makes use of concrete estimates of odds, based on the notion of "expected value" and "certainty equivalence." Here is an introduction to the tool, using as examples a chocolate bar masquerading as a lottery, and a more weighty decision: whether or not to acquire rights to a patent.

PAYDAY

I was once taught an important lesson about risk by a lowly 40-cent peanut bar. The name of the bar is Payday. The reason for its name is that it offers prizes, as well as peanuts.

Win instantly! Game piece inside! the wrapper screams. Each wrapper has one letter. To win a prize, you need to collect the letters N-U-T-T-Y. I would guess there are plenty of Ns, Us and Ts—but rare Ys. The odds of winning a prize are one in 105,111, or 49,999 prizes out of some 95 million chocolate bars. Payday promised a chance to win stereo systems, 10-speed bikes, cameras, telescopes, and personal stereos.

Payday's intrinsic peanut-bar value was, in my view, low. Toblerone it isn't. But it had added value that other bars lacked—a "free" lottery. How much was that lottery worth? Its value was the probability of winning a prize, multiplied by the value of that prize, added up over all possible prizes. For instance, the grand prize was a $1,800 Akai system 7 stereo. The chances of winning it were 1 in 19,004,000 (five such prizes for every 95,020,000 bars). The "expected value" is simply the odds of winning times the value of the prize if won. In this case, it is (1/19,004,000) times $1,800 or 0.0095 cents, a value so small it is hard to put in words (less than one one-hundredth of one penny).

The lottery value of Payday is the expected value of all the prizes. That comes to 0.08 cents—just under one-tenth of one cent. This is a very tiny fraction of Payday's retail price—40 cents. The estimated cost of the prizes provided by Hollywood Brands is about $177,810, on estimated revenues of $38 million (95 million

TABLE 9.1
The Expected Value of Payday
(Computing the expected value of Payday as a lottery ticket.)

Prize	Probability of Winning	Value of Prize	Prob. x Value (cents)
Apple IIe			
computer	1/19,004,000	$1,800	. 0095¢
Stereo system	1/7,309,231	$ 600	. 0082
10-speed bike	1/1,484,688	$ 150	. 010
telescope	1/637,718	$ 100	. 016
camera	1/332,238	$ 60	. 018
personal stereo	1/245,530	$ 50	. 020
Total:			.082¢

peanut bars at 40 cents each). For the seller, Payday's cost-value logic makes offering the lottery a good deal. For the buyer, one wonders.

The expected value of the Payday lottery, in which buyers of 95 million chocolate bars win some 50,000 prizes, is 0.082 cents. The law requires Payday to list the odds of winning and number of prizes on the wrapper, to enable buyers to make an informed choice. It is unlikely that many leap at the opportunity to do so.

GRAPHING EXPECTED VALUE

Expected value is always the product of the magnitude of the probability and the magnitude of the prize or payoff. This can be shown graphically as the area of a rectangle, with the base of the rectangle measuring the size of the prize, and the height of the rectangle measuring the probability of winning it (on a scale of zero to one, with zero representing "no chance" and one representing certainty). See figure 9.1.

FIGURE 9.1
Expected Value. The expected value of an outcome is the product of the likelihood, or probability, and its value; this is the area of the rectangle shown below.

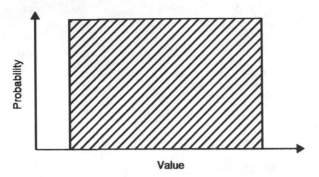

The expected value of a decision is the *sum of the individual expected values for each outcome*. For instance, the Payday lottery's expected value, when portrayed graphically, would look like figure 9.2.

The total value of the Payday lottery is simply the area of all six rectangles—about 0.082 cents.

If the "prize" is in fact a loss, then the rectangle's area should be subtracted, rather than added. The total expected value of a risky decision is portrayed as the total area of all the individual "expected value" rectangles.

Once this expected value is quantified, it can be shown as a single, many-sided figure. The area encompassed by this figure yields the numerical value of the risky decision, as shown in figure 9.3.

Here is a somewhat more weighty example of expected value in a business context. In 1974, a division of what is now Eaton Corp. was offered the chance to buy the defense market rights to a new flight-safety system patent. The market for the product was quite uncertain. The inventor asked the company to make up its mind quickly. The company used the "expected-value" tool.

They foresaw three possible outcomes, if the patent were purchased:

- a 60 percent chance of losing $700,000;
- a 29 percent chance of losing about $125,000;
- a 11 percent chance of earning an average of $5.25 million.

FIGURE 9.2

Graphic View of the Expected Value of Payday Lottery

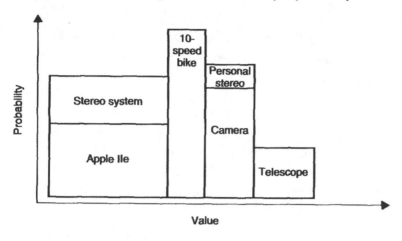

FIGURE 9.3

Graphic portrayal of "expected value."

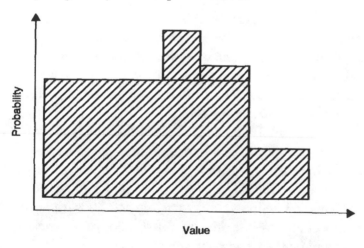

The expected value (taking into account the fact that future dollars are, in present value, less valuable than ones earned immediately), works out to:

- Loss:
  0.6 times $700,000 plus 0.29 times $125,000 = $456,250
- Gain:
  0.11 times $5,250,000 = $577,500

• Net expected value:
Gain minus Loss = $577,500 minus $456,250 = $121,250.

This average, or expected, gain of $121,250 had high risk attached to it. The likelihood of loss was some 89 percent. The profit was substantial, but it was also quite unlikely, with probability of only 11 percent.

The company had another alternative. It could wait, not buy the patent license, see how the market developed, then offer to buy a sublicense from the licensee. Ninety-four times out of a 100, the patent would prove valueless. Six times out of a 100, it would be of value, yielding profits of about $830,000.

This would involve the following expected value:

• No gain or loss:
(in the event the patent was worthless) 94 percent times zero
• Gain: (6 percent likelihood):
0.06 times $830,000 = $49,800.

A unanimous decision was made by the company: the president and vice-presidents for business development and operations chose the second, less risky strategy—the sublicense. Though it offered less than half the expected value of the first alternative, it was far less risky. The added risk of the licensing strategy was just not worth its return, or value, they decided.[7]

Even simple choices often involve a bewildering variety of possible outcomes. The key to good decision making under uncertainty is to follow Einstein's advice: Simplify as much as possible—but not more so. Simplify the outcomes down to the main ones and evaluate the likelihood and value of each. Be sure not to leave out an important possible outcome; if you do, your expected value rectangle will be the wrong size and will seriously mislead. If you try to include every possible development, the decision calculation will be hopelessly complicated and tangled. For instance, the company debating the license had to worry about possible legislation about to be enacted, and the likelihood of a plane crash in the ensuing months that would affect the value of the patent. The rule of thumb is: boil things down so they can be portrayed in a single chart.

While charts are helpful, they sometimes need to be discarded, when intuition speaks strongly. Akio Morita's Sony Corp. licensed the transistor from AT&T's Bell Labs, where it was invented by physicists William Shockley, John Bardeen, and Walter Brattain in 1948. They paid $25,000 for the license, at a time when it was utterly unclear what the market value of the device might be. The transistor became the foundation of a huge new electronics market. At the time, it was unlikely that the probability of this happening could be estimated with any degree of confidence.[8] AT&T's own vision of the transistor's usefulness, at that time, was limited to such devices as hearing aids. Morita realized that the expected value of his risk-taking choice was almost unknowable, but he sensed that it was very large compared to the small sum he risked to buy the license. He was right.

Quantifying risk—insisting that prognosticators attach a likelihood value to their predictions, in the same way that weather forecasters have come to do—is crucial. Yet even when hard numbers are used, not all the fog is dispelled. Take this example of the assessment of cancer risk to persons exposed to radiation after the Chernobyl disaster.

By one calculation, the risk of cancer caused by Chernobyl radiation is very high.

- 24,000 people between 3 and 15 kilometers from the plant (2 to 9 miles) will ultimately receive a million man-rems of radiation. It takes 8,000 man-rems to cause one case of cancer. Hence: a million divided by 8,000 yields 131 cases of cancer caused by radiation. This is a relatively large number, compared to the 31 people within the power plant itself who died of radiation sickness within two months of the accident.
- Yet by another type of reasoning, the risk is quite low. In any event, 5,000 cancer deaths would occur to this same population of 24,000 people, from other causes. So, 131 added deaths is only a 2.6 percent increase in cancer incidence—rather low, compared to the 30 percent of all cancer deaths that are caused by lung cancer induced by smoking and hence are preventable.
- Moreover, there are 75 million people in Byelorussia and the Ukraine, who together will receive 29 million man-rems of

radiation. The 3,500 "extra cancers" that Chernobyl radiation will cause is itself a large number—but only 0.0047 percent of the 15 million cancers that this population will incur from other causes.

So—is the added risk of cancer caused by Chernobyl radiation high—or low? It is both, depending on how one frames the calculation.[9]

CERTAINTY EQUIVALENCE

Economic choices are always comparisons of alternatives. Sometimes, unhappy alternatives look good when compared to even worse ones. Asked how he felt on turning 80, Winston Churchill said, "quite good—when I consider the alternative." Many business choices are like Churchill's perception—poor, but better than anything else available at the time.

Often, a risk-ridden choice can be compared with a no-risk or "certainty equivalent" one. Executives should ask:

What is the smallest value of money that I would accept, without risk, in return for the risky choice, whose expected value is as shown?

This is the "certainty equivalent" of the risky choice. For those who dislike risk, it is generally smaller than the expected value, reflecting the important fact that risk is aversive and often requires us to pay money to others in return for their agreement to accept that risk. The difference between the "certainty equivalent" sum, and the expected value, is the "risk premium"—the money cost of the uncertainty, as perceived by the person about to bear it.

Suppose, after completing college, you are offered a job by a leading firm of consultants. They offer you two alternate wage contracts. One calls for a certain wage, $X, that does not vary year-in year-out. The second calls for an incentive contract, that pays you $80,000 in good years and $40,000 in bad ones. One year out of two, you are told, is a good one; one year out of two, a bad one.

What, for you, is the smallest value of $X, that leaves you quite indifferent between the certain $X and the risky incentive contract?

The expected value of the risky contract is (1/2) times $80,000, plus (1/2) times $40,000, or $60,000. On average, with this contract, you earn $60,000, or half-way between $80,000 and $40,000.

Many people would offer values of $X somewhere in the range of $50–$55,000, reflecting a "certainty premium" (a value of certainty over uncertainty) of between 8 and 16 percent. That means that in return for knowing their wage with utter certainty, they would be willing to give up, on average, between 8 and 16 percent of their annual wage, as a kind of "insurance premium." (Some people who enjoy risk-taking might actually suggest $X is more than $60,000.)

Figure 9.4 shows a risk premium for a hypothetical subject who chose $X as $50,000.

A risky wage contract is worth an expected value of $60,000; this individual is willing to accept, in its place, a $50,000 wage paid with absolute certainty. The person's risk premium is $10,000, or about 20 percent of the expected value of the risky contract.

CERTAINTY AND CAPITAL MARKETS

Figure 9.4 has major applications in capital markets. Contrary to common belief, it is not stocks and bonds and other assets that are bought and sold in capital markets—well over $1 trillion a day, worldwide. Instead, it is risk—the willingness to bear risk and uncertainty, in return for payment, and the desire to get rid of risk and pay someone else to bear it. Capital markets are places where individuals and institutions come to trade in risk. Those who are successful in capital markets are those who are best at correctly perceiving and evaluating the risk attached to various assets. Such evaluations involve considerable independent thinking, because at a given moment there is often a "consensus" in capital markets, about whether asset prices are about to rise or fall, and this consensus gives the false appearance of a riskless gain. Independent thinking about risk premiums is one of the most important characteristics of smart decision making under uncertainty.

The episode of junk bonds is a good example. A young University of California student named Michael Milken read, in the

FIGURE 9.4

Certain versus risky wage. A risky wage contract is worth an expected value of $60,000; this individual is willing to accept, in its palce, a $50,000 wage paid with absolute certainty. The person's risk premium is $10,000, or about 20 percent of the expected value of the risky contract.

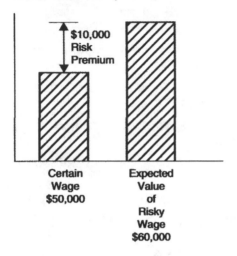

mid-1960s, an abstruse study by economist W. Bradford Hickman, published in 1958. Hickman studied every corporate bond issued between 1900 and 1943. He found that for low-rated debt—small or risky companies—the risk premium bonds paid was "greatly exaggerated" compared to the true underlying riskiness of the bonds. In other words, such bonds were good value because they overpaid for the amount of risk-bearing entailed in holding them, compared to the going price of risk. As a summertime bond trader, Milken discovered firsthand the fallibility of the credit market in wrongly pricing low-grade bonds. "There was something seriously wrong with traditional credit analysis," he concluded, analysis based on the notion that capital markets are super-efficient and always quantify and price risk accurately.

After earning his M.B.A., Milken got a job with an investment-banking firm named Drexel Harriman Ripley. Milken used his knowledge of faulty risk pricing in the bond market craftily. He reasoned that a bond market that overrated risk, might also be prone to underrate it. His meteoric career was built on *selling* low-grade high-risk bonds ("junk bonds," they came to be known) rather than buying them. His buyers were investors attracted by the high rates of interest such bonds paid. Those high yields reflected the high risk such bonds entailed —risk far greater, as we now know by hindsight, than in fact the risk premium or price paid for bearing such risk. Milken's insight, learned in college, was that even very smart and experienced people operating in capital markets can make utterly wrong calculations in evaluating risk. During 1900–43, they overvalued it; in the 1970s, under his guidance, they undervalued it.[10]

Highly sophisticated investors bought junk bonds, including large insurance companies. Many of those bonds became worthless, as their issuers became unable to pay the principal and interest on them. During the rapid inflation of 1973–81, paying off debt was easy, because you paid principal and interest in cheap, easy-to-acquire inflated dollars. Suddenly, after 1981, inflation turned into deflation. Debt repayment became terribly burdensome, because debt is paid off with hard-to-get dollars whose value is constant.

In one sense, capital markets are just huge insurance markets, where people with money accept the risk inherent in lending in return for a "two-part tariff," comprised of: (1) compensation for giving up money for a year, 10 years, or 30 years, rather than having it to enjoy now—this is a so-called "agio," Latin for "premium," or time premium; and (2) compensation for the risk of possibly having the borrower default and not pay back interest and principal. This risk premium, like any sum of payment, is the product of a "price" (the going price for bearing one unit of risk) and the amount (the quantity of risk inherent in the deal).

GAMBLING AND INSURANCE

One of the paradoxes of business is that Americans hate risk and spend large amounts of money to avoid it by insuring against it. At the same time, Americans also love risk. They spend large amounts of money to gamble and seem to think every penny is worth it. Often, the same people who spend large amounts of their incomes on *avoiding* risk, spend similar sums in *taking* risk.

The industries built on gambling and insurance are both large and growing. While the following figures are somewhat dated, they do give some indication of the enormous size of both the insurance and gambling industries.

Life is risky. Car accidents alone cost about $76 billion annually. Theft causes another $11 billion in damage. Fires cause about $8 billion in damage. Many companies that insure against such risks lost large amounts of money in the 1980s on their insurance business, yet ironically, by making high-risk high-return investments of the income from the sale of insurance, managed to make a large profit.

In 1991 Americans had $10 trillion in life insurance in force. There were over 6,000 insurance companies, with assets over $1.5 trillion, and the industry employed over 2 million people. Purchases of life insurance in that year amounted to $1.6 trillion. Some 65 percent of the U.S. population is covered by life insurance.[11] In other words, not only is life full of very real risks, but we are sufficiently scared by them to pay for a lot of insurance.

But at the same time, Americans bet about $200 billion a year on lotteries, sports, and Las Vegas. In 1984, casino operators made $5.1 billion, charitable games and bingo operators $1.4 billion, and illegal gambling bookies and operators $5.2 billion. A slot machine that costs about $5,000 typically earns over $100,000 a year—paying for itself in 18 days.[12] Slot machines have the additional advantage of avoiding sick days, benefits, scheduling problems, or cheating. They account for about two-thirds of all Las Vegas gambling action.

Las Vegas generated $14 billion in gambling revenues in 1989 alone. The seven largest hotels in the world are all in Las Vegas, from Excalibur (4,032 rooms) through the Imperial Palace (2,637 rooms).[13]

So, even though we hate risk, we also love it. Today, 28 states plus the District of Columbia run lotteries. Even the federal government is considering getting into the act. In 1988 Americans bought $15 billion worth of state lottery tickets. They got back about half that sum in prizes—$7.5 billion. About 15 percent of the $15 billion went for administration and a third of it was net profit for the states. In large states, lotteries gross $100 a year per adult.[14]

The immense popularity of state lotteries is somewhat inexplicable, in terms of cold "expected value" computations. The reason is that only half the money raised in the lotteries is given back in prizes. State governments skim the other half for operating costs and revenue. This means that the expected value of a lottery ticket is only half the price it costs to buy one. If someone offered to sell you an object, and told you up front that its price was twice what it was worth—would you buy it? That is what state lotteries do, with enormous success. There must be something about this type of "calculated risk" that makes it especially attractive. Perhaps it is the fun value of buying the dream of becoming a multi-millionaire for the negligible price of a one dollar ticket. And while the dream is improbable—highly improbable—the enormous odds against it are perceived as implying not impossibility, but possibility—it could happen, a perception that advertising carefully cultivates by trotting out actual winners on television.

ODD BEHAVIOR TOWARD ODDS

Researchers who explored how people perceive risk and behave toward it have found a rich and fascinating region of human behavior.[15] Probability is by nature a complicated and abstract notion. Few decisions are like Payday, with Life providing one with a neat set of odds or chances on the decision's inside wrapper. Mostly we guess at the odds on our own. A large variety of biases, errors, and mistakes exists in the way people treat uncertainty and executives are certainly subject to most or all of these. Here is a selection of just a few of the probability errors people have been found to make, with applications to executive decision making.

• ARE YOU BEING FRAMED?

Imagine the United States is gearing up for an increase in the incidence of AIDS, expected to kill 600,000 people. A drug company has a new and unproven vaccine. The only alternative to it is a public health program of education, testing, and free sterile needles. Because of budget limitations, resources allow only one of the two alternatives to be implemented. Table 9.2 shows two ways the choice could be presented.

In terms of probabilities and facts, *Frames A and B are identical*, because "200,000 people saved" is the same as "400,000 people die," given that there is a 1-in-3 chance that 600,000 people will

TABLE 9.2

Frame A	Frame B
If the public health program is adopted, 200,000 people will be saved.	If the public health program is adopted, 400,000 people will die.
If the vaccine is adopted, there is a 1-in-3 chance that 600,000 people will be saved and a 2-in-3 chance that no people at all will be saved.	If the vaccine is adopted, there is a 1-in-3 chance that nobody will die, and a 2-in-3 chance that 600,000 people will die.

be saved. Yet experiments by psychologists show that more than three persons in four, when faced with Frame A, choose the public health program [because, how can one gamble with human lives, when 200,000 could be saved with certainty]. Yet facing Frame B, the same individuals—three out of four—pick the vaccine, for precisely the same reason—at least there's a fighting chance to save 600,000. When shown the conflict between their choices, subjects feel uncomfortable, yet do not feel inclined to alter either of their choices. This inconsistency is as common among sophisticated educated respondents as it is among uneducated ones. (A British scholar, D. E. Bell, once went to the United States to study probability as an undergraduate. "When I first went to the U.S. and heard of a probability of precipitation of 10 percent," he reports, I went out with my mackintosh on thinking it would rain. If they had said a probability of 90 percent of no rain, I would have gone out wearing my sunhat.")

Framing is used daily by retailers and advertisers. Economist Richard Thaler has observed that consumers are pleased to get a 5 percent discount on cash purchases (compared with credit card), but would be disgruntled, to say the least, if charged 5 percent extra for using a credit card—even though the two setups are identical.

• NOTHING IS NOISE, OR "EVERYTHING HAS A REASON"

There is a great deal of random "noise" in the world, especially in busy markets. Not every event has a purposeful cause. Yet experts and analysts somehow manage to find such a cause for nearly every happening. This so-called "overfitting"—attribution of meaning to randomness—is in a sense a denial of risk and uncertainty. For example: after good economic news is printed, a rise in stock prices is attributed to the news, while a fall in stock prices is explained as "the market already discounted the news previously." The cure for this particular error is far easier to say than to take. It is: Try not to find (false) reasons for events that are simply noise, or randomness. If you do find such causes, test your hypothesis carefully, to see whether it checks out.

• MY BROTHER-IN-LAW'S VOLVO

"We think in the abstract," mathematician Alfred North Whitehead once said, "but live in the concrete." Often, however, we both live and think in the concrete. Judging risk is often a matter of drawing conclusions, or inferences, from a number of examples, or samples. Often, even trained scientists draw unwarranted conclusions from very small samples. This can occur when a very small sample—perhaps only one instance—is particularly vivid and concrete. For instance, *Consumer Reports* surveys tens of thousands of user-reported repair frequencies for cars and may find that Volvo is not exactly as durable as a Rolls-Royce. But if my brother-in-law owns a Volvo, finds it a superb, flawless, and tough-as-nails car, I am likely to find his evidence far more persuasive than reams of statistics. As Bertrand Russell observed, popular induction depends on the emotional interest of the instances, not upon their number.

"For instance is not a proof, " says a Yiddish proverb. While we may know this cognitively, a powerfully vivid "for instance" can defeat batteries of statistics. Hearing something firsthand from someone has been shown to be far more persuasive than printed statistical facts.[16] For example, people tend to underestimate the likelihood of common causes of death, such as stroke, cancer, accidents, at roughly one-tenth of their true value. They also overestimate the frequency of very rare causes of death (botulism poisoning, for example) by as much as a hundred or a thousand times. These mistakes apparently result from the fact that people often judge the likelihood of an event in terms of how easily they can recall (or imagine) examples. We learn of death from stroke only when a friend or relative dies. But cases of death from botulism are all reported by the media. They are rare, yet very concrete through media reporting.[17]

• A BIRD IN THE HAND

Cervantes, in *Don Quixote*, cited the popular proverb that a bird in the hand beats two in the bush. It is as true now as it was then. Individuals ascribe high value to absolute 100 percent certainty, far more than, say, 99.9 percent. While we may know that 99.9 percent means failure only one time in one thousand, what it may tell us is that disaster is possible, if improbable—and that is cause for worry. This excess weighting of certainty explains in part the rising importance of quality in products among consumers. "Near-perfect" has to come to mean, "likely to let us down sometime."

• OVERCONFIDENCE

Experts tend to attach far more certainty to their predictions and estimates than their knowledge permits. Moreover, this overconfidence is fairly resistant to a wide range of attempts to alter or correct it. Ask people how long the Nile River is, and they may profess uncertainty. Ask them to provide a range—longest and shortest length—such that the odds are 50/50 the true length lies inside their range, and generally, the range is far too small. Studies have revealed such overconfidence among bankers, managers, civil engineers, and clinical psychologists.[18]

• EXAGGERATING SMALL PROBABILITIES

Human beings have great difficulty perceiving, with accuracy, very large numbers, and very small numbers, and fully grasping their meaning. This is well exploited by some state lotteries—recently, a seven-state combined lottery—that merge their top prizes to create enormous sums, up to $10 million. Because the number of contestants is equally large, however, the odds of winning this huge sum are proportionately tiny—perhaps one in 10 million. Suppose you lived in metropolitan New York City. Your chances of winning are equivalent to being the one person, out of all ten million New Yorkers, chosen. But generally, lottery-ticket buyers focus on the huge prize rather than on the tiny odds of winning it.

The one-in-10-million odds, in our mind's eye, tend to seem larger than reality. This "overweighting" of small odds holds for probabilities up to around 10 percent. Above that, the tendency reverses itself—we tend to underweight odds greater than one in ten, especially in the upper range of near-certainty (see above).

Courage, Ernest Hemingway once said, is grace under pressure. The pressure of making tough decisions in the face of great uncertainty may reveal courage as well as other characteristics in decision makers, in the same way that high heat and pressure in a materials testing lab tell experts much about the substance being tortured. Executives face such tests daily. A major risky decision executives face is introducing new products. Companies that lead their industries in profitability and sales growth get about half of their revenues from products developed in the past five years. The least successful get only about 10 percent of their sales from new products.[19]

Skill at taking calculated risks of this type can mean the difference between high profitability and average or below-average returns. A condition for making smart choices under risk is knowing yourself—your own biases, tendencies and weaknesses. While improved self-knowledge may be a *result* of decision making under uncertainty, it is probably one of the profoundest causes of, or preconditions for, good decisions toward risk. As "Adam Smith" (business writer George Goodman) once noted: If you don't know who you are, you can find out by making risky decisions—for instance, in the stock market—but it will a very expensive lesson.

Or, as gambler Nick the Greek phrased it: Remember this. The "house" doesn't beat a player. It merely gives him a chance to beat himself.

Chapter Ten

COMPETING BY COOPERATING

Some economists might sum up the core message of their discipline thus: Spirited competition in open markets makes for efficient firms, great products, and good prices. In the struggle for survival among competing firms and their products, competition for the hearts and minds of consumers leads the best goods and companies to survive, while others wither or perish.[1]

I think they may have got it all wrong. The economists' claim that wealth and profit flow from the "invisible hand" of competition needs updating and revision. It is not competition but *cooperation and collaboration* that is the fundamental source of a company's profits and of society's economic well-being. Providing another person with a product or service made with pride and care, far from being a deed of greed, is an act expressing concern and sensitivity for others, concern from which ultimately society gains its wealth, and individuals and companies large and small make their living.

Consider these two examples from the financial services industry—GE Capital and Donaldson, Lufkin, and Jenrette. GE Capital, a subsidiary of General Electric, is one of America's largest nonbank financial institutions. It builds profitable deals by putting together coalitions of business partners. Part of GE Capital's business is leasing airplanes. Some of its planes were leased to Eastern Airlines. When that company went bankrupt, GE Capital was stuck with a handful of Boeing 757s. It found that USAir wanted the 757s, but already had some McDonnell-Douglas MD-80s leased from GE. GE leased USAir the 757s, took back the MD-80s, and then leased them again to a Chinese carrier. The motive behind the deals was profit. What created the deals, however, was the fact that they benefitted all concerned. GE built a coalition among itself and other airlines, filling all their needs while doing so. One can argue about whether GE Capital is rapacious or altruistic—but it is hard not to argue that their profits are driven by their provision of quality services to their clients.[2]

Another example of competing by cooperating is Donaldson, Lufkin, and Jenrette (DLJ). In the 1960s, DLJ rose to a prominent position in the U.S. securities market. Its three founders were young men just out of business school. Within five or six years their firm rose to seventh place among Wall Street houses, then became the first Wall Street firm to sell shares to the public, altering the New York Stock Exchange from a private club to a public institution.

DLJ recognized that so-called "institutional" investors—pension funds, insurance companies, and mutual funds—were growing in importance, as more and more individuals channelled their savings through them rather than directly into the capital market. DLJ defined their business as cooperating with these "new capitalists" through provision of financial services, advice, and management to them.[3] They found a niche that quickly became a major market.

The tool this chapter offers is a concept: *Executives who cooperate best, compete best.* This concept of competing by cooperating calls on business decision makers to ask persistently: *How can I join with those who share my interests and goals, to achieve our mutual goals?* Executives can make their firms more competitive by exploring ways to build coalitions with those who share common interests—workers, managers, suppliers, customers, even fierce rivals. I will use this conept as a kind of lens through which business strategies can be viewed and evaluated. Each of the nine tools described in the preceding chapters will be enlisted in turn, to show how collaboration and alliances can help build strong competitive strategy.

There are at least three reasons why competing by cooperating is becoming increasingly important for business decision making:

1. In many industries, major firms no longer compete solely in local or domestic markets. The playing field has become the entire global market. Even purely domestic competitors increasingly meet competition from foreign imports. Commanding sufficient resources, size, and muscle to compete at the world level often means that even large firms need allies. Few industrial firms are larger than General Motors—yet even GM found it wise to join forces with a competitor, Toyota, in its NIEMI plant in California. Joint ventures—enterprises formed by two or more companies who want to broaden their activities—are one way such cooperation is undertaken. Increasingly, such ventures are informal ones without equity investment. There were fewer than 100 joint ventures in the United States in all of the 1960s; in the 1980s, according to the Cambridge Corp. of Boston, there were on average over 200 such ventures *annually*, many with foreign partners.[4]

2. Products and services are becoming increasingly knowledge-based and information-intensive. Such products emerge best from a collaborative environment in which knowledge is broadly shared, rather than a jealously competitive one. An important example is "mechatronics"—the combination of mechanical engineering and electronics. Modern machines rely heavily on electronics. Each of the two technologies, mechanical engineering and electronics, is complex. Melding them together requires close collaboration among experts and companies to succeed. Companies who want be more competitive through mechatronics can achieve this only by initiating and managing a high degree of collaboration, both internally (among their mechanical and electronic engineers) and externally, with other firms who have the needed expertise.

3. It is becoming the rule that new products and services embrace a whole portfolio of technologies rather than a single major one. Few firms command sufficiently broad expertise in their core competencies to deal with all the needed technologies

on their own. Most require outside help with at least some of them. Perhaps the exception that proves this point is the DC-3—called the best plane ever built. The first DC-3 prototype was made in 1936. Research, development, evaluation, and testing costs came to only $130,000! In today's prices, that is perhaps $1.0 million, about a hundred-thousandth the cost of developing the Lockheed Tristar, for example, or the Boeing 767. The DC-3 embodied over 30 major technological advances. All of them were known and used previously—such as folding landing gear and variable-pitch propellers—but the DC-3 packaged them together for the first time. The day it appeared, the DC-3 made all its competitors utterly obsolete. It wasn't the fastest, cheapest, biggest, or longest plane available—it was simply the best. Nearly half of all DC-3s ever made are still flying. And no DC-3 ever crashed because of structural weakness. In one stroke, the new aircraft cut the cost of flying one passenger seat-mile to one-fifth that of its competitors. It gave Douglas Aircraft Corp. a major advantage over its competitors, one that lasted for years or decades.

Douglas could handle the 30 major technological advances—but today, it probably would need to find at least one strategic ally. Sixty years have passed since the first DC-3 flew. Today, new products that package and integrate many different technological improvements—including aircraft—require high-level managerial skill to orchestrate the varied talents required. They are now the rule rather than the rare exception. As a result, it makes increasing sense to find knowledgeable partners who can save you time and money.

The result of these three forces—global markets, knowledge-based products and technology portfolios—is to create a paradox. Increasingly, firms that compete best are those that find innovative ways to cooperate and collaborate, often even with their bitterest rivals. Woody Allen once quipped that the lion will indeed lie down with the lamb, but the lamb won't get much sleep; yet even such fractious lambs, lions, and tigers as IBM, Apple, and Motorola "lie down" together, by creating a new and powerful microprocessor chip "Power PC," and their executives appear to sleep very well.

One result of all this cooperation has been to make much of

America's antitrust legislation, conceived a century ago in the age of huge cartels and trusts, obsolete. For example, when a smallish conglomerate known as National Intergroup—close to the bottom of *BusinessWeek*'s Top 1,000 U.S. companies—tried to sell off some of its National Steel properties to giant U.S. Steel, the Department of Justice quashed the sale on grounds it would limit competition. Undaunted, National Intergroup sought out an international joint venture between National Steel and the Japanese steelmaker Nippon Kokan. The Justice Department grudgingly approved. The deal kept National in the steel business and made U.S. steel more competitive globally.

THE STRATEGY OF COOPERATION

The word "strategy" comes from two Greek words meaning "army" (stratos) and "to lead" (agein). Strategos is Greek for army general. As generals lead armies, so executives lead their businesses. They do so by establishing a clear vision of where their companies ought to be in the next 5 or 10 years and then showing how they will get there.

In his famous best-seller on competitive strategy, Harvard professor Michael Porter shows how to analyze the competitive structure of an industry, by analyzing firms' relationships with four other entities: buyers, suppliers, potential competitors, and existing competitors.[5] A close reading of Porter's theory reveals, I believe, that the essence of competitive strategy is *the development of collaborative links* with all four.

Firms collaborate with *buyers* by learning their needs and meeting them. They cooperate with *suppliers* by integrating them in the process of production and distribution very early in the product life cycle, starting from design. In a sense, firms even collaborate with existing and potential competitors. Firms compete/cooperate with potential entrants to their industry by keeping their prices low enough to make such entry unattractive, thus avoiding bitter price wars stemming from "overpopulation" in thin markets. This is the so-called contestable markets theory, pioneered by economist William Baumol, which suggests that even if one firm dominates an industry, it still must behave *as if* it had competition, because if its acts greedily in hiking prices and profits—it soon will.[6] And firms even collaborate with competitors, legally, by making their products sufficiently different from others to build separate markets, customer loyalty, and demand, to *diminish* competition.

In building a strategy of cooperation, executives need to find appropriate answers to a checklist of searching questions: In what business environment and markets does my firm compete, or, what business am I in? What resources are available to sustain my company? Who are my competitors? What are their skills and resources? How do my products compare with theirs? Who are my collaborators? With whom can I profitably cooperate? What will give my company a sustainable advantage over my competitors, in the competition for sales revenue and market share? How will we survive, endure—and prevail?

As we review our previous chapters' tools, the cost-price-value tool, our first, serves as a kind of organizing principle for the rest. (See figure 10.1.) By remembering where each tool sits on the chart, and bearing in mind how it focuses on collaboration, not just competition, readers gain a framework for decision making that can yield immediate, positive dividends.

Tool #1: Cost-Price-Value

Rapid economic growth is, for business, like stage makeup on an aging actor or actress—it conceals blemishes that ultimately must reveal themselves. During the 1980s, when America, Europe, and Asia all had rising output, spending, and employment, eager consumers who had money and the will to spend it caused many firms to weaken the links among their prices, their costs, and the value they created for their buyers. America's recession in 1990, and later Europe's, tightened consumers' purse strings. Businesses returned to the fundamentals—giving consumers value for money at costs that permit reasonable profits.

Marketing experts call the 1990s the decade of value for this reason. An age-old social contract between seller and buyer—one that always existed but was neglected by many firms in the 1980s—has returned with greater force. The contract says: You, seller, give me good value for my money, and I, buyer, on my part

FIGURE 10.1
Nine Approaches to "Competing by Cooperating"

will purchase your product repeatedly. Managers can jigger costs and prices, but unless they keep the collaborative concept of value creation in mind, the crucial links among cost, prices, and profits will be incomplete.

McDonald's is an example. Its vice-chairman and chief financial officer, Jack Greenburg, admits that "we got spoiled by our success." McDonald's raised its prices too high, and lost sales and profits. Executives attacked the problem with a three-pronged cost-price-value plan. Prices were slashed. That alone was no solution—lower prices, with no other strategy, would have meant lower profit.[7] McDonald's linked its lower prices with value—so-called Extra Value Meals that sold "combos" (hamburger, fries, and drink) together for less than the sum of their individual prices. At the same time, it addressed seriously soaring costs that had boosted the cost of developing a restaurant by 60 percent in five years. It did this by learning from franchise operators in European cities. There, space was tight and expensive, making efficient use of land crucial. From them McDonald's learned how to assemble 2,000-sq. ft. restaurants from factory-built modules. McDonald's now enjoys record 20 percent profit margins as a result. The secret of its success was its drive to compete by building collaborative links, first of all with its customers, and second, with franchise managers abroad.[8] Creating and increasing value is one of the ultimate acts of cooperation, because it demands that producers of a good or service be closely in tune both with those who make the product—workers and suppliers—and those who consume it—buyers—in efforts to raise value while reducing cost and price.

Tools #2 and #3: Tradeoffs, Hidden Costs, and Comparative Advantage (cost versus value)

The classic example of rugged individualism in business is that of the innovative entrepreneur, who dares to risk reputation and fortune by creating a startup firm to compete against well-established existing companies. But even in entrepreneurship, the earliest stage of business decision making, collaboration is essential. There are tradeoffs and hidden costs (tools #2 and #3) that can best be discovered and managed through cooperative alliances.[9]

Nobel Laureate Isaac Bashevis Singer once said that a writer should write a story only if three conditions are fulfilled: the story is unique, only the writer can tell it, and the writer has a passion to tell it. The same advice applies to creating value. Managers should attempt to bring a new or redesigned product or service into the world only if it is in some way unique or special, only the innovator can create it, and has a burning passion to do so. These are the three necessary conditions that build attractive cost-price-value triangles, with substantial profits nestled right in the center.

Innovating new products is a major element of competitive strategy. Innovation has been called the "attacker's advantage." It is based on developing new products quickly and getting them to market. But speed can be overdone, if it trades off for hasty design, low quality in production, and poorly conceived marketing. How fast is "too fast"? And how can the speed-quality tradeoff be managed and improved?

A new study co-authored by Thomas M. Hout, vice-president of the Boston Consulting Group, surveyed 553 global manufacturers. He found that it takes Japanese manufacturers only 17.7

months to introduce a new product, compared with 19.7 months for American firms. The two-month lag is more important than one might think, for Hout notes that speed in new product development is the single most important factor in determining market share and its rate of growth. The question that arises is, how can speed in new-product introduction be achieved without incurring damaging costs? Hout believes that the answer lies in cooperation and collaboration. "Fast and innovative companies have a better staffing balance, suggesting more interaction among the functions during the development process, with the design engineer getting more input, context and support from the other functions. Such interaction increases the odds that the product will work, sell and make a profit."[10] This type of cooperation depends less on particular types of organizations than on how well the existing organization is managed, Hout found.

One of the important spinoffs of tradeoff analysis is the notion of comparative advantage (tool #3). Entrepreneur Howard Head made powerful use of this tool. He built two highly successful firms—Head Ski Co., which made the first aluminum skis, and Prince Manufacturing Co., which innovated oversize tubular aluminum tennis rackets—and in doing so showed how cooperating with suppliers can be a key factor for success. Rather than try to build the rackets itself, Prince contracted with a Taiwanese firm, Kunnan Lo, who had expertise in working with high-strength aluminum alloy tubing, to make the rackets. This partnership let Prince concentrate on marketing and distribution, and left Kunnan Lo to work out complex production problems related to "stress corrosion." Head had earlier created a similar partnership with Maark Corp., experts in aluminum fabrication, in building his aluminum skis and early Prince aluminum rackets. It was a real-world application of the principle of comparative advantage, in which Prince, Maark, and Kunnan Lo each focused on what it did best, to their mutual gain.[11] In the end, shareholders of all the collaborating companies benefitted from the synergy that made Head Skis and Prince tennis rackets highly competitive.

One of the major "hidden costs" discussed in an earlier chapter was the nearly invisible cost of shareholders' capital. It was shown, in the case of Coca-Cola, that operating divisions should charge themselves 16 percent opportunity-cost "interest" on their own capital, to reflect true costs and make correct decisions about the use of that capital.

A curious reverse example, now having powerful impact on world markets, is Russia and its "costless" and "ownerless" capital. Russia is a major industrial power, with huge capacity in such products as copper, steel, aluminum, and oil. Enormous amounts of capital are in place to produce these products. But who are the shareholders? To whom does the capital belong, and what is the opportunity cost? With a shift in system from command-economy to free enterprise, state-owned factories are being privatized— sold to individuals—but the process is a long and complex one. Meanwhile, millions of Russians are employed in huge plants whose ownership is in a strange twilight zone, between state and private ownership. To keep their heads above water, plant managers are selling their goods on world markets at bargain-basement prices—prices which do not include charges for capital that capital-intensive Western firms are burdened with. As a result of heavy Russian sales, the current price of aluminum is at a historic (inflation-adjusted) low of 49 cents a pound. American aluminum producers have slashed payrolls and cut output by 20 percent. Nor is the problem confined to aluminum. It is estimated that fully a third of Russia's current industrial output is unprofitable, if the true unsubsidized costs of labor and capital were taken into account.[12] But their products are being sold at (or below) their variable cost, ignoring the fixed opportunity cost of capital. It is as if Russia's huge reserves of raw materials and massive industrial capacity are waiting for the second shoe to drop—even if it never does, expectations that it will make markets jumpy and unstable. By one estimate, if all Russian output of oil, gas, gold, iron, and other metals were exported at world prices, it could more than double Russia's per capita income. Russia's cost and price advantage is not solely the "free" capital, but also unrealistically low domestic energy prices—perhaps half those in Western countries.

The competitive price war that ignores hidden costs in aluminum and other products may benefit consumers in the short run—by making cars, which now contain 191 pounds of aluminum on average, cheaper, for instance—but in the long run it makes the aluminum industry unstable. The same price-war phenomenon among airlines, for instance, has made airfares fluctuate greatly. One solution may be a cooperative agreement among Western and Russian producers, now under discussion. While consumers sometimes rub their hands in glee when price wars erupt among producers, more than once they later find that casualties of that war are numerous and the remaining survivors jack up their prices steeply to recoup their wartime losses. In such wars, there are few, if any, victors.[13]

Tool #4: Cost Functions (cost versus value)

Western companies find themselves in the opposite situation to those in Russia. Rather than ignore fixed costs, increasing numbers of firms are desperately seeking ways to lower costs of all kinds. Among costs that have risen especially rapidly in recent years are those incurred in expensive research and development projects. More and more firms are finding ways to lower R&D costs by sharing them, through international collaborative ventures. Such partnerships are the *result*, rather than the *cause*, of intensified international competition. In the competitive jungle, survival of the fittest now means surviving *with* the fittest. The objective is to cut high and growing fixed costs, related to research and development, by sharing them among collaborating partners.

When should your firm engage in such ventures? How and with whom? In what area—R&D, marketing, manufacturing? Should your partner be big or small, foreign or domestic, public or private? And above all—do collaborative ventures really work? Recent research provides some helpful answers.

Soaring costs and high risk in basic and applied research point to that area as a natural candidate for joint ventures. Deepak Sinha and Michael Cusumano, of MIT's Sloan School of Management, built a theoretical model of research joint ventures (RJVs).[14] An RJV should confer two main benefits, they claim:

- *Complementarity.* Joint research among firms with largely similar research abilities has few advantages over unbridled rivalry. Look for companies whose brainpower complements, rather than duplicates, your own.

- *Cost.* An RJV should make research cheaper for its participants, either by economies of scale or through spreading one facility's costs over a wider range of projects.

As Nobel Laureate Albert Szent-Gyorgi once said, research is four things: brains, eyes, machines, and money. Pooling the first three can boost research efficiency, and ultimately save a lot of the fourth. Sinha and Cusumano show that cooperation among firms is more likely and desirable when the technology in question is highly "appropriable" —that is, its profits can be protected and captured by the innovator. Competition is a furious plagiarism, G. K. Chesterton once wrote. Only when research can be largely protected from plagiarism will it prove worthwhile.

Most of the successful Japanese collaborations, they write, were in *applied* (rather than basic) research and involved large companies. It is a fallacy that small firms have most to gain from cooperation. Large companies are best positioned to apply research results and thus can gain most from working with their industry rivals. U.S. government policies that seem to favor RJVs for small firms are unlikely to work.

Some RJVs fail because big firms like to latch onto smaller ones, in order to limit the benefits and profits they will share. This strategy is misguided. Several studies show mismatches between big and small firms in joint ventures lead to failure. Whales and minnows mate poorly, both in nature and in business.

Sinha and Cusumano suggest that because of fierce interfirm rivalries, cooperative R&D is often "not an ideal form of research partnership." Instead, they claim firms are better off looking for partners in an RJV "among universities, non-profit research institutions, or firms outside their industry." Perhaps for that reason, more firms are looking to federal labs for ideas. They are aided by new legislation and policies. U.S. government laboratories spend up to $21 billion yearly, generating world-class research. Of that, $12 billion is for defense and $9 billion for civilian purposes. Access to this brainpower by private industry is now helped by the 1986 Federal Technology Transfer Act. Its purpose was "to facilitate technological collaboration at a far earlier stage, by granting intellectual property rights in advance to collaborators for inventions made by Federal employees, in return for access to far larger resources." Prior to the 1986 Act, there was no exclusive licensing of any patent belonging to the federal government. This curtailed industry's cooperation with federal labs, because the fruits of such work were hard to capture. The Act changed that. The idea was to encourage technology transfer without giving away taxpayer-funded research results. It does this mainly through CRADAs (Cooperative Research and Development Agreements). There are now over 500 CRADAs between federal labs and industry. Industry is now being offered the chance to buy in. Many firms are now taking advantage of that offer.

Another form of cooperative R&D is that of informal trading of know-how, in which one company's engineers exchange information about production processes with those of another company, even a rival one. A study by Eric von Hippel examined 11 firms in the U.S. minimill steel industry. (Minimills are plants that melt steel scrap with an electric arc furnace, then cast and roll it into various shapes. They tend to be small and cheap to build, and the best U.S. minimills are more cost-efficient than their Japanese competitors.) He found that many of the firms routinely traded proprietary process know-how, "sometimes with rivals." In an informal way, von Hippel concludes, "participants appeared to strive to keep a balance in value given and received." Bartering knowledge makes good sense, because it makes both parties better off—each gains knowledge it would not otherwise have. Other studies indicate that such informal markets in knowledge exist in other industries, too, and date back as far as the nineteenth century.[15] The key role played by such cooperation, even among rivals, contrasts sharply with the caricature of no-holds-barred capitalism that some economists laud. It is often this cooperation, rather than competition, that creates opportunities for reducing costs.

Tools #5 and #7: Learning Curves as Friends and Foes (cost versus price) and the Saving Grace of People, Machines, and Knowledge (value versus price)

The force of collaborative competition in rapidly driving down prices is sometimes phenomenal. Consider the first IBM PC computer, introduced in August 1981. It had 64 KB of random-access memory, a 160-KB floppy drive, and a monochrome monitor. It cost $2,600. Today that $2,600 is worth about $4,600 and will buy a computer with several hundred times the computing power of the original IBM PC. Once, computers were severely limited in their calculating power by a shortage of memory. In 1973, the cost of dynamic random-access memory was about a cent per bit, in 1K chips. By 1986, 256K RAM chips were available, and the cost of memory per bit had fallen to 1/1,000 its 1973 level.

PC learning curves bear an important lesson. Even though IBM was the major innovator of personal computers, it did not capture the lion's share of their benefits—imitators did. Business evolution requires not only that innovators create some small or large improvement in existing products—but also that they learn quickly to turn them to their own advantage with speed and alacrity. One of IBM's problems was that other divisions of the company did not treat the personal-computer product as a serious partner, nor learn from its successes and achievements. The PC innovators could have been superb allies for other divisions, but instead were regarded like the early Volkswagen—producers of playthings. The solution, as should by now appear obvious, would have been more and better collaboration.

Learning curves are not always friendly, especially when production runs are not long enough. Airbus Industries, the European consortium, has designed and produced seven different aircraft. While these planes share some common parts, they differ widely in size, capacity, and design. All in all, Airbus has sold over 2,000 planes. That works out to an average of 285 per model. This relatively small average output is not big enough to permit savings through learning curve effects. It is thus not surprising that only in the past couple of years, after over two decades of operation, has Airbus managed to turn an operating profit. European governments bore the losses that piled up until that point—had they not, Airbus would have gone under long ago. The soaring costs of developing new models of aircraft have driven such fierce no-holds-barred competitors like Boeing and Airbus to discuss joint ventures; when survival sometimes depends on cooperation, even rivalrous enemies can become close allies.

Not every organization is eager to learn and to improve. Sometimes learning curves can be threatening because the cost savings and efficiency gains they bring may imperil some people's jobs, making them redundant. Overcoming this threat can sometimes prove next to impossible. Here is an example of how a young naval officer linked people, machines, and knowledge (tool #5) to introduce a huge mechanical improvement—continuous-aim firing—on warships, despite fierce opposition. It is a case study of how to persuade an organization to cooperate in doing what is best for it, even though some individuals in the organization may ultimately be harmed.

Before 1898 gunfire at sea was highly inaccurate. A gun pointer would wait until the roll of his ship brought the gun sights on target, then press the firing button. The process was hit or miss, and it was most often miss. In 1898, major technological change occurred with the introduction of continuous-aim firing. Elevating gears and telescopic sights were developed, enabling the gun pointer to compensate for his vessel's roll by rapidly elevating and depressing the gun, thus keeping the target permanently in the gun sights and improving gunnery accuracy by 3,000 percent in six years!

This remarkable invention was the product of the imaginative mind of British admiral Sir Percy Scott in 1898. In 1900, in China, Scott met a junior American officer, William S. Sims, who had long been upset with the inefficiency of his own navy. Sims learned from Scott all there was to know about continuous-aim firing. Sims altered his own ship's gear and tried out the new system; within a few months, his ship's experimental batteries achieved remarkable records at target practices.

Sims then set out to educate and change the U.S. Navy. He wrote 13 official reports, documenting the case for continuous-fire aiming with masses of data. Both the Bureau of Ordnance and the Bureau of Navigation responded by not responding at all. Too many persons stood to lose from the sweeping structural changes that would result from Sims's learning curve.

Sims then changed his tactics. He sent copies of his reports to other officers in the fleet. His gunnery claims were circulated and discussed. More persons saw that they stood to gain from the innovation. But—still nothing happened. The chief of the Bureau of Ordnance told Sims, our equipment is as good as that of the British; the problem therefore must lie with the gun pointers, whose training is the responsibility of the ships' officers; and anyway, continuous-aim firing was impossible. Sims was ridiculed as a crackbrained egoist and falsifier of evidence.

Sims, a lowly lieutenant, was caught in the intricate web of a precisely organized society and took extraordinary measures. He wrote to the President of the United States, Theodore Roosevelt, his commander-in-chief. Those who have served in the military realize what consequences such behavior, in bypassing the chain of command, can have for the perpetrator. But Roosevelt's reaction was positive. Roosevelt brought Sims home from China and made him inspector of target practice, a job Sims held until Roosevelt left office, and one at which he could introduce and test all the continuous-aim firing he wished. In one stroke, through the support of the most senior officer of all, a critical mass for change was created. When Sims left his post six years later, he was universally acclaimed as "the man who taught us how to shoot."[16]

In introducing and managing learning curves, most executives cannot call on the President of the United States as an ally. In his absence, they need to create partnerships with those whom the learning curve will ultimately benefit—their workers. The opposition to learning should never be underestimated, nor should managers ever give in to it.

Tool # 6: Scale and Scope (cost versus price)

For students of management, the excitement and fascination of watching huge new markets form must resemble astronomers' absorption with watching gas clouds in space create new galaxies. Since the beginning of time, the act of creation is unequalled in its drama and importance. The newest market now undergoing its "Big Bang" creation is "digital media"—a potentially huge industry that could quickly reach hundreds of billions of dollars a year in sales. Digital media convey huge quantities of pictures, sound, and text, in the form of digital information, across telephone lines and satellite links. They provide people, in their own homes, with interactive television (TV they can alter or respond to), home shopping, video movies, database information, and a variety of other services yet to be invented.

Digital media are by nature an industry built on economies of scope—once phone or cable links to homes are in place, the marginal cost of delivering another TV channel or home-shopping service to the consumer is very small. It is an industry that could only be created by close cooperation among large firms, as it combines industries that until recently operated quite separately—broadcast and movies, printing and publishing, computers and communications.[17] Its birth was forecast over a decade ago by a visionary scholar, Nicholas Negroponte.

In the late 1970s, Negroponte proposed establishing what he called the MIT Media Lab. In raising funds among industry worldwide, Negroponte showed a single powerful diagram to make his case for the Lab. His figure showed three industries—computers, entertainment, and printing—that at that time were slightly interconnected, but operated mainly as separate entities. By the year 2000, Negroponte prophesied, the three circles would nearly coincide.[18] (See figure 10.2.)

The Lab he proposed would focus on researching the processes—technologies, products, ideas, innovations—that would bring the three circles together. The year 2000 is still years away but the three industries are quickly merging. The merger of technologies is accompanied by sweeping mergers of large companies—the most recent being the abortive fusion of Bell Atlantic, a telecom firm, and TCI, a huge cable TV company. This is a new industry whose birth is dependent on an incredible mix of partners, that include major players in computers, home electronics, communications, TV, and media. Among the collaborating players: TCI, Bell Atlantic, AT&T, Matsushita, Motorola, Philips, Sony, Apple, AT&T, Toshiba, Sears, IBM, Time Warner, and Columbia. Like a guest list to a high-society ball, hardly a major figure is missing.

Negroponte got his funding and built the Media Lab. Some of its futuristic research may one day become new digital products. And as for Negroponte's merging circles—they have counterparts in nearly every other industry, as innovation increasingly demands the linking of widely differing technologies and expertise.

Industries built on scope in products and services require scope in expertise and facilities, which in turn requires executives to seek

FIGURE 10.2
Diverse Industries Converge

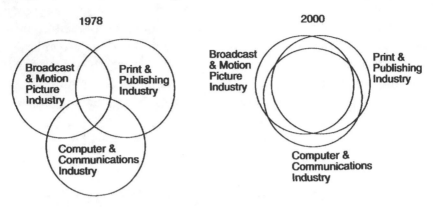

willing partners with whom to collaborate. Innovating by cooperating in newborn industries like digital media is not only the best way to compete, it is probably the only way.

Tool #8: Markets and Demand (price versus value)

The Porsche 911, first produced and sold in 1963, is believed by many experts to be the best sports car ever made. The saga of how Porsche is revamping its 911, after slumping sales, and staking the company's future on it, serves to highlight how managers' understanding of markets and the forces of demand that propel them can be crucial for their firms' survival.

Porsche's high-priced high-performance cars met with great market success in the 1980s, because they matched their customers' needs. Doctors buy Mercedes, it was said, lawyers drive BMWs, and Wall Street experts zip around in Porsches. At its peak, Porsche sold 50,000 cars worldwide, and 30,000 in America alone. But times, and the tastes and needs of customers, changed quickly. In 1992, Porsche sold only 4,000 vehicles in America, and 23,000 worldwide.

Porsche executives may have been puzzled by the slump. After all, their product had improved in quality and performance over the years. But the point was, *demand* had changed. The conspicuous consumption that Porsche exemplified was no longer fashionable.

Indeed, the market for sports cars in general had contracted, as the maturing Yuppies gave way to the value-conscious Yiffies. At the same time competition had stiffened. There were now less-costly substitutes for the Porsche 911, including the Nissan 300ZX and Mazda RX-7.

Porsche executives returned to their drawing boards. They re-examined market demand and completely changed their design and production process. In the past, Porsche engineers had first designed new models, then other experts worked out their cost and how they would be produced. Now, using cost-value logic, Porsche executives reversed the process. They *began* with a cost target—produce a new model of the 911 that could be sold at a profit, for $64,990 (not by chance, the going price of the old 911 model). Buyers would thus get more value for the same price. To achieve this price target, Porsche had to slash the number of labor person-hours per car by one-fourth. This was achieved by improving collaboration with their parts suppliers, involving them in the project right from the outset. Internal collaboration within Porsche was also radically changed. Design engineers worked closely with production engineers right from the outset to ensure that the new 911 could be produced at low cost and without serious hitches.

Will the new Porsche 911 enjoy good sales, especially in the U.S. market? I think it will. It is "apt," or suited to its market—faster and more comfortable. It matches demographic patterns, appealing to older groups who as young people wanted a Porsche but perhaps could not afford one. Its price takes into account the increased price-sensitivity of demand among sports car buyers. It seeks to re-capture old loyalty to the Porsche name. But whether or not the new 911 sells as well as, or better than, the old one, it conveys a lesson—managing demand is primarily a collaborative exercise, weaving tacit or explicit bonds with buyers, with suppliers, and with the company's workers and managers, with the goal of achieving a product that suits its market, and the resulting profit a direct result of the quality and quantity of those collaborative bonds.

The emphasis on cooperation and concern for others as the basis of profit, rather than competition and self-interest, does not jibe well with conventional economics. Consider Adam Smith's endlessly quoted statement that "it is not from the benevolence of the butcher, the brewer or the baker, that we expect our dinner, but from their regard to their own self-interest." It *is* from the butcher's benevolence that we dine, because this benevolence (value for money) determines how well he or she dines.

Successful businesses create value by understanding their customers' needs and by satisfying those needs. Whatever the *motive* of the business, the *objective* is not just to help oneself but at the same time to help others, the customers—and the rewards in a market system are proportional to how well businesses succeed in doing that. This holds true, even in industries —such as financial services—where the central product or service—bearing or selling risk—stubbornly defies attempts to quantify it accurately.

Tool #9: Expected Value (value versus price)

One of America's most important industries involves the mediation between those who have capital—individual savers and those who represent them, like pension funds and insurance companies—and those who want to borrow it, such as corporations and government. During 1990–93, interest rates in the United States fell. The result was to slash the incomes of those who live in part or in full off their capital savings.

One response of Americans has been to seek higher rates of return, by shifting investments from low-risk assets like bonds into higher-risk (and higher-return) assets like stocks, or mutual funds, which are diverse bundles of different stocks. Americans hold nearly two-thirds of their personal wealth in financial assets, and of that, a growing proportion is being diverted to stocks, mainly through mutual funds managed by professional investors.

Is this shift toward stocks wise? The question, in other words, is one of *expected value*. The answer involves, in part, the issue of collaboration. Is the added risk that stocks entail worth the higher expected value of their return? And are the mediators—brokerages and investment bankers—truly serving the interests of their consumers, by catering to their wish for higher rates of return, yet recognizing the added risks such a move on the financial trade-off curve involves? Are Americans properly valuing the added risk they are incurring? Or are the higher risks not being fully considered?

It does appear in part that the recent shift toward stocks corrects in part a long-term irrational bias against them. As experts have pointed out, over the long haul, since 1926, bonds have paid only around 1 percent return a year, while stocks on average returned 8 percent profit. The gap between them is far too large to justify the relatively tiny proportion of their assets that people hold as stocks (directly, only about 20 percent of American households' financial assets). One of the problems of capital markets is that its real product, or service—risk-bearing—is quite distinct from its ostensible products—stocks, bonds, options, foreign exchange, and so forth, and the attributes of risk-bearing are often very difficult to assess.[19]

Making good cost-value judgements under uncertainty requires executives to make accurate assessments of risk—assessments that may fly in the face of what experts and advisors claim. This is one economic tool where the accompanying warning—use with great care—is as important as the tool, expected value, itself. Collaboration with experts is important, but in this case, executives must consider whether the experts—who have counselled that a mixed, diversified portfolio is the most desirable—may have been collectively wrong for many years.

AMERICAN CAPITALISM: DYNAMO OR DINOSAUR?

Modern societies are built on people who care about one another, who work well together, who talk to one another, who build durable teams and keep them together, and who put together coalitions at the drop of a hat to achieve mutual goals. They compete by collaborating. This is especially true of knowledge-based economies. Knowledge, unlike labor, goods, wealth, or capital, expands, the more of it you share and give away. Societies better at sharing will over the long haul do better than their more avaricious rivals.

In *The Wealth of Nations*, Adam Smith spoke about how people are driven by two forces: passions and interests. Competition is propelled by passion. Cooperation is energized by interests. I would argue that the intensity of thought and effort driven by people working together to attain common interests is in general a more effective, controllable tool for executives than the passion motivated by the need or desire to do better than a rival.

While a large part of the world is bent on learning and imitating America's free-enterprise system built on competition—including Eastern Europe, the ex-USSR, and perhaps to some extent China—it may be true that America's version of capitalism, built on laws and values that stress competition and which worked well in the earlier industrial era, is less and less suited to the postindustrial global business environment. America's economic fate could well be like that of Britain, which faded at the turn of the century because it did not adapt to changing circumstances.

Business historian Alfred D. Chandler, Jr., noted the huge differences in the way capitalism operates in America, Britain and Germany.[20] America, Chandler observed, practices "competitive *managerial capitalism,*" *in which firms run by a professional man*agerial class compete fiercely with one another for market share both at home and abroad. The UK's brand was "personal capitalism," in which a small number of upper-class individuals, often members of firm founders' families, controlled major corporations—and often were unfit and untrained to do so, failing to make investments, recruit managers, and develop organizational capabilities needed to obtain and retain market share in many industries. Germany has yet another system: "cooperative managerial capitalism." While in the United States, industrial leaders act as if they were in a demolition derby, with good cars smashing up bad ones, in Germany, Chandler notes "they often preferred to negotiate with one another to maintain market share at home and in some cases abroad."

Despite Germany's current deep recession, its version of capitalism, shared by Japan, Singapore, and even France, seems far more suited for success in today's global markets. Take Toshiba, for example. For decades Toshiba has fashioned a circle of nearly 20 corporate allies in several different industries and a half-dozen countries, with whom it develops, distributes, and markets innovative products. Those allies are helping Toshiba weather current tough times and slow markets in Japan.[21]

The argument that a company's ability to compete will depend far more on its cooperative skills than on its competitive juices is the consensus view of a majority of respected thinkers about management. Each of them has his own term for cooperation. Peter Drucker speaks of firms as "symphony orchestras," with the CEO serving as conductor. Quinn Mills talks of "clusters." Robert Waterman speaks of "ad hocracy." Mel Horwich has analyzed the "networked corporation." Jon Katzenbach writes of "the horizontal organization." All of these notions refer to organizations built to foster communication, teamwork, integration, and cooperation.

A new study by management consultants Charles Hampden-Turner and Alfons Trompenaars, *The Seven Cultures of Capitalism,* provides hard evidence on how individualistic American capitalism really is, in its stress of competitiveness. Hampden-Turner, a Chicago-based management consultant and Trompenaars, head of the Netherlands' Center for International Business Studies, argue that wealth creation—the avowed objective of managers and acid test of an economic system—derives from moral values, which they say "are the bedrock of national identity and the source of economic strengths and weaknesses." To compare and contrast such values, they surveyed 15,000 managers in seven countries—the United States, Japan, Germany, France, Britain, Sweden, and the Netherlands. They found that American managers differ sharply from their counterparts in other countries. Americans tend to be far more individualistic than managers in Japan or even France.

- Two-thirds of American managers believe that if you let businesses cooperate with one another, they usually collude against consumers and the larger society. In contrast, less than a quarter of Japanese managers and only 41 percent of German managers agree. The Japanese and Germans mostly believe businesses that cooperate with each other pass on to their customers enhanced effectiveness and economies of operations.
- 92% of American managers picked "individual ability" when asked whether in hiring a new employee it matters more that he or she "fit into the group" or has the exact "skills, knowledge and record of success necessary for the job." Fewer than half of

the Japanese opted for individual skills, and only 57 percent of the French.

Japanese, German and French managers, say Hampden-Turner and Trompenaars, "will found their value system first on the welfare of their group and then, only after the needs of the group are met, will attention be paid to individual needs. Other managers, especially Americans, British, Dutch and Swedes, will found their value systems on the welfare of the individual, and then, only later, form these persons into effective groups."[22]

Is American capitalism a dynamo, as it is portrayed especially by those eager to imitate it? Or is it in fact a dinosaur, built on principles of Darwinian competition that no longer hold? The answer rests with top management—their wisdom in imitating cooperative systems that seem better adapted to their present environment. American executives *can* learn and change—a trick the brontosaurus never did get the hang of, with fatal consequences.[23]

CONCLUSION AND SUMMARY: TEN TOOLS—A CHECKLIST

- Have you dissected your production process, from start to finish, to make sure all parts of it are vital for creating value, all costs are as low as they can be without impairing product quality, your product or service is optimally designed to create value, and your prices are well positioned, in comparison with what your product costs and the value it generates for its buyers?
- Have you audited your operations to detect hidden costs, and made them more visible and less transparent, or eliminated them where possible? Do all costs, including hidden non-out-of-pocket ones, have a "parent"—someone who bears responsibility for them, and sees them in a bottom-line calculation?
- How well do you manage tradeoffs? Have you identified the major tradeoffs your company faces? Can you quantify them, at least roughly, knowing what you gain and what the pain is for such gain? Can you justify the choice, in terms of gain and

pain? Have you considered other, perhaps better, spots, on your tradeoff curves? And most of all, are you sure you face tradeoffs—or could you achieve greater gain, with absolutely no pain (economic cost) at all, by better organization and management?

- Do you know how your costs change as your output rises? Do you know the cost of producing one more unit of output (good or service), as well as the historical average cost for previous units? Can you split your costs into fixed (overhead) and variable (production) components?

- Do you know how productive your labor, capital, materials, and information all are, relative to what they cost you? Is your production mix just right? Or should you alter it, because some of your resources are highly productive, relative to their cost, while others simply do not earn their keep? In particular, do you have the people/machine mix right? Do you need more machines, or fewer? More people, or fewer?

- Can you lower costs by achieving higher volumes of production (scale)? Or by broadening the range of products and services that your firm provides (scope)? Or perhaps by both?

- Is your organization able to learn? Can this ability be demonstrated by continually falling costs as experience builds and cumulative production rises? Have you managed the learning process to take full advantage of its innate potential?

- Do you know precisely how your product creates value for customers? How price sensitive they are? Do you know how each of the 13 demand factors plays out in your industry and for your own product?

- Do you evaluate risk appropriately, avoiding the many pitfalls that probability-based decisions involve? Are you overly cautious, or overly bold? Do you have a system for measuring risk, by comparing it with equal-value riskless alternatives?

- Have you built an organization whose parts cooperate and collaborate internally? Have you explored all legal ways of cooperating with those who share your common goals and interests, who have knowledge you need, and who can gain from working with you?

THE EXECUTIVE OF THE FUTURE

Your company, a major player in telecommunications and electronics, has in the past fallen on its face in making and selling personal computers. Your marketing people tell you a major corporate market niche is developing, in the booming notebook computer market. Despite past failures, you assemble an entire new Division and give it the green light. Engineers and marketing experts work together closely to define the performance characteristics of a new machine that would create substantial value for its buyers. A Japanese strategic ally is acquired which provides a valuable network of low-cost high-quality manufacturing sources in the Far East. A top U.S. industrial designer is hired to give the new machine a distinctive look. Arrangements are made to assemble the machine in the United States. Laws of physics are broken— working at speeds faster than light, the project brings a high-quality working prototype to a major trade fair only four months after the decision to undertake it. And only six months after that, the product is shipped. It is an unqualified success—your first success in personal computers—bringing market prices and volume sales *that generate substantial profits. Speed got you to market before* others found and exploited the niche. Quality created an enduring market, rather than a transient one. Efficiency made the whole effort profitable. And cooperation within your division, with other divisions, and with other companies worldwide was the glue that stuck it all together.

The future is already here. The product described above is a real one.[24] There are already many similar examples. Its message is a paradoxical. Executives will in future manage their companies in very different ways than they do at present, using futuristic technologies (such as wireless communications with anyone, from any place on the globe to any other place, at any time) and teams and alliances that assemble and then self-destruct for each new product or idea. At the same time, one can say with reasonable certainty that the nature and aims of the decisions executives make, and the bedrock foundations of their businesses, will in the year 2194 be the same as those that prevailed in 1794, 1894, or 1994—making goods and services that create substantial value for buyers, at as low a cost as possible, selling for a price that permits reasonable and stable profit. Cost, value, price, the three pillars of profit, offer executives who master them a simple, enduring framework for competing successfully in the ever-changing global economy.

Notes

Preface

1. My thanks and apologies to Axel Leijonhuvd, from whose "Life with the Econ" (*Western Economic Journal*, Sept. 1973, pp. 327—37) I borrowed the tribal totems.

Chapter 1. Cost, Value, Price

1. *International Business Week*, "Portrait of a CEO," Oct. 11, 1993, p. 64.
2. Shlomo Maital, "What Do Economists Know That Managers of Technology Find Useful?" *Journal of Economic Education*, Spring, 1992, pp. 175–80.
3. Guisseppi A. Forgionne, "Economic Tools Used by Management in Large American Operated Corporations," *Business Economics*, April 1984, pp. 5–14.
4. "Portrait of a CEO," p. 65.
5. T. George Harris, "The Post Capitalist Executive: An Interview with Peter Drucker," *Harvard Business Review*, May–June 1993, pp. 115–122.
6. I am grateful to Prof. Mel Horwitch, of the MIT Sloan School of Management and Theseus Institute, for sharing his insights on the rise of the general manager and the "simultaneous corporation." For an account of his views, see Shlomo Maital, "The General Manager

Rides Again," *Across the Board,* May 1992, pp. 47–48.

7. "Payday, Payday," *Fortune,* June 14, 1993, pp. 56–61.

8. Strassman is a former Xerox Co. vice-president. The example is taken from his book: Paul A. Strassman, *The Business Value of Computers: an Executive's Guide* (Information Economics Press: New Canaan, Conn.; 1990).

9. They are: Fujitsu, 25.8%; Hitachi, 47.8%; NEC, 13.9%; Sony, –44.1%; and Toshiba, 66.4%. Source: Strassman, *The Business Value of Computers,* pp. 122–23.

10. Harris, "The Post Capitalist Executive," p. 120.

11. "Dinosaurs," *Fortune,* May 3, 1993, pp. 32–39.

12. "Rethinking IBM," *International Business Week,* Oct. 4, 1993, p. 48.

13. From "The Fortune 500: The Largest U.S. Industrial Corporations," *Fortune,* April 19, 1993, p. 106.

14. Motorcycles are an even more vivid example. Japanese motorcycle firms—Honda, Suzuki and Yamaha—began by making small motorbikes with small engines. In the mid-1960s, the board chairman of a major British manufacturer, BSA, said that "the success of Honda, Suzuki and Yamaha in the (United) States has been jolly good for us.... people here start out by buying one of the low-price Japanese jobs. They get to enjoy the fun and exhilaration of the open road and frequently end up buying one of our more powerful and expensive machines." The problem was, people soon ended up buying more expensive Japanese motorcycles, rather than British or American—as they did with automobiles, too. Harvard Business School Case Study 9–384–049.

15. David Halberstam, *The Reckoning* (Avon: New York, 1986), pp. 12–14.

16. "The World's Best Brand," *Fortune,* May 31, 1993, p. 25.

17. Ibid.

18. Akio Morita, *Made in Japan* (Fontana: New York, 1987), p. 82.

19. Coke and Sony are curiously linked in another cost-value-price decision. Roberto Goizueta decided to buy Columbia Pictures in 1982 for $692 million. Movies was not a business Coke understood and the price of Columbia may well have exceeded its value to Coke. Coke sold its stake in the movie business to Sony in 1989 for a price of $1.55 billion, a healthy profit. Some observers believe Sony overpaid.

Chapter 2. Hidden Costs

1. Susan Lee, *ABZ's of Business* (Poseidon: New York, 1988), pp. 156–57

2. "The World's Best Brand," *Fortune,* May 31, 1993, p. 31.

3. A rough rule of thumb for figuring out the number of years needed for something growing at $x\%$ a year to double, is: 69 divided by x.

4. Why do companies ever distribute profits at all, as dividends? Shareholders who earn dividends pay personal income tax on them. If the profits were left in the company, they would help the company's stock rise in value and accrue to the shareholders as capital gains—increases in stock value. Generally capital gains are taxed at lower rates than dividends, creating a strong incentive not to pay dividends. Companies do it anyway, for a variety of reasons, none of which seems adequate under cost-value logic. Japanese companies pay proportionately far lower dividends than do U.S. or European firms.

5. That is less attractive than it seems, however; the dollar was losing its value at the time at about 6 percent year, the rate of inflation. The inflation-corrected rate of interest was close to zero. Most information about prices and costs are provided without being adjusted for inflation. Managers need to become accustomed to altering price and cost data to take inflation into account, as second nature, to avoid being misled.

6. Robert H. Hayes and William J. Abernathy, "Managing our way to Economic Decline," *Harvard Business Review,* July–Aug. 1980.

7. "Portrait of a CEO," *International Business Week,* Oct. 11, 1993, p. 65.

8. Paul A. Strassman, *The Business Value of Computers: An Executive's Guide* (Information Economics Press: New Canaan, Conn., 1990), p. 375.

9. The value of another very large chunk of time is equally invisible—time spent producing services in the home, including care of children, cleaning, and preparing meals. Because the services this time generates are not bought and paid for in the marketplace, it is not valued as a cost or a service in a country's national output of goods and services. A study by the OECD estimates that the value of housework, for five large countries that it studied, would add between one-third and one-half to their Gross Domestic Product if taken into account! (*Economist,* July 4, 1992, p. 58).

10. Michael Schrage, *Los Angeles Times,* Feb. 10, 1991, p. F1.

11. Richard Thaler, *Quasi-Rational Economics* (Russell Sage Foundation: New York, 1992).

12. "The L1011 debacle... [is] a spectacular example of organizational failure to 'bail out.'" Barry M. Staw and Jerry Ross, "Knowing When to Pull the Plug," *Harvard Business Review,* March–April 1987, pp. 68–74.

13. "Sony Corp: Globalization," Harvard Business School Case Study 391–071, 1990, p. 23.

14. Staw and Ross, "Knowing When to Pull the Plug," pp. 73, 74.

Chapter 3. Tradeoffs

1. *Business Week,* June 12, 1989, p. 62.
2. Yoko Shibata, "Restructuring, Japanese Style." *Global Finance,* Summer 1993, p. 56.
3. Harvey Leibenstein, "Allocative versus "X" Efficiency," *American Economic Review,* 56, 1966, pp. 392–415.
4. See historian Paul Kennedy's account of how the burden of armies and empires drag down wealthy nations and turn them into poor ones: *The Rise and Fall of the Great Powers 1500-2000* (New Haven, Conn., Yale University Press: 1988).
5. The half-million dollar Robodoc machine provides robotic assistance to surgeons in hip-replacement operations. Like most people-machine choices, this machine complements surgeons' skills rather than completely replacing them. ("A Surgeon Whose Hands Never Shake," *International Business Week,* Oct. 4, 1993, p. 76.)
6. Shibata, "Restructuring, Japanese Style," p. 55.
7. The equation is : $R\ C^{0.5}\ D^{0.33}$ = constant, where R is resolution, C is contrast, and D is dosage.
8. "Budget Ax Lops Off Entire Departments at San Diego," *Science,* vol. 256, June 26, 1992, p. 1757.
9. *New York Times,* May 16, 1991.
10. Schieber and Pullier, "Datawatch, International Health Spending: Issues and Trends," *Health Affairs,* Spring 1991.
11. *Washington Post,* Feb. 10, 1991, p. F-1 (emphasis in original).
12. "You can't say it often enough: never lose touch with your customers." "The Computer Revolution," *Fortune,* June 14, 1993, p. 20.
13. Peter Drucker, *Management: Tasks, Responsibilities, Practices* (Harper and Row: New York, 1974), pp. 43–44.
14. *Economist,* Oct. 21, 1989, p. 26.
15. Drucker, *Management,* op. cit.
16. See Edward Roberts, *Entrepreneurship: Lessons from MIT and Beyond* (Oxford University Press: New York, 1992).
17. Gary Hofbauer, Institute for International Economics, Washington, cited in *Fortune,* April 19, 1993, p. 53.
18. This example was suggested in John A. Walgreen, "Babe Ruth and Comparative Advantage" in Ralph J. Burns and Gerald W. Stone, *Great Ideas for Teaching Economics* (Scott Foresman: Glenview, Ill., 1981), p. 15.
19. Cited in *Business Week,* Aug. 2, 1993, p. 35.
20. Samuel Brittan, "Myth of European Competitiveness," *Financial Times,* July 1, 1993.

Chapter 4. Do You Know Where Your Costs Are?

1. Paul Kennedy, *The Rise and Fall of the Great Powers, 1500-2000* (Yale University Press: New Haven, Conn., 1988).
2. Akio Morita, *Made in America* (Fontana: New York, 1987).
3. David Halberstam, *The Reckoning* (Avon: New York, 1987), p. 106.
4. *BusinessWeek,* May 31, 1993, p. 15.
5. Nam P. Suh, "The Future of the Factory and the Factory of the Future," in *Global Technological Change: A Strategic Assessment* (MIT Industrial Liaison Program, Cambridge, MA, 1983).
6. America's 20 highest-paid executives in 1992 all made more than 10 times their weight in gold, ranging from number 20, Wheelabrator Technologies' Phillip B. Rooney, at $11.216 million, up to number 1, Thomas F. Frist, Jr., CEO of Hospital Corporation of America, at $127 million.
7. Noted in David Halberstam, *The Reckoning,* chapter 4, "The Founder."
8. Herbert Simon, interview, in *Challenge,* Nov.–Dec. 1986, p. 24.
9. "The Computer Revolution," *Fortune,* June 14, 1993, p. 30.
10. Theodore Levitt, *Thinking about Management* (Free Press: New York, 1991), pp. 125, 129.

Chapter 5. People, Knowledge, and/or Machines

1. *International Business Week,* "Doctor! Doctor! This Company Needs a Doctor." July 26, 1993, p. 20.
2. This example is based on Leslie Cookenboo, *Crude Oil Pipe Lines and Competition in the Oil Industry* (Harvard University Press: Cambridge, Mass., 1955).
3. David Halberstam, *The Reckoning* (Avon: New York, 1987), p. 70.
4. Adam Smith, *The Wealth of Nations* (1776), Book I, chapter 1.
5. Clifford F. Pratten, "The Manufacture of Pins," *Journal of Economic Literature,* March 1980, pp. 93–96.
6. Halberstam, *The Reckoning,* pp. 60, 71–73.
7. This argument is made most forcefully in Lester Thurow's book *Head to Head: The Coming Economic Battle Among Japan, Europe and America* (Warner Books: New York, 1993).
8. Howard Head, in "Howard Head and Prince Manufacturing, Inc.," Harvard Business School Case Study 9-388-079, 1988.
9. *Financial Times,* June 26, 1992, p. 30, based on survey "Top Management Remuneration."
10. See "Global Reach," *Across the Board,* Sept. 1992.
11. Ibid.
12. Based on: Michael A. Cusumano, "Manufacturing Innovation and Competitive Advantage: Reflections on the Japanese Automobile

Industry," MIT Sloan School of Management, May 9, 1988; and John F. Krafcik, "Triumph of the Lean Production System," *Sloan Management Review* 30, (1988–89), pp. 41–52.

13. "Why Joe's Dream-car Matters," *Economist*, July 24, 1993, p. 66.

14. Boston Consulting Group, "Strategy Alternatives for the British Motorcycle Industry" (HM Stationery Office, London, 1972).

15. *International Business Week*, Aug. 10, 1992, p. 53.

16. Yoko Shibata, "Restructuring, Japanese Style," *Global Finance*, Summer 1993, p. 54.

17. *Fortune*, June 14, 1993, pp. 64–65.

18. Studies by Daniel Mitchell, David Lewin, and Edward Lawler; Martin Weitzman and Douglas Kruse; and Michael Conte and Jan Svejnar, Brookings Institution: March 1989 conference.

19. Thomas Hout, "International New Product Survey: Review of Findings," Boston Consulting Group, August 1993.

20. "Make Better Things... or Make Things Better?" *Across the Board*, Nov. 1990, pp. 9–10.

21. This point was expressed forcefully to me by management consultant Charles Hampden-Turner.

22. "Global Reach," *Across the Board*, Nov. 1992.

23. Cited in *Fortune*, May 17, 1993, p. 36.

24. *MIT Management*, Spring 1992, p. 50.

25. "Is Information Systems Spending Productive?" *MIT Report*, July–Aug. 1993, p. 1.

26. Alan B. Krueger, "How Computers Have Changed the Wage Structure: Evidence from Microdata, 1984-89," Working paper, Princeton University, Dept. of Economics, Aug. 1991.

27. Paul Strassman, *The Business Value of Computers* (Information Economics Press: New Canaan, Conn., 1990).

28. Robert Hayes, Steven Wheelwright, Kim Clark, *Dynamic Manufacturing* (The Free Press: New York, 1988), p. 270.

Chapter 6. From Volume to Variety

1. Alfred Chandler, Jr., *Scale and Scope: The Dynamics of Industrial Capitalism* (Harvard/Belknap: Cambridge, Mass., 1990).

2. "Trust" was short for Trustees; the company was a large holding company, run by trustees.

3. See also "Standard Oil Trust," Harvard Business School Case Study 391-244.

4. Chandler, Jr., *Scale and Scope*, p. 26.

5. "When Wal-Mart Starts a Good Fight, It's a Doozy," *International Business Week*, June 14, 1993, p. 68.

6. "Circuit City Stores Inc," Harvard Business School Case Study 9-191-086, p. 1.

7. Kenneth Small, *Road Work: A New Highway Pricing and Investment Policy*. Brookings Institution: Washington, D.C., 1989, p. 113.

8. H. Youn Kim, "Economies of Scale and Scope in Multiproduct Firms: Evidence from U.S. Railroads," *Applied Economics* 19, June 1987, p. 739.

9. B. Joseph Pine II, *Mass Customization: The New Frontier in Business Competition* (Harvard Business School Press: Boston, Mass., 1993).

10. Ibid., pp. 197–98.

11. Theodore Levitt, *Thinking about Management* (Free Press: New York, 1991), p. 107 (emphasis added).

12. Akio Morita, *Made in Japan* (Fontana: New York, 1987), p. 207.

13. See B. Joseph Pine II, Bart Victor, and Andrew C. Boynton, "Making Mass Customization Work," *Harvard Business Review*, Sept.–Oct. 1993, p. 108.

14. Based on: Global Reach column, *Across the Board*, November 1991.

Chapter 7. Racing Down the Learning Curve

1. "The New Computer Revolution," *Fortune*, June 14, 1993, p. 20.

2. Ibid., p. 24.

3. R. Rosenbloom and M. Cusumano, "Technological Pioneering and Competitive Advantage: The birth of the VCR industry," *California Management Review* 4, Summer 1987, pp. 51–76. Also: "The World VCR Industry," Harvard Business School Case Study 9-387-098, Jan. 23, 1990.

4. Uwe Reinhardt, "Break-even Analysis of Lockheed's Tristar: An Application of Financial Theory," *Journal of Finance* 28 (4), Sept. 1973, pp. 821–838.

5. "Collision Course in Commercial Aircraft: Boeing-Airbus-McDonnell-Douglas 1991," Harvard Business School Case Study 9-391-106, July 23, 1991.

6. T. P. Wright, "Factors Affecting the Cost of Airplanes," *Journal of Aeronautical Science* 3, Feb. 1936, pp. 122–128.

7. Alfred Chandler, Jr., *Scale and Scope: The Dynamics of Industrial Capitalism* (Harvard/Belknap: Cambridge, Mass., 1990), p. 24.

8. For a learning-curve coefficient of 0.77, for instance, marginal costs are 64 percent of average variable costs.

9. These calculations are only illustrative. A full-blown break-even analysis would of course not treat the first and the five hundredth Tristar as if they were equally valuable to the company's sales revenues, but would take into account the cost of time through present-value calculations.

10. I am indebted to Frank Robbins, U.S. Air Force, for supplying this unpublished (and unclassified) information. Robbins was one of AMRAAM's main directors.

11. See Boston Consulting Group, "Perspectives on Experience" (Boston, Mass., 1972).
12. Boston Consulting Group, "Strategy Alternatives for the British motorcycle industry" (HM Stationery Office, London, 1972).
13. "Note on the Motorcycle Industry—1975," Harvard Business School Case Study 578-210, August 1987.
14. This section is based on the following sources: J. A. Wolff and D. D. Baker, Harley Davidson: How Long Can the Eagle Stay Afloat," Washington State University Case Study, 1990; "Note on the Motorcycle Industry—1975," Harvard Business School Case Study 578-210; *New York Times,* Aug. 12, 1990, p. F-5.
15. See Chris Argyris, "Strategy Implementation: An Experience in Learning," *Organizational Dynamics,* Autumn 1989, 18, 4–12. See also by the same author, *Overcoming Organizational Defenses: Facilitating Organizational Learning* (Allyn and Bacon, Boston, Mass., 1990) and "Teaching Smart People How To Learn," *Harvard Business Review,* May-June 1991, pp. 99–109.
16. Argyris, *Overcoming Organizational Defenses,* p. 115.
17. Based on a study published in *Industrial Relations* (1988), cited in S. Maital, "Are People Assets or Costs?" *Across the Board,* Sept. 1992, p. 48.
18. Cited in William Abernathy and Kenneth Wayne, "Limits of the Learning Curve," *Harvard Business Review,* Sept.-Oct. 1974, p. 114.
19. Michael Hergert, "Market share and profitability: Is Bigger Really Better?" *Business Economics,* Oct. 1984, pp. 45–48.
20. "Tristar Production Costs Lockheed Profits," *Aviation Week & Space Technology,* Oct. 15, 1979, p. 32.
21. Based on: "Pentagon Cutbacks on Lockheed's F-22 Would Make Fighter's Cost Soar 50%," *Wall Street Journal,* July 13, 1993, p. A4.

Chapter 8. Markets and Demand

1. Shlomo Maital, "What Do Economists Know That Managers of Technology Find Useful?" *Journal of Economic Education* 23 (2), Spring 1992, pp. 175–80.
2. Michael Siconolfi and Randall Smith, "Jumping the Track: How First Boston Lost Capital, Morale and Many Key Players," *Wall Street Journal,* July 19, 1993, p. A1.
3. This account of Sears, Roebuck is taken partly from Richard S. Tedlow, *New and Improved: The Story of Mass Marketing in America* (Basic Books: New York, 1990), chapter 5.
4. Joel Mokyr, *Lever of Riches* (Oxford University Press: New York, 1990).
5. See Harvey Leibenstein, "Bandwagon, Snob and Veblen Effects in

the Theory of Consumer Demand," *Quarterly Journal of Economics* 64, 1950, pp. 183–207. See also S. E. G. Lea, "The Psychology and Economics of Demand," *Psychological Bulletin* 85, 1978, pp. 441–66.

6. "It's a Scream," *Economist*, June 12, 1982, p. 89.

7. Drawn from Stanley Schachter, Donald C. Hood, Paul B. Andreassen, and William Gerin, "Aggregate Variables in Psychology and Economics: Dependence and the Stock Market," in B. Gilad and S. Kaish, *Handbook of Behavioral Economics*, vol. B (JAI Press: Greenwich, Conn., 1986), pp. 243–44.

8. Charles Schultze, *The Private Use of the Public Interest* (The Brookings Institution: Washington, D.C., 1977), pp. 76–77.

9. *TWA Ambassador* magazine, Feb. 1991, pp. 44–47.

10. Alan Blinder, "Why Are Prices Sticky?" *American Economics Association Papers and Proceedings*, May 1991, pp. 89–96; and "The Price Is Wrong," *Wall Street Journal*, Jan. 2, 1991, p. B1.

11. David Halberstam, *The Reckoning* (Avon: New York, 1987), p. 4.

12. H. E. Frech III and William C. Lee, "The Welfare Cost of Rationing by Waiting Across Uses: Empirical Estimates from the Gasoline Price Controls," working paper no. 212, University of California at Santa Barbara, June 1982.

13. Letter to *National Geographic*, Sept. 1988, unpaged, by T. W. Schillhorn-Van Veen.

14. "A Car Is Born," *BusinessWeek*, Sept. 13, 1993, p. 40.

15. *What the Customer Wants: the "Wall Street Journal"'s Guide to Marketing in the 1990s* (Dow-Jones Irwin: Princeton, N.J., 1990), p. 106.

16. Paul Krugman, *The Age of Diminished Expectations: U.S. Economic Policy in the 1990s* (MIT Press: Cambridge, Mass., 1990).

17. The comparison of Yuppies and Yiffies is drawn in part from my Global Reach column, *Across the Board*, May 1991.

18. See "The Upside of America's Population Upsurge," *International Business Week*, Aug. 9, 1993, p. 12.

19. *Wall Street Journal*, July 10, 1992, p. B1.

20. Gerard Russo, "The Demand for Physicians' Services and the Price of Cigarettes," working paper no. 90-24, Dept. of Economics, University of Hawaii at Manoa, April 11, 1990.

21. E. J. Working, "What Do Statistical Demand Curves Show?" *Quarterly Journal of Economics* 41, 1927, pp. 212–35.

22. In a 1973 *Playboy* interview, Professor Friedman asked rhetorically, "What society isn't based on greed?"

23. Cited by Albert J. Hettinger, "Director's Comments," in Milton Friedman and Anna Schwartz, *The Great Contradiction, 1929–33* (Princeton University Press: Princeton, N.J., 1965), p. 127.

24. See Gary Becker, "Habits, Addictions and Traditions," Nancy L. Schwartz Lecture, Northwestern University, May 15, 1991, p. 19.
25. G. Becker, M. Grossman, and K. M. Murphy, "An Empirical Analysis of Cigarette Addiction," N.B.E.R. working paper no. 3322, April 1990.
26. *Time* magazine, Economics: 1923–1989, special edition (Scott Foresman: undated), p. 9.
27. *What the Customer Wants*, pp. 57–59.
28. The answer to question (a) is X/Y, where X is purchases of some good X and Y is income. The answer to question (b) is ΔX/ΔY, where the Δ indicates the change in purchase of X, following a small change in income. The ratio is (ΔX/ΔY)/(X/Y), which translates into (ΔX/X)/(ΔY/Y), the percentage change in X divided by the percentage change in Y, which is the definition of income-elasticity of demand for X.
29. "Wireless World," *International Business Week*, April 12, 1993, pp. 40–43.
30. "How Williams Co. Turned Oil Pipelines to Conduits of Data," *Wall Street Journal*, Aug. 11, 1991, p. A1.
31. "The Computer Revolution," *Fortune*, June 14, 1993, p. 20.
32. "Flops," *International Business Week*, Aug. 16, 1993, pp. 34–39.
33. "America's Fastest Growers," *Fortune*, Aug. 9, 1993, p. 44.
34. Taken from Christopher Bartlett and Sumantra Ghoshal, *Managing across Borders: The Transnational Solution* (Harvard Business School Press: Boston, Mass., 1989).
35. "Brands on the Run," *International Business Week*, April 19, 1993, p. 26.
36. Robert Kuttner, "Why Business Is at a Loss in a Free Market," *BusinessWeek*, Sept. 28, 1987, p. 10.
37. "Sticking it to Japan with Sticker Shock," *International Business Week*, Sept. 6, 1993, p. 34.
38. "Shoot Out at the Check-out," *Economist*, June 5, 1993, pp. 65–66.
39. "Grand Met's Chief Executive Plans to Turn Brand Loyalty into a World-Wide Strategy," *Wall Street Journal Europe*, Oct. 7, 1993, p. 5.
40. Based on calculations for 1979 food basket, updated to 1993; see S. Maital, *Minds, Markets and Money: Psychological Foundations of Economic Behavior* (Basic Books: New York, 1982), p. 11.

Chapter 9. Calculated Risks

1. cited in S. Maital, *Minds, Markets and Money: Psychological Foundations of Economic Behavior* (Basic Books: New York, 1982), p. 202.
2. Carol J. Loomis, "Dinosaurs?" *Fortune*, May 3, 1993, p. 36.
3. "Corporates' New Trait: Volatility," *Wall Street Journal*, July 19, 1993, p. A1.

4. Karen Pennar and G. David Wallace, "The Economy: Uncertainty Isn't about to Go Away," *International Business Week*, Feb. 22, 1988, p. 53.
5. P. G. Moore, "The Manager's Struggle with Uncertainty," *Journal of the Royal Statistical Society* A, 1977, 140, Part 2, pp. 129–65.
6. Ibid., p. 129
7. Jacob W. Ulvila and Rex V. Brown, "Decision Analysis Comes of Age," *Harvard Business Review*, Sept.–Oct. 1982, pp. 130–41.
8. "Adam Smith" (George Goodman), *The Roaring 80's* (Summit Books: New York, 1988), p. 121.
9. Richard Wilson and E. A. C. Crouch, "Risk Assessment and Comparisons: An Introduction," *Science*, April 17, 1987, p. 270.
10. Noted in Anthony Bianco, *Rainmaker: The Saga of Jeff Beck, Wall Street's Mad Dog* (Random House: New York, 1991).
11. Louis Rukeyser, *Business Almanac* (Simon and Schuster: New York, 1988), pp. 332–33.
12. Ibid., p. 506.
13. *USAir* magazine, June 1991, pp. 51–55.
14. *International Business Week*, April 10, 1989, p. 73.
15. Many of the following behaviors are drawn from D. Kahneman, A. Tversky, and P. Slovic, *Judgment under Uncertainty* (Cambridge University Press: Cambridge, 1982).
16. Richard E. Nisbett, Eugene Borgida, Rick Crandall, and Harvey Reed. "Popular induction: Information Is Not Necessarily Informative," in Kahneman, Tversky, and Slovic, *Judgment under Uncertainty*, pp. 101–16.
17. M. Granger Morgan, "Risk Analysis and Management," *Scientific American*, July 1993, pp. 24–30.
18. Kahneman, Tversky, and Slovic, *Judgment under Uncertainty*, p. 439.
19. Thomas P. Hustad, editor of *Journal of Product Innovation Management*, cited in *International Business Week*, Aug. 16, 1993, p. 39.

Chapter 10. Competing by Cooperating

1. There are close links between this model and Charles Darwin's biological model that explains the origin of the earth's several million species. In *The Origin of Species*, Darwin wrote: "multiply, vary, let the strongest live and the weakest die." He was speaking about species, but today one could substitute "firms" or "products" with ease. Darwin apparently was inspired by the famous 1798 essay of economist T. R. Malthus, who wrote that people, too, struggle for survival, when population growth outstrips the supply of food.
2. *International Business Week*, March 8, 1993, p. 40.
3. Peter Drucker, *Management Tasks, Responsibilities, Practices* (Harper and Row: New York, 1974), p. 87.

4. See S. Maital, Global Reach column, *Across the Board,* June 1991.
5. Michael Porter, *Competitive Strategy* (The Free Press: New York, 1980).
6. William Baumol, "Contestable Markets: An Uprising in the Theory of Industry Structure," *American Economic Review,* March 1982, pp. 1–15.
7. A cut in price of only one cent on each of the 700 million servings McDonald's sells daily means a decline of $2.5 billion a year in pretax profit. Warren Buffett, cited in *Fortune,* Nov. 29, 1993, p. 11.
8. "Look Who Learned about Value," *Fortune,* Oct. 18, 1993, pp. 39–40.
9. Edward Roberts, an expert on high-tech entrepreneurship, has shown that startup firms founded by three entrepreneurs—with balanced skills in technology, management, finance and marketing—have a significantly higher chance of succeeding than firms founded by only a single entrepreneur. See his *Entrepreneurs in High Technology: Lessons from MIT and Beyond* (Oxford University Press: New York, 1991).
10. Thomas M. Hout, Boston Consulting Group, *International New Product Development Survey: Review of Findings* (Boston Consulting Group: Boston, Mass., 1993), p. 2.
11. "Howard Head and Prince Manufacturing Co.," Harvard Business School Case Study 9-388-079, 1988.
12. "Russia's Value Gap, *Economist,* Oct. 24, 1992, p. 69.
13. "Aluminum Everywhere," *International Business Week,* Oct. 25, 1993.
14. Deepak Sinha and Michaal Cusumano, Working paper, MIT Sloan School of Management, 1992.
15. Eric von Hippel, *The Sources of Invention* (Oxford University Press: New York, 1988), pp. 76–84.
16. Taken from Elting Morison, *Men, Machines & Modern Times* (1966), cited in H. Leibenstein and S. Maital, "Organizational Foundations of X-Inefficiency," *Journal of Economic Behavior and Organization,* forthcoming, 1994.
17. "Digital Media Business Takes Form as a Battle of Complex Alliances," *Wall Street Journal,* July 15, 1993, p. 1.
18. Taken from: Stewart Brand, *The MIT Media Lab* (Viking Penguin: New York, 1987).
19. *Economist,* Oct. 9, 1993, p. 88; S. Benartzi, working paper, Cornell University, 1993.
20. Alfred D. Chandler, Jr., *Scale and Scope: The Dynamics of Industrial Capitalism* (Belknap, Harvard University Press: Cambridge, Mass., 1990).

21. "How Toshiba Makes Alliances Work," *Fortune*, Oct. 4, 1993, pp. 40–43.

22. Charles Hampden-Turner and Alfons Trompenaars, *The Seven Cultures of Capitalism* (Currency/Doubleday: New York, 1993), pp. 4, 13.

23. An early hint of change comes from the Mecca of hard-nosed business competition, Harvard Business School's newly reformed MBA program. Up to a quarter of course requirements would involve collaborative work in teams. Little such teamwork existed under the old curriculum, in which students were encouraged to compete as individuals. See *International Business Week*, Nov. 15, 1993, p. 33.

24. In the spring of 1990, AT&T created a Safari Computer Division, which hired industrial designers Henry Dreyfus Associates, joined with the Japanese trading firm Marubeni (who in turned contracted with Matsushita as manufacturer), brought a notebook computer prototype to the Comdex trade fair in fall 1990, and started shipping its product in the spring of 1991. Source: *21st Century Manufacturing Enterprise Strategy* (Iacocca Institute, Lehigh University, Bethlehem, Pa., 1991), vol. 1, p. 39.

Acknowledgments

My first editor on this project was Peter Dougherty, now with Princeton University Press, who thought up the title and gave me the winning, secret formula: "Tell stories." My current editor, Bruce Nichols, found ways to rescue chapters other editors would have shredded instantly. He helped wean me from a nearly-incurable addiction to graphs and maths, and stuck with the book despite my erratic writing and missed deadlines. All authors know copyeditors are the unsung heroes of publishing. Mine, Ann Hirst, did an especially fine job, earning my thanks and admiration.

I am especially grateful to Edward Roberts, Sarnoff Professor of Management of Technology at MIT Sloan School of Management. Ten years ago, Ed gave me the opportunity to teach, as a summer visitor, in the Management of Technology M.Sc. program he founded. Despite my rocky start, Ed gave me time and space to learn how to teach managers economics. This book is mainly due to that wonderful opportunity.

My home university, Technion-Israel Institute of Technology, has for 14 years offered me a stimulating environment in which technology, economics, and management blend together in exceptionally interesting, applied contexts. And finally, my country, Israel, half a decade younger than me, vibrant and dynamic, on the eve of long-sought peace, has given my life and work meaning and purpose, a gift of which there is none greater.

Index

Abedi, A. H., 87, 115
Abernathy, William, 163
Accountants, Ford's view of, 69–70
Ad hocracy, 249
Addiction, 193
Advantage. *See* Comparative advantage
AIDS, 221–22
Air Force. *See* United States Air Force
Air to air missiles, 150–51, 152
Airbus Industries, 146, 240
Aircraft industry, 26–27, 38–40, 109, 142–50,164–67, 230
Airline industry, 83–84, 126, 199, 228, 237
Allen, Woody, 56–57, 230
Allocative inefficiency, 44–46
Aluminum production, 236
American Airlines, 199
American Express, 65
AMF Inc., 155
Ampex, 141
AMRAAM missile, 150–52
Anderson, Roy, 26, 164
Anheuser–Busch, 164

Anthony, Robert N., 86
Apple, 140, 230, 243
Aptness and demand, 172–74
Argentina, 200
Argyris, Chris, 157–61
Army. *See* United States Army
AT&T, 12, 196, 215, 243, 267n24
Australia, 197, 198, 202
Automobile industry, 14–16, 59–60, 69–70, 76–78, 92–95, 102, 105–107, 113, 128, 162–63, 180, 184, 188–90, 199, 229, 244–45
Average costs, 71–72, 83, 86, 92
Average product, 92, 103
Average variable cost, 71–72
Avro Arrow fighter aircraft, 166

B-2 bomber, 166
Baby-boomers, 181
Baby bust, 181–82
Bandwagon effects, 174–76
Bank for Credit and Commerce International (BCCI), 115

Banker's Trust, 202
Banking, 160, 171–72, 201–204
Bardeen, John, 66, 215
Barker, J. M., 192
Baseball, 32, 58
BASF, 119–20
Baumol, William, 176, 231
Bayer, 119–20
BCCI. *See* Bank for Credit and Commerce International (BCCI)
BCG. *See* Boston Consulting Group (BCG)
Beals, Vaughn, 155–56
Becker, Gary, 35, 193
Beer industry, 164
Bell, D. E., 222
Bell Atlantic, 243
Bell Labs, 215
Belmonte, Norman, 183
Benchmarking
    cost benchmarking, 76
    price sensitivity, 187–88
    productivity tracking, 102
Berkshire Hathaway, 17, 107
Betamax system, 142
Bicycle production, 117–18, 121, 128
Bird in hand proverb, 224
Black Death, 180
Blake, Jules, 36
Blinder, Alan, 178
Blumenthal, Michael, 127
BMW, 76, 184
Boeing, 109, 143, 165, 228, 230, 240
Bond market, 207, 247
Boston Consulting Group (BCG), 103, 108, 151–54, 234–35
Boston Federal Reserve Bank, 173
Boston Red Sox, 32, 58
Brand names, 198–200
Brattain, Walter, 66, 215
Bravo pagers, 129–30
Break-even points, 149–50
Britain
    bubonic plague in, 180
    capital in, 96

capitalism in, 118, 248
characteristics of managers in, 249–50
devaluation of sterling in, 203–204
gunnery invention from, 241
missiles sold to, 150
motorcycle production in, 151–54
pin factory in, 93–95
population of, 185
productivity in, 99
ratio of marginal product to wage costs in, 103–104
South Sea Bubble in, 175–76
tariffs in 18th century, 60
Brittan, Samuel, 63
Brooke, Geoffrey, 113
Bubbles, financial, 175–76, 191–92
Bubonic plague, 180
Budweiser, 164
Buffett, Warren, 17, 107–108
Bull, George J., 200
Bulova, 66–67
Burroughs 127–28
Business cycle and mass customization, 130–33
Business value added, 9
Byrnjolfsson, Erik, 113

Cajoline, 198
Calculated risks
    bird in hand proverb and, 224
    certainty and capital markets, 217–219
    certainty equivalence and, 216–18
    crazy markets, crazy governments and, 208
    exaggerating small probabilities and, 224–25
    examples of, 205–207
    expected value and, 207, 210–16
    framing and, 221–22
    gambling and insurance, 219–21
    odd behavior towards odds, 221–25

[Calculated risks]
odds in, 209–10
overconfidence and, 224
overfitting and, 222–23
quantification of, 215–16
types of risks, 208
California State University, 48
Cambridge Corp., 229
Canada, 166
Cancer, 215–16, 223
Capital
computer capital, 112–115
cost of, 107
productivity and, 96
shareholders' capital, 235–36
Capital markets, 217–19, 247
Capitalism as dynamo or dinosaur, 247–50
Caroline's Cookies, 28–29
Carrs Supermarkets, 177
Caspian Sea oil fields, 119
Census Bureau. *See* United States Census Bureau
CEOs. *See* Executives; and specific executives
Certainty and capital markets, 217–19
Certainty equivalence, 216–18
Cervantes, Miguel de, 224
Chandler, Alfred, Jr., 118, 120, 146, 248
Chemical industry, 119–20, 121
Chernobyl disaster, 215–16
Chesterton, G. K., 238
China, 194–95, 204, 241, 248
Chrysler, 65, 95, 105
Churchill, Winston, 216
Cigarettes, 188, 193, 198, 199
Circuit City Stores, 124, 125–126
Clark, Kim, 114
Clemens, Roger, 32
Clothing industry, 175, 183–84, 193–94
Clusters, 249
Coca-Cola, 16–17, 21–25, 29, 32, 33, 44–45, 172, 235–36, 256n19

Coccolino, 198
Cohorts, 182
Cold war, death of, 65–66
Colgate-Palmolive Co., 36
Collaboration. *See* Cooperation
Collective bargaining, 98
Colleges. *See* Higher education
Columbia, 243
Columbia Pictures, 256n19
Comfort, 198
Commodore, 140
Compact-disk (CD) recorders, 96
Compaq, 141, 185–86
Comparative advantage, 57–64, 103–104, 105, 235
Competition, 227, 247. *See also* Cooperation
Computer industry, 70–75, 78, 84–85, 96–97, 112–115, 127–28, 140–41, 185–86, 206, 230, 239–40, 267n24
Computer tomography (CT), 47–48
Construction industry, 182–83
Consultants, 55, 88, 103, 151–52, 234–35, 249
Continental Airlines, 199
Continuous improvement, 109
Cooperation
American capitalism and, 247–50
checklist of tools for, 250–51
comparative advantage and, 235
cost functions and, 237–39
cost-price-value and, 232–34
examples of, 227–28
expected value and, 246–47
hidden costs and, 234–37
importance of, 228–29
learning curves and, 239–41
markets and demand and, 244–46
reasons for competing by cooperating, 229–30
and saving grace of people, machines, and knowledge, 241–42
scale and scope and, 242–44
strategy of, 231–247
tradeoffs and, 234–35

Coors, 164
Cost
    average costs, 83, 86, 92
    cooperation and cost functions,
        237–39
    cost-price-value in cooperation,
        232–34
    in cost-value-price triangle, 6–19
    definition of, 6
    example of shutting down CPU
        factory, 70–75, 84–85
    examples of hall of fame cost cut-
        ting, 77–79
    fickleness of cost efficiency, 75–77
    five pairs of cost numbers for five
        different levels of produc-
        tion, 70–75
    fixed costs, 82, 85, 86
    General Motors and, 14–16
    hidden costs, 21–40, 235–37
    hidden elements in, 179
    of higher education, 34–36
    IBM and, 13
    large-scale production and cost-
        savings, 79–80
    less as more, 66–70
    management costs, 10–11
    and managers' worth, 8–12
    marginal costs, 82–86, 88, 89, 92
    marginal product and, 88–95,
        103–104, 105
    and markets and demand, 176–79
    of meetings, 34
    occupancy costs, 30–33
    opportunity cost, 22–25, 34–36,
        73–74
    overhead, 82
    Simon on, 79–80
    sunk costs, 37–40, 80–82, 86
    tension between value and, 46–47
    time as money, 33–38
    U-shaped cost curve, 67–69,
        71–72, 79–80
    variable costs, 71–72, 82, 86, 139
    volume and/or variety matrix,
        121–126
    zero-output cost numbers, 70–75
Cost benchmarking, 76

Cost efficiency, fickleness of, 75–77
Cost matrix, 121–126
CRADAs (Cooperative Research and
        Development Agreements),
        239
Crazy markets, crazy governments,
        208
Cross-price elasticity, 188
CT. *See* Computer tomography (CT)
Customers
    aptness and, 172–74
    bandwagons and bubbles, 174–76
    costs and prices and, 176–79
    demand function and, 170–71
    demographics of, 179–85
    and economists on markets and
        demand, 169–72
    and elasticity, or sensitivity to
        price, 185–90
    fashion and, 190, 191
    forces shaping market demand,
        171
    greed and, 190–92
    habit and, 192–93
    income of, 193–96
    jazz and, 196–97
    knowledge about, 197–98
    loyalty and, 198–200
    and meeting of minds and money,
        200–204
    tradeoffs and customer psycholo-
        gy, 52–54
Customization. *See* Mass customiza-
        tion
Cusumano, Michael A., 102, 237–38

Darwin, Charles, 265n1
Davidson, William, 153, 156
Davis, David E., 14–15
Davis, Evan, 32–33
Day, Thomas, 48
DC-3 aircraft, 230
Decision making. *See also* Calculated
        risks
    employee participation in compa-
        ny decision making, 108
    in tradeoffs, 46–49

[Decision making]
uncertainty and, 207
Defense Department. *See* United
States Department of
Defense
Defensive behavior, 157–59, 161
Dell, Michael, 141
Dell Computer Co., 141
Demand. *See* Markets and demand
Demand curve, 188–90
Demand function, 170–71
Demographics and demand, 179–85
Depressions, 130–31, 193
Dershowitz, Alan, 49–50
Deutschman, Alan, 181
DFD (design for disassembly) pro-
jects, 184
Dickens, Charles, 65
Diet Coke, 16–17
Digital Equipment, 65
Digital media, 242–43
Diversification, 132
Divorce, 183
DLJ. *See* Donaldson, Lufkin, and
Jenrette (DLJ)
Donaldson, Lufkin, and Jenrette
(DLJ), 227, 228
Double-loop learning, 159, 160
Douglas Aircraft Corp., 230
Dow-Jones Industrial Average,
206–207
Downsizing, 87
Downy brand, 198
Drexel Harriman Ripley, 218–19
Drucker, Peter, 4, 12, 17, 25, 30, 35,
55–56, 190, 249
Drug abuse, 193

Earphones, 132
Eastern Airlines, 228
Eastern Europe, 110, 179, 248
Eastman Kodak, 12, 65
Eaton Corp., 212–14
Econ and Exec stories, vii–ix, 70–75,
84–85, 169
Economic efficiency. *See* Efficiency
Economic inefficiency, 44–46

Economic profit, 24–25
Economic rent, 31–33
Economics. *See also* specific economic terms
competition in, 227
managers' use of, 2–8
on markets and demand, 169–72
reasons for class in, for managers,
1–2
three pillars of profit, 6–7
Economies of scale. *See* Scale and
scope
Economies of scope. *See* Scale and
scope
Education, 101
Effectiveness, 56
Efficiency
definition of, 43
economic notion of, 43–57
fickleness of cost efficiency,
75–77
reasons for inefficiency, 43–46,
157–58
Einstein, Albert, 178–79, 214
Eisenhower, Dwight D., 46
Elasticity, or sensitivity to price,
185–90
Electronics industry, 8–11, 17–18,
66–69, 80, 96–97, 128–30,
141–42, 190, 191, 215
Eliot, T. S., 115
Emerson, Ralph Waldo, 3
Emerson Electric, 106
Employee stock ownership plans
(ESOPs), 108
Employment. *See* Human resources;
Unemployment
Entrepreneurship, 266n9
Environmentally safe products, 184
EPZ. *See* Export Processing Zone
(EPZ)
Equity capital, 23–24
ERM. *See* Exchange Rate Mechanism
(ERM)
Errors, 158–59
ESOPs, 108
Estes, Pete, 14–15
Ethics versus tactics, 49–50

Exchange Rate Mechanism (ERM), 203
Exec and Econ stories, vii–ix, 70–75, 84–85, 169
Executives. *See also* Managers; and specific executives
characteristics of, in different countries, 249–50
financial and accounting backgrounds of, 27–28
and firms as symphony orchestras, 249
of future, 252–53
main jobs of, 140
salaries for human-resource executives, 97, 98
salaries of, 259n6
status of human-resource executives, 97–98
Expected value
cooperation and, 246–47
definition of, 207, 212
graphing of, 211–16
Payday candy bar as example of, 210–11
Experience curves, 139, 140
Experimenting organization, 39
Export Processing Zone (EPZ), 100
Exxon, 118, 120

F-22 aircraft, 166
Factories. *See* Manufacturing
Fads, 190, 191
False choices and tradeoffs, 54–55
Farnsworth, 174
Fashion and demand, 190, 191
Federal Technology Transfer Act, 238–39
Financial bubble, 175–76
First Boston Corp., 171–72
Five pairs of cost numbers, 70–75
Fixed cost shirking, 82
Fixed costs, 82, 85, 86
Fleming, Alexander, 174
Flower sales, 177–78
Food service industry, 195–96, 197, 233–34

Ford, Henry, 69–70, 77–78, 92–95, 105–106, 110, 128, 153, 162–63, 172
Ford Motor Co., 14, 69–70, 77–78, 92–95, 102, 105–106, 110, 162–63, 165, 188–90, 199
Foreign exchange market, 200–204, 206–207
Forgionne, Guiseppe A., 2–3
Framing, 221–22
France, 60, 98, 135–37, 185, 198, 248, 249–50
France Telecom, 135–37
Franklin, Benjamin, 34
Free trade, 57–58, 60–63, 100
Friedman, Milton, 177, 190, 246
Frist, Thomas F., 259n6
Frito snacks, 198

Galbraith, John Kenneth, 93
Gambling, 219–21, 225
Gasoline shortage, 179
GE. *See* General Electric
GE Capital, 227–28
Geneen, Harold, 36
General Electric, 4–5, 106, 184, 207, 227–28
General Foods, 160
General Motors, 14–16, 65, 78, 95, 102, 162, 229
Gerber babyfoods, 198
Germany, 75–76, 96, 98, 118–20, 121, 185, 198, 248–50
Gerstner, Lou, 13
GM. *See* General Motors
Goelman, Daniel, 49
Goizueta, Roberto, 16–17, 18, 21–25, 32, 33, 44–45, 256n19
Gold, 191–92
Goldwyn, Samuel, 201
Goodman, George, 25
Grand Metropolitan PLC, 200
Graphing of expected value, 211–16
Greed, 190–92
"Green" products, 184

Greenburg, Jack, 233
Gulf War, 207

Haagen-Dazs ice cream, 200
Habit and demand, 192–93
Halberstam, David, 14–15
Hampden-Turner, Charles, 249–50
Harley-Davidson, 153, 154–57
Harvard Business School, 267n23
Hatsopolous, George, 173–74
Hayes, Robert, 114
Head, Howard, 97, 235
Head Ski Co., 235
Health care, 49, 188, 221–22
Hemingway, Ernest, 225
Henderson, Bruce, 103, 152
Henry Dreyfus Associates, 267n24
Hergert, Michael, 163
Hickman, W. Bradford, 218
Hidden costs, 21–40, 235–37
Higgins, Miller, 58
High-tech entrepreneurship, 266n9
Higher education
    cost of, 34–36
    tradeoffs in, 48–49
Hirohito, Emperor, 192
Hoechst, 119–20
Honda, 103, 105, 152, 153, 155,
        156, 180, 256n14
Hong Kong, 97, 98–99, 101
Horizontal organization, 249
Horwich, Mel, 249
Hospital Corporation of America,
        259n6
Housework, value of, 257n9
Housing, 182–83
Hout, Thomas M., 108, 234–35
Huggy, 198
Human resources
    in agriculture, industry, informa-
        tion, and services, 109–10,
        111
    cooperation and, 241–42
    crisis decisions and, 87–88
    and employee participation in
        company decision making,
        108
    employment crisis and, 104–109
    hidden unemployment in Japan,
        42
    hiring of new employees, 164–65
    importance of, 95–99
    information technology and,
        112–15
    knowledge, productivity and,
        109–12
    layoffs and, 76, 107, 114
    marginal product of labor and
        capital, 88–95
    marginal productivity in Mauri-
        tius and Hong Kong,
        99–101
    pay for performance, 107–109
    productivity and, 87
    salaries for human-resource exec-
        utives, 97, 98
    status of human-resource execu-
        tives, 97–98
    teamwork, 108–109
    tracking productivity and,
        102–104
    tradeoff decisions on people ver-
        sus machines, 47

Iacocca, Lee, 105
IBM, 1, 4, 12–14, 16, 36, 65, 78,
        127, 135, 140, 141, 206,
        208, 230, 239–40, 243
Immigration, 185
Income, 193–96
Income elasticity of demand, 195–96
Income-sensitivity of demand,
        195–96
Incremental cost, 82–86
Indonesia, 97
Inefficiency, reasons for, 43–46. *See
        also* Efficiency
Information technology, 110,
        111–15, 134–37, 229
Innovation
    in competitive strategy, 234–35
    perils of, 162–63
Innovative versus mature industries,
        76–77

Insurance business, 219–20
Integrated services digital network.
    See ISDN (integrated ser-
    vices digital network)
Intelligent organization, 137
International Monetary Fund, 100
International Trade Commission,
    155–56
Inventions, 174, 241–42
Investment in human capital, 35
ISDN (integrated services digital net-
    work), 136–37
Italy, 185, 198, 203, 204
ITT Corp., 36

J&B Scotch, 200
Japan
    automobile industry in, 102, 107,
        133, 164
    bicycle production in, 117–18,
        128
    capitalism in, 248
    characteristics of managers in,
        249–50
    cost of capital in, 107
    electronics industry in, 96, 117,
        141–42
    exports from, 76
    hidden unemployed in businesses
        in, 42
    land prices in, 192
    layoffs in, 107
    manufacturing costs in, 76
    motorcycle industry in,
        103–104, 152, 153–55,
        256n14
    new products from, 234–35
    population of, 185
    production of pagers in, 129
    ratio of marginal product to wage
        costs in, 103–104
    robotics in, 47, 107, 118, 128
    salaries in, 98, 104, 105
    steel industry in, 231
    unemployment in, 42–43
Jazz and demand, 196–97
Jelassi, Tawfik, 135, 136

Joint production, 121
Joint ventures, 229, 237–38
Jordache Enterprises, 175
Junk bonds, 217–19
Justice Department. *See* United
    States Department of
    Justice
JVC, 141–42

Kaiser, Henry J., 173
Katzenbach, Jon, 249
Kawasaki, 103, 155
Kay, John, 32–33
Kelvin, Lord, 7
Kelvin's Law, 7
Kennedy, John F., 181
Kerosene production, 118–19
Kim, H. Youn, 127
Knowledge
    cooperation and, 229, 241–42
    cost of, 115
    creation and dissemination of,
        115
    information technology and,
        112–15
    markets and demand and,
        197–98
    network economies of scope and,
        134–137
    productivity and, 96–97, 109–12
    products and services based in,
        229
    sharing and use of, 114–15
Kochan, Thomas, 97–98
Kodak, 12, 65
Kondratiev, Nikolai, 131
Korea, 150
Kraft, 198, 200
Kroger Co., 125
Krueger, Alan, 113
Krueger, Hank, 79
Krueger Vertical Automatic Cham-
        bering Machine, 79
Krugman, Paul, 184
Kunnan Lo, 97, 235
Kuschelweich, 198
Kuttner, Robert, 199

Labor. *See* Human resources
Labor-management relations, 98
Las Vegas, 220
Layoffs, 76, 107, 114
Learning
 definition of, 158
 double-loop learning, 159, 160
 single-loop learning, 159–60
Learning curves
 for air to air missiles, 150–52
 in aircraft industry, 142–50
 in computer industry, 140–41
 cooperation and, 239–41
 defensive behavior and, 157–59
 description of, 139–40
 double-loop learning, 159, 160
 enemies of, 157–61
 language of, 151
 in motorcycle industry, 151–57
 perils of, 162–65
 political economy of, 165–67
 single-loop learning, 159–60
 truthful organization and, 157–61
Lease agreements, 199
Lee, Susan, 22–23
Legal system, 49–50
Leibenstein, Harvey, 43–44
Lenor, 198
Less as more, 66–70
Levitt, Theodore, 18, 65, 81–82,
 131–32
Life cycle analysis of products, 190
Life insurance, 220
Lighting controls, 128–29
Linden, Lawrence H., 36–37
Lockheed Corp., 26–27, 38–39,
 52–53, 142–50, 164–65,
 230
Lotteries, 220–21, 224–25
Loyalty and demand, 198–200
Lutron Electronics, 128–29

Maark Corp., 235
Machine tools, 79
Madogiwa-zoku, 42
Mail-order business, 172–73,
 196–97

Malaysia, 96, 97
Malthus, Thomas, 99–100, 265n1
Management, definition of, 87
Management costs, 10–11
Management value added, 8–11
Managers. *See also* Executives
 backgrounds in finance and accounting or marketing, 4
 characteristics of, in different
 countries, 249–50
 and choice over time, 55–56
 competencies needed by, 4–6
 defensive behavior and, 157–59,
 161
 functions of, 25
 general manager, 4, 5
 information technology and, 114
 and measurement, 8
 need for class in economics, 1–2
 and three pillars of profit, 6–7
 use of economics by, 2–8
 worth of, 8–12
Mankiw, N. Gregory, 182
Manufacturing. *See also* specific
 companies and products
 of air to air missiles, 150–52
 of bicycles, 117–18, 121, 128
 in Germany, 75–76
 in Japan, 42, 47, 76, 117–18,
 121, 128
 joint production, 121
 mass customization, 128–33
 mass production, 92–95,
 105–106, 128, 153
 of Model Ts, 78, 92–95, 105–106
 offshore production, 76, 97
 robotics in, 47, 107, 118, 128,
 130
 salaries in, 105, 106
 Smith's pin factory, 92, 93–95,
 120
 of Tristar, 142–50, 164–65
 in United States, 76
 U-shaped cost curve in, 67–69,
 71–72, 79–80
Marginal costs, 82–86, 88, 89, 92
Marginal product, 88–95, 103–104,
 105

Marginal profit, 149
Markets and demand
  aptness, 172–74
  bandwagons and bubbles, 174–76
  cooperation and, 244–46
  costs and prices, 176–79
  demographics and, 179–85
  economists on, 169–72
  and elasticity, or sensitivity to
     price, 185–90
  fashion and, 190, 191
  forces shaping market demand,
     171
  greed and, 190–92
  habit and, 192–93
  income and, 193–96
  jazz and, 196–97
  knowledge about, 197–98
  loyalty and, 198–200
  and meeting of minds and money,
     200–204
  paucity of economic tools for de-
     mand analysis, 170–72
Marlboro cigarettes, 198, 199
Marlboro Friday, 199
Marriage, 183
Marubeni, 267n24
Marx, Karl, 111
Marxist economics, 111
Mass customization
  business cycle and, 130–33
  as new paradigm, 128–130
Mass production, 92–95, 105–106,
    128, 153, 162–63
Mathematica, 55
Matsushita, 117, 141, 243, 267n24
Mature versus innovative industries,
    76–77
Mauritius, 98–101
Mazda, 133, 245
McDonald's, 233–34
McDonnell-Douglas, 146, 228
McKinsey & Co., 36
MCI, 196
Measurement
  of income elasticity of demand,
    195–96
  of prices, 178–79
  tradeoffs and, 48, 49–52

Mechatronics, 229
Meeting Meter, 34
Meetings, cost of, 34
Mercedes-Benz, 76
Meteorology, 209
Mexico, 57–58, 60–63, 105, 106
Milco Industries, 183–84
Milken, Michael, 217–19
Miller, Arjay, 69
Miller beer, 164
Mills, Quinn, 249
Mimosin, 198
Minimills, 239
Minitel, 135–137
Missiles, 150–52
MIT Media Laba, 243
MIT Sloan School of Management, 1
Mitsubishi, 133
Model T, 78, 92–95, 105–106, 110,
    118, 128, 162–63, 176,
    188–90
Mokyr, Joel, 174
Moore, P. G., 209
Morita, Akio, 17–18, 66–68, 71, 72,
    80, 132, 215
Motorcycle industry, 102–104, 140,
    151–57, 256n14
Motorola, 97, 129–30, 133, 230,
    243
Movie industry, 18–19, 39–40

NAFTA, 57
Nakash, Joe, 175
National Association of Realtors,
    182
National Bicycle Industrial Co.,
    117–18, 121, 133
National Intergroup, 231
National Steel, 231
Navy. *See* United States Navy
Negative synergies, 127
Negroponte, Nicholas, 243
Netherlands, 177–78, 200, 249–50
Network economies of scope,
    134–37
Networked corporation, 249
New York Stock Exchange, 191, 228
New York Yankees, 58

New Zealand, 202
Niche firms, 163–64
Nick the Greek, 225
NIEMI plant, 229
Nippon Kokan, 231
Nissan, 102, 107, 133, 245
Noonan, 201
North American Free Trade Agreement (NAFTA), 57
Northrop, 52
Norton, Teresa, 193–94
Norton-Villiers-Triumph, 103, 105, 152–54
Norway, 150

Object of utility, 111
Occupancy costs, 30–33
Odds, 209–10, 221–25
Offshore production, 76, 97
Oil industry, 90–92, 118–19, 120, 121
Opel, 102
Opportunity cost
    description of, 22–25
    example of, 73–74
    of higher education, 34–36
Opportunity costs, failure to acknowledge, 36–37
Osborne, 140
Outback Steakhouse, 197
Outsourcer, 101
Overconfidence, 224
Overfitting, 222–23
Overhead, 82

Pagers, 129–30
Patton, General George Smith, 154, 205, 208
Payday peanut bar, 210–11
PCs. *See* Computer industry
Penicillin, 174
People resources. *See* Human resources
Pepsi-Cola, 4
Personnel. *See* Human resources
Per-unit costs, 71–72, 86
Per-unit variable cost, 71–72

Philip Morris, 164, 199
Philips, 96, 243
Pin factory, 92, 93–95, 120
Pine, B. Joseph, II, 128, 129
Plague, 180
Point-of-sale computers, 184
Political economy of learning curves, 165–67
Pontiac, 78
Population, 99–101, 179–85
Porsche, 244–45
Porter, Michael, 154, 231
Pratten, Clifford, 94
Predatory pricing, 199
Price sensitivity, 185–90
Price wars, 236–37
Prices
    change of, 178
    competitive price war, 236–37
    cost-price-value in cooperation, 232–34
    in cost-value-price triangle, 6–19
    definition of, 6
    elasticity, or sensitivity to price, 185–90
    General Motors and, 14–16
    habit and, 193
    hidden elements in, 179
    IBM and, 14
    jazz and, 196
    marginal product and, 88–95
    marginal-cost pricing, 84–85
    and markets and demand, 176–79
    measurement of, 178–79
    predatory pricing, 199
    as social fact, 176
    value pricing, 196–97
Prince Manufacturing Co., 235
Printers, 78
Probabilities, 209–10, 221–25
Procter & Gamble, 198
Prodigy, 135
Productivity
    in automobile industry, 102
    consultants and, 88
    continuous improvement and, 109
    and employee participation in company

[Productivity]
  decision making, 108
  employment crisis and,
    104–107
  in Germany, 76
  importance of human resources
    in, 95–99
  information technology and,
    112–15
  knowledge and, 96–97, 109–12
  marginal product and, 88–95
  marginal productivity in
    Mauritius and Hong Kong,
    99–101
  in motorcycle industry, 102–
    104
  pay for performance and,
    107–109
  as ratio, 104
  restructuring and, 87–88
  rise in, 99
  team work and, 108–109
  tracking of, 102–104
  in U.S., 112–13
Productivity paradox, 113
Products. *See also* specific products
  DFD (design for disassembly)
    projects, 184
  jazz and, 196–97
  as knowledge-based and informa-
    tion-intensive, 229
  life cycle analysis of, 190
  multiproduct economies of scale,
    124, 126–27
  new products, 197, 234–35
  portfolio of technologies in,
    229–30
  single-product economies of scale,
    122, 126–27
  versus services, 111–12
Profit
  break-even points and, 149–50
  cost-value-price triangle of, 6–19
  economic profit, 24–25
  marginal costs and, 83–86
  marginal profit, 149
Proprinter, 78

Quality circles, 156
Quality control, 158–59
Quantum Fund, 203
Quinn, James Bryant, 112

R&D. *See* Research and Develop-
    ment
Radios, 190, 191
Railroads, 18, 19, 127
Reagan, Ronald, 202
Recycling, 184
Redesign, 130
Reebok, 30
Reece, James S., 86
Re-engineering, 112
Reinhardt, Uwe, 142, 143, 148
Rent, 30–33
Research and Development, 26,
    37–39, 78–79, 80, 128,
    237–39
Research joint ventures (RJVs),
    237–38
Restructuring, 66, 87–88,
    104–105
Retail sales, 121–126
Retained earnings, 26
Return on investment, 11
Return on management, 11–12
Ricardo, David, 60, 63
Risks. *See* Calculated risks
RJR Nabisco, 4, 200
RJVs. *See* Research joint ventures
    (RJVs)
Roads, 127
Roberts, Edward, 266n9
Robodoc, 258n5
Robots, 47, 107, 118, 128, 130,
    258n5
Rockefeller, John D., 118–19
Rooney, Phillip B., 259n6
Roosevelt, Theodore, 242
Ross, Jerry, 39, 40
Rowntree, 200
Russia. *See* USSR and ex-USSR
Russo, Gerard, 188
Ruth, Babe, 58S-curve, 190

Safari Computer Division, 267n24
Saginaw Steering, 78
Salaries
  in automobile industry, 106
  cutting of, in face of competition,
    106
  of executives, 259n6
  of human-resource executives, 97,
    98
  in Japan, 104
  in manufacturing, 105, 106
  pay for performance, 107–109
  of workers using computers, 113
Salomon Brothers, 65, 107–108
San Diego State University, 48
Savage, Leonard, 209
Scale and scope
  in bicycle production, 117–18
  cooperation and, 242–44
  definition of, 120–121
  intelligent organization and, 137
  mass customization and business
    cycle in, 130–33
  mass customization as new para-
    digm in, 128–30
  Minitel as example of, 135–37
  multiproduct economies of scale,
    124, 126–27
  network economies of scope,
    134–137
  origins of, 118–121
  single-product economies of scale,
    122, 126–27
  vices and virtues of variety,
    126–128
  volume and/or variety matrix,
    121–126
Schachter, Stanley, 176
Schools. *See* Education; Higher edu-
    cation
Schultze, Charles, 176–77
Scope. *See* Scale and scope
Scott, Sir Percy, 241
Sears, Richard Warren, 172, 196–97
Sears, Roebuck, 65, 135, 172–73,
    196–97, 243
Sears Watch Co., 172

Services
  as knowledge-based and informa-
    tion-intensive, 229
  knowledge-based services,
    134–37
  portfolio of technologies in,
    229–30
  production of, at home, 257n9
  versus products, 111–112
Shareholder equity, 9, 235–36
Shareholder value added, 9–10
Shaw, Barry, 39, 40
Shockley, William, 66, 215
Short-termitis, 55–56
Shrage, Michael, 36
Silver, 192
Simon, Herbert, 79–80
Sims, William S., 241–42
Singapore, 96–97, 106, 248
Singer, Isaac Bashevis, 234
Single-loop learning, 159–60
Sinha, Deepak, 237–38
Skil Corp., 130
Sloan, Alfred P., 162
Smirnoff vodka, 200
Smith, Adam, 60, 63, 92, 93–95,
    120, 245–46, 247
Smoking, 188, 193, 198, 199
Smoot, Senator, 193
Smoot-Hawley tariff, 62, 193–94
Snuggle, 198
Solow, Robert, 112
Sony Corp., 8–11, 17–18, 66–69,
    80, 142, 215, 243,
    256n19
Sony Electric, 107
Soros, George, 203
South Sea Bubble, 175–76
South Sea Co., 175–76
Soviet Union. *See* USSR and ex-USSR
Space shuttle project, 54–55
Spain, 175, 198
SPC. *See* Statistical process control
    (SPC)
Speed
  economies of, 146
  speed-quality tradeoff, 234–35

Sperry, 127–28
Spira, Joel, 129
Springfield Arsenal, 79
Sprint, 196
SRI International, 109–10, 111
Stalin, Josef, 45
Standard Oil Company, 118–19
Standard Oil Trust, 119, 120, 121
Statistical process control (SPC), 156
Steel industry, 231, 236, 239
Stereos, 190, 191
Stevenson, Adlai, 41, 46
Stock market, 191, 206–207, 246–47
Strassman, Paul, 8, 11–12, 34, 113–114
Stroke, 223–24
Suh, Nam, 76–77
Sullivan, Chris, 197
Sunk costs, 37–40, 80–82, 86
Supermarkets, 32–33, 125
Suzuki, 155, 256n14
Sweden, 249–50
System/360, 206, 208
Szent-Gyorgi, 238

Tactics versus ethics, 49–50
Taiwan, 97, 235
Tariffs, 57–58, 60–63, 100, 156, 193–94
TCI, 243
TDK, 107
Teamwork, 108–109
Technology. *See also* Computer in-
    dustry; *and other specific*
    industries and products
    companies built around problem-
        solving technologies, 174
    high-tech entrepreneurship,
        266n9
    information technology, 112–15
    jazz and, 196
    mechatronics, 229
    network technology, 134–37, 201
    productivity and, 96–97

products and services embracing
    portfolio of technologies,
    229–30
    waves of emergence of, 130–31
Teerlink, Richard, 155, 156–57
Telecommunications industry,
    134–37, 243
Telephone service, 196
Teletel, 135
Television, 18–19, 134, 174, 190,
    191, 198–99, 242–43
Texas Instruments, 140
Thailand, 96, 97
Thaler, Richard, 38, 222
Thermo Electron, 173–74
3M, 184
Thurber, James, 12
Time as money, 33–38
Time Warner, 243
Toshiba, 11, 243, 248
Total quality movement, 112
Toyota, 102, 133, 229
Toys-R-Us, 124
Trade, international, 57–58, 60–63
Tradeoffs
    choice over time in, 55–56
    comparative advantage and,
        57–64
    cooperation and, 234–35
    customer psychology and, 52–54
    decision making concerning,
        46–49
    description of, 41–43
    efficiency and, 43–57
    failure to acknowledge, 56–57
    false choices and, 54–55
    in health care, 49
    in higher education, 48
    in legal system, 49–50
    measurement problems in,
        49–52
    people versus machines, 47
    and reasons for inefficiency,
        43–46
Trajtenberg, Manuel, 47–48
Transistor, 66, 215
Transistor radio, 66–69

Transportation. *See* Airline industry;
     Railroads; Roads
Tristar, 142–50, 164–65, 230
Trompenaars, Alfons, 249–50
Truthfulness, 157–61
Turkey, 150

U-shaped cost curve, 67–69, 71–72,
     79–80
Unemployment, 42–43, 104, 114,
     130, 193
Unilever, 198
Unisys, 128
Unit costs, 71–72, 86
United Kingdom. *See* Britain
United Parcel Service, 109
United States Air Force, 52–53, 150,
     165
United States Army, 78
United States Census Bureau,
     184–85
United States Department of De-
     fense, 52–54, 165–66
United States Department of Justice,
     231
United States Navy, 241–42
Universities. *See* Higher education
UPS. *See* United Parcel Service
U.S. Steel, 207, 231USAir, 228
USSR and ex-USSR, 45, 96, 110,
     111, 179, 207, 215–16,
     236, 248
USX, 207
Utility function, 170

Value
     cost-price-value in cooperation,
          232–34
     in cost-value-price triangle, 6–19
     of creating value, 16–18
     customer psychology and, 52–54
     definition of, 6
     General Motors and, 14–16
     IBM and, 13–14

     tension between cost and, 46–47
Value added
     business value added, 9
     definition of, 8–9
     management value added, 8–11
     in motorcycle industry, 104
     shareholder value added, 9–10
Value pricing, 196–97
Variable costs, 71–72, 82, 86, 139
Variety. *See* Scale and scope
Variety and/or volume matrix,
     121–126
Varley, Eric, 103, 152
VCRs, 96, 132, 140, 141–42, 190,
     191
VHS technology, 141–42
Victor Co. of America, 141
Victor Corp. of Japan, 141–42
Videocassette recorders (VCRs), 96,
     132, 140, 190, 191
Videotex, 135–37
Volume. *See* Scale and scope
Volume and/or variety matrix,
     121–126
Volvo, 223
Von Hippel, Eric, 239

Wages. *See* Salaries
Walkman, 17–18, 80
Wal-Mart, 121–125, 128
Walton, Sam, 121
Watergate, 181
Waterman, Robert, 249
Wayne, Kenneth, 163
Wealth. *See* Income
Weil, David N., 182
Westinghouse, 4, 65
Wheelabrator Technologies, 259n6
Wheelwright, Steven, 114
Whirlpool, 184
Whitehead, Alfred North, 223
Wilde, Oscar, 19
Williams Co., 196
Wolfe, Tom, 207
Working, E. J., 189
World Bank, 100

World War II, 45, 78–79, 174, 182,
    205
Wright, T. P., 143–44

X-efficiency, 45, 53, 157–58
X-inefficiency, 43–46
Xerox, 98

Yamaha, 103, 155, 256n14

YF-22 next-generation fighter air-
    craft, 165
Yiffies, 181–84, 199, 245
Yugoslavia, 207
Yuppies, 181, 182, 184, 199

Z1 automobile, 184
Zelig syndrome, 56–57
Zero-output cost numbers, 70–75
Zworykin, Vladimir, 174

Printed in the United States
By Bookmasters